Murat Halstead
and the
Cincinnati Commercial

Murat Halstead in 1874.

Murat Halstead
and the
Cincinnati Commercial

Donald W. Curl

A Florida Atlantic University Book

UNIVERSITY PRESSES OF FLORIDA

Boca Raton

University Presses of Florida is the central agency for scholarly publishing of the State of Florida's university system. Its offices are located at 15 NW 15th Street, Gainesville, FL 32603. Works published by University of Presses of Florida are evaluated and selected for publication by a faculty editorial committee of any one of Florida's nine public universities: Florida A&M University (Tallahassee), Florida Atlantic University (Boca Raton), Florida International University (Miami), Florida State University (Tallahassee), University of Central Florida (Orlando), University of Florida (Gainesville), University of North Florida (Jacksonville), University of South Florida (Tampa), University of West Florida (Pensacola).

Library of Congress Cataloging in Publication Data

Curl, Donald W.
    Murat Halstead and the Cincinnati commercial.

    "A Florida Atlantic University book."
    Bibliography: p.
    Includes index.
    1.   Halstead, Murat, 1829–1908. 2.   Journalists—United States—Biography. 3.   Cincinnati Commercial gazette. I. Title
PN4874.H222C8   070.4'1'0924 [B]   80-12046
ISBN 0–8130–0669–4

Typography by Business Graphics Incorporated
Albuquerque, New Mexico

PRINTED IN USA

Contents

Preface

Newspapers and their reporters, editors, and publishers have long held the interest of historians. The newspaper is a prime source for historical research, and every major library boasts of its extensive files of newspapers, either in bound volumes or on microfilm. Although historians using these files may have many differing purposes—some see the newspaper as a chronicle of an era, others as a reflection of popular sentiment, and still others as a principal molder of public opinion—all agree that the newspaper is a major tool in writing history. Some historians are attracted to the newspaper because a particular reporter, editor, or publisher influenced the course of history.

My own interest in Murat Halstead and the *Cincinnati Commercial* grew out of a seminar paper on the Liberal Republican party convention. Most of the party leadership had newspaper connections. With the exception of Halstead, I found biographies, autobiographies, special studies, and articles detailing the place of these men in the Liberal Republican movement and on the American scene. Hardly a study of the Civil War or of the late nineteenth century existed in which Halstead was not mentioned or quoted, but no one had investigated his life or written a study of his newspaper.

As one of the most important newspapers in Ohio's largest city in the late nineteenth century, the *Commercial* and its opinions were respected in Cincinnati, in the state, and across the nation. Under Halstead's leadership, it pioneered in new methods of gath-

ering and printing news and in the creation of the modern newspaper we know today. Although strongly Republican most of his
adult life, Halstead also promoted and became a chief spokesman
for independent journalism. As president of the Western Associated
Press, he was instrumental in the formation of the national organization. His friends included almost every major journalist, publisher, and author in the country.

A much respected political reporter, Halstead attended every
Republican national convention from the first in 1856 through that
of 1904 and many of the Democratic conventions during those
years. In 1860 he became the only correspondent to report all of the
many national party conventions. As a close personal friend of
Presidents Rutherford B. Hayes and Benjamin Harrison, he was
often consulted on public and political policy. Moreover, Halstead
knew every American politician of national importance in the Gilded
Age. In 1876 he spoke across the country on the money question,
and in 1884 he edited the *Extra,* a special Blaine campaign newspaper published in New York City.

In 1889 President Harrison appointed Halstead minister to Germany; the Senate, however, reacting to charges of corruption he
had made against several senators, refused to confirm him. Although chiefly known as a political reporter and editor, Halstead
also acted as a war correspondent, reporting several battles in the
Civil War, the Franco-Prussian War, and the Spanish-American
War. In his sixties he traveled to the Philippines and interviewed
several rebel leaders. Finally, in his last years Halstead wrote over
twenty volumes on politics and current affairs. One of these, *The
Illustrious Life of William McKinley: Our Martyred President,* sold over
700,000 copies.

As a reporter and editor, Halstead recorded his opinion on most
public issues of the era. Unfortunately, the details of his private life
are almost all unavailable. Although his correspondence with many
public figures can be found in their papers, the subjects discussed
are nearly always political. He did leave several unpublished stories about his early years, but never wrote an autobiography. As a
consequence, little can be said about Halstead's private life; lacking
the intimate details of his life, a study of Halstead makes him
appear somewhat one-dimensional. To a large extent, I suspect
that he was, for his devotion to career, newspaper, and politics left
little time for a truly private life.

The research and writing of this manuscript profited from the aid and counsel of many individuals. I am particularly appreciative of the aid given by the staffs of the Cincinnati Historical Society Library, the Ohio Historical Society Library, the Rutherford B. Hayes Library and Dr. Watt Marchman of its staff, the Manuscript Division of the Library of Congress, the Public Library of Cincinnati and Hamilton County, the Kent State University Library, the Ohio State University Library, and the Florida Atlantic University Library. A faculty development grant from Florida Atlantic University also provided time for completion of the manuscript. Although I cannot express my appreciation to each individual who so generously gave of their time and knowledge, I would like to thank Dean Jack Suberman, Mrs. Thelma Spangler, Professors Richard R. Duncan, Raymond A. Mohl, Robert Schwarz, Eugene H. Roseboom, Robert H. Bremner, and, especially, Francis P. Weisenburger.

1

The Young Man from Paddy's Run

Murat Halstead, a child of nineteenth-century midwestern America, typified his era in almost every respect save his first name. He received this unusual name from his father, a colonel in the local Paddy's Run unit of the Ohio militia and a devotee of military history. "Colonel Griff," as the people of Butler County called Halstead's father, admired Napoleon's commander of cavalry, Joachim Murat. During the 1820s Murat's two sons came to the United States. American newspapers published accounts of their travels, further arousing the colonel's interest in the French family. Thus the name of the colonel's first son became that of the illustrious Murats.

The Halsteads were an ancient English family. The name Halsteede or Halsteade appeared in the Domesday Book of the late eleventh century. The first American Halstead, Henry, emigrated from England in 1651 and became the owner of a slave plantation near the present site of Norfolk, Virginia. Murat Halstead's immediate family can be traced from his grandfather John Halstead, of Currituck County, North Carolina. John married Ruth Richardson, a young woman of similar southern gentry background. The birth of their son—Murat's father—occurred in Orange County, North Carolina, in 1802. Dissatisfied with his land in North Carolina, John joined the growing numbers seeking a new life in the Blue Grass country of Kentucky. Although the region surpassed all of his expectations, by 1810 land titles in Kentucky had become confused. Afraid to risk a purchase, John decided to cross the river into Ohio at Cincinnati. [1]*

Unimpressed with the "Queen City," a village of a thousand people living in a few hundred houses along the northern bank of the Ohio, John later said he would not have traded all he owned for the entire town. Moving on to the area known as Paddy's Run in Butler County, he paid $700 for 281 acres: a sizable farm considering the methods of cultivation of that time. Paddy's Run Valley in 1810 presented the picture of almost unbroken wilderness. Near a spring, about one hundred yards from the north line of his untamed land, John built his family a square log house. In this house Griffin grew to manhood. In 1827 he married Clarissa Willet, the daughter of a Hamilton County family. Two years later, on September 2, 1829, Murat's birth occurred in the same log house. [2]

Murat retained no boyhood memories of the early log house. Two years after the boy's birth Griffin built a new house, more befitting a prosperous young farmer—a substantial two-story structure, the first floor was built of stone, the second of frame. This new house was the scene of the birth of Murat's sister Helen on November 11, 1831, and of his brother Benton on March 11, 1834.

Although raised on a pioneer farm in an isolated community, the young Halsteads did not live in need or deprivation. By the time of Murat's birth, the more onerous tasks of pioneering had been completed. His parents could provide the amenities of rural life. Moreover, John Halstead's bank account showed a surplus, which he loaned to neighbors at the prevailing 10 percent rate of interest. [3]

Less than twenty miles from Paddy's Run, Cincinnati was already a manufacturing and trading center, and soon became a literary and intellectual center that attracted many bright young men from the surrounding countryside. Murat's parents considered subscriptions to newspapers and periodicals a necessity. Living near Cincinnati gave the Halsteads the advantage of the budding literary activity of that city. As soon as Murat could stand by her side, his mother read him articles from newspapers and taught him his letters from their headlines. As the Halsteads, like most of the citizens of Butler County, supported the Democratic party, the *Hamilton Telegraph* became Murat's first primer. Constant readers themselves, Murat's parents encouraged his interest in literature and history. [4]

*Notes begin on page 145.

Although Murat received his early education from his mother, at ten he attended a school run by B. W. Chidlaw, a young Congregational minister, in New London, Ohio. During his days in Chidlaw's school Murat developed a strong aversion to his Christian name. The Anglo-Saxon sounding names of his schoolmates prompted them to tease him by mispronouncing his name. As a consequence, he used "M. Halstead" as his signature all his life. Nonetheless, when he became prominent his unusual, "yet euphonious full name 'Murat Halstead,' was an asset, like a well-chosen stage name, in establishing and spreading his fame." Although in later years other newspaper men debated the correct pronunciation, Halstead offered no clues until 1889. Testifying before a congressional committee, he gave his name as " 'Mu-raw' Halstead."[5]

As young Halstead's school days drew to a close, he thought about a college education. John Halstead, unenthusiastic about this plan for his eldest grandson, wished him to remain on the farm, since he believed a college education a waste of time and money. However, Murat found his parents willing accomplices in thwarting the will of his grandfather. They believed in their son's abilities and encouraged him to seek a wider range for his talents than the Butler County farm.[6]

Fortunately, the 1840s saw the establishment of an institution that overcame John's objections to a college education for his grandson. In 1832, Freeman G. Cary, a graduate of Miami University at Oxford, opened a high school in a room of his house at Pleasant Hill, near Cincinnati. Cary's school expanded rapidly, and by the mid-forties it outgrew the small campus of two brick classroom buildings and several frame dormitories. Cary, unwilling to invest more of his own money in further additions to the physical plant of the school, asked a number of former patrons for additional aid. This group formed a corporation and received a charter from the state for a college with Cary as its president. Adopting the name Farmers' College of Hamilton County (Cary proposed to establish an agricultural education curriculum), the patrons formed a board of directors and sold stock in the new corporation. This stock's unusual feature was the payment of interest in college tuition.[7]

The directors visited the farmers of the surrounding counties, urging them to buy a share (or "scholarship") in the new college. For only $30, a farmer could ensure the establishment of an institu-

tion for his sons based on the newest reforms in agricultural education.[8]

When the directors reached Paddy's Run Valley, all thoughts
that young Halstead had of attending Miami, Marietta, Kenyon, or
any of the other older, more established institutions instantly van-
ished. This college removed all of John's objections to higher education for farmers' sons. By 1847 the board of directors reported a
subscription of $13,000.[9] A large brick building with a chapel, class-
rooms, and student's rooms stood completed on the rainy autumn
day in 1848 when young Halstead and about 200 other students
arrived for their first day at the new college. The old academy
buildings and the frame dormitories completed the small campus.[10]

Of all Halstead's college teachers, Robert Hamilton Bishop, professor of history and political economy, had the most lasting influence. Bishop, in the twilight of a distinguished career, had served
the cause of higher education since 1804. Scottish by birth and
education, he came to the United States as a very young man. He
first taught at Transylvania University, and then for sixteen years
served as president of Miami University. An intrauniversity debate
centering chiefly on the slavery issue led to his dismissal by the
board of trustees from the Miami post. Cary, a former student of
Bishop's, invited him to join his faculty along with John W. Scott,
who also had been dismissed.[11]

Bishop's wide knowledge, his enthusiasm for learning, and his
obvious love for teaching made him one of those rare instructors
whose influence can be seen in his students' development. Time
and again in later life, Halstead stated that he had been guided in
decisions and responses to important issues by the principles
Bishop had instilled in his classes in biography, history, and political economy.[12]

Bishop believed that the purpose of government and the "avowed
object of all modern political economy" should be to reconcile differences between social classes. Although men uniting in commu-
nities discarded some of their freedoms for the good of the whole,
those they retained became even more valuable. Thus Bishop taught
that government must diligently protect the civil and religious liberty of every citizen.[13] Halstead echoed these essentially nineteenth-
century, laissez-faire, liberal views of government throughout his
public life. As an editor, he used his position to fight for the rights
and freedom of individuals. His philosophy upheld the right of the

individual to acquire and hold property and to have it protected by the government, although he believed that government should never interfere in a situation that individuals could handle. He used his editor's position also to demand honesty in government and to attack and condemn corruption. Finally, he supported the right of everyone, black and white, to the political and legal rights of voting, officeholding, and recourse to court.

Both Professor Bishop and George Ornsby, the teacher in charge of the college's preparatory school, held antislavery views. Thus Halstead found his own childhood proslavery sentiments challenged time and again during his college career. As an editor, his hostility to slavery and the power of the slaveholding South became well known.[14]

At its annual commencement exercises in September 1851, Farmers' College conferred the degree "American Scholar" upon the student from Paddy's Run. The faculty believed that Halstead's successful completion of courses in mathematics, English composition, rhetoric, logic, sacred history, chemistry, history, and political economy, and his writing of a graduation thesis on "Suppressed Thought," prepared him to seek his fortune in the world. Absent from the graduation, which included two future attorneys, two future editors, and a future railroad president, was one of Halstead's early college friends and the college's most illustrious student. Benjamin Harrison left the school for Miami University the end of his junior year. Professor Scott had already returned to Miami, and Harrison, wishing to be close to Scott's daughter—Harrison's future wife—also transferred.[15]

Some years later the college made Halstead a "Master of Arts" for engaging in literary pursuits for a period of "at least three years." In 1890, at its last commencement, Halstead received an honorary "Doctor of Laws." In a humorous report, the *New York Sun* said that although the then well-known journalist had the age and dignity for such a degree, it hoped he would not call himself "Dr. Halstead."[16]

As John Halstead feared, the young college graduate had no desire to return to the farm in Paddy's Run. As his interests in college had been largely literary, Halstead decided to seek a career in Cincinnati. By the fall of 1851 the city had grown to almost 120,000. Although still "Porkopolis" to wags across the country, its citizens engaged in businesses ranging from wool picking to iron production. Meat packing remained the largest single industry, accounting for almost $8 million of the city's annual production. Allied industries, such as oil and lard production, soap and candle making, and luggage manufacturing nearly equaled the parent industry in the value of their products. By 1857 Procter and Gamble, candle and soap manufacturers, had annual sales exceeding $1 million. Already some of these firms were bringing in raw materials from packing centers farther west. [17]

The many daily and weekly newspapers and monthly periodicals published in the city in 1851 concerned Halstead more than its industrial output. Besides six English and four German dailies, Cincinnati boasted forty-three other publications ranging from General Samuel F. Cary's Christian temperance journal, the *Western Fountain,* to the *Hachwaechter* of the radical Forty-Eighter Frederick Hassaurek, which one critic described as "Socialist and infidel of the deepest dye." In addition, there were many professional and business periodicals, such as the *Journal of Homeopathy,* the *Dental Register,* and *Dye's Counterfeit Detector,* as well as many devoted exclusively to literature. [18]

Wealthy, and with a cultural life unequaled in the Midwest, Cincinnati nevertheless remained a city of contrasts. It was a focal point for German migration, and hundreds of immigrants arrived yearly. Many, living in the "over the Rhine" district, found themselves condemned by low wages to years of poverty. On the other hand, young and cultured college graduates such as Halstead also sought the city, hoping to prosper with its growth. Although the expanding wealth produced spacious public buildings, elegant homes, lofty churches, and lush parklands, these existed side by side with vile and unsightly packing plants and some of the worst tenement conditions in the country.

Halstead arrived in Cincinnati in the fall of 1851 determined to make his mark as a writer. Years of outdoor life and wholesome farm food made the Queen City's new citizen strong and healthy. Although tall like his father, his coloring—light brown hair, fair skin, and blue eyes—came from his mother. Self-confident, energetic, and almost always cheerful, he found easy acceptance in the small set of young intellectuals who, drawn by the numerous newspapers with their large literary departments, made Ohio's largest city the literary center of the Midwest. [19]

During most of his college career, Halstead bombarded the city's newspapers with stories of Indians and frontier life. Although he continued to submit articles which the newspapers often accepted, the newspapers had meager budgets and could pay their contributors very little. As Halstead desperately needed a regular source of income, he eventually sought employment on a newspaper staff. William D. Gallagher, the editor of the small afternoon daily *Atlas,* offered him the $5-a-week post of exchange editor, one of the lowest-paid men on a newspaper staff, who carefully read the newspapers received "in exchange" for a free copy of his own newspaper, clipping articles of interest to local readers. Headed with a phrase such as, "From the *New York Tribune,*" the newspaper printed these articles verbatim. Though it was hardly an enviable position, the ambitious young man promptly accepted. Unfortunately, a few weeks later Halstead lost his job when a new economy-minded editor decided the paper did not need a "scissors man." He next found a temporary position with the *Cincinnati Enquirer* during a leave of absence of a staff member. At the end of this eight-week stint, he decided to make newspaper life his career. With the confidence found only in a novice, he and a printer friend founded a Sunday newspaper, which they named the *Cincinnati Leader.* There was little public response to this new venture. Moreover, with only two issues published, and one side of the third printed, Halstead's printer-partner went on a drinking spree that consumed the small capital collected for the project. With no capital, few readers, and a missing printer, the new editor abandoned the newspaper.[20]

The young man's initiative struck a responsive chord in William B. Shattuck, editor of the *Columbian and Great West,* a flourishing literary weekly. When the *Leader* failed, Shattuck offered Halstead the assistant editorship of his paper. He remained on the *Columbian* until March 8, 1853. On that day, Halstead began his nearly forty years' association with the *Cincinnati Commercial,* the city's leading morning journal. He had enjoyed the position on the *Columbian,* where his duties combined writing with editing. Nonetheless, the offer from the *Commercial,* with its $12-a-week salary, could not be resisted.[21]

The *Commercial,* owned in 1853 by Martin D. Potter and Richard H. Lee, had been founded in October 1843 by the firm of Curtis and Hastings. Potter, a printer turned publisher, bought control of the paper in 1851 and shortly thereafter sold a half-interest to Lee.

Potter handled the financial and printing aspects of the business; Lee acted as editor-in-chief. A prosperous paper, its large circulation supported a growing staff of editors and reporters.[22]

In the 1850s Cincinnati journalism was a leisurely occupation. The various newspapers competed for advertising, not news. Although the newspapers had a few local reporters, news gathering consisted mainly of clipping items from the exchange papers. Moreover, the reporters on the morning newspapers ended their work at ten o'clock at night. Halstead discovered that by waiting until two o'clock in the morning, he could meet the train from the east with its late-edition newspapers, clip the important articles, and have his copy ready before the paper went to press.[23]

The telegraph had just been introduced. Although the Cincinnati papers joined forces to purchase one short dispatch a day, for complete news they still waited for the eastern papers. For several years the telegraph only speeded Halstead's composition. The telegraphic dispatches told him what to look for in eastern journals. He could accept the reproaches showered upon him by his fellow reporters "for being in such an atrocious hurry" when the *Commercial*'s sales proved that the citizens of Cincinnati preferred a morning paper with the latest news. His initiative also found an appreciative response from his employers.[24]

When Halstead joined the *Commercial* staff, the newspaper contained four pages. An average edition had more literary material than news of the day; Saturday's edition usually devoted a whole page to a chapter of a serialized novel. Later, when Halstead decided to use longer telegraphic dispatches, he dropped the literary features. He discovered that these served mainly to fill the newspaper's pages, and no one noted their omission. The young journalist found life on the staff of a major daily newspaper extremely demanding. At his desk to write his own stories soon after noon, he often returned to his room at four or five o'clock the next morning.[25]

During this early period on the *Commercial* he began many lifelong friendships that had great importance for his career. Several of these came from contacts made at meetings of the Cincinnati Literary Club. The club had been formed in 1849 as a protest against an older literary group known as the Semi Colon Club. The Semi Colons held their meetings in private houses, necessarily limiting the choice to those with large drawing rooms. The gatherings tended to be sedate and, according to the Literary Club members, boring affairs.

The Literary Club abandoned the tea and cakes of the Semi Colons for pickled oysters, crackers, Rhine wine, and cigars. Often the meetings formally adjourned to continue informally in a nearby saloon. The new organization hoped to break the confining bonds of the old group and, in more congenial surroundings, to discuss controversial questions of the day. [26]

The Literary Club soon found private rooms for its meetings, and began a ritual, still continued over a century later, of gathering on Monday evenings for dinner and for a paper read by a member. After the formal presentation, members discussed the paper. When Halstead joined the group in 1853, serious debates often followed the papers. These led to many angry comments and sometimes fights. As the sixties approached and the papers often dealt with questions of slavery, abolition, and states' rights, the debates grew more heated. Cincinnati, a city in a northern state with many strong antislavery citizens and institutions, also enjoyed a booming trade with the South. Moreover, lying just across the Ohio River from a slave state, it had many residents of southern heritage. Since the intensities aroused by some of the debates threatened its continuance, the club adopted a rule in the late fifties that no public comments should follow the papers. Halstead by this time had become sympathetic to the antislavery cause, and he also loved a good debate. Although he agreed with the majority that the club had more value than the debates, he regretted the decision.

The club greatly widened Halstead's circle of friends. His early acquaintances had been limited to the literary and journalistic fields. Now he met the city's young professionals and businessmen, such as attorneys Stanley Matthews, later an associate justice of the United States Supreme Court, and Rutherford B. Hayes, the future president. Both of these men, and many others from the organization, remained lifelong friends. [27]

A few months after Halstead began working on the *Commercial*, he started to write short articles about various issues of the day which Lee published on the editorial page. His vigorous style and the initiative he showed in scooping other papers on late news prompted Lee to give him greater editorial responsibilities. Lee fell ill in the late summer of 1853. As Potter had gone east on vacation, Halstead, relieved of local reporting duties, submitted a news summary and lead editorial every day. Lee's illness proved fatal. When Potter returned in August, he found the paper virtually under the direction of the young reporter who had been on the staff just six months. Impressed with Halstead's capabilities, when Potter organized M. D. Potter and Company in the spring of 1854, he made Halstead a one-sixteenth partner. Increased circulation and advertising revenues allowed the young editor to pay for his $5,000 interest from his share of the profits in just four years.[28]

As Potter worked alongside the new assistant editor, his admiration for the young man grew. Potter had no sons, but in many ways Halstead filled this void. Thus Potter began to groom Halstead as his successor. The young man learned the financial management of the newspaper from Potter, while the new editor, A. R. Spofford, later librarian of Congress, supervised his editorial training. Possessed of a comprehensive and searching mind, Spofford produced an endless supply of informative and interesting editorials. By emulating his devices, Halstead became the master editorial writer known by later generations of Cincinnatians.[29]

Halstead's antislavery professors had weakened his youthful support of all things Democratic. Writing editorials on political questions of the day convinced him that the southern wing of the Democratic party seemed bent on destroying the Union. Thus the Republican party gained an early convert in the young editor. Moreover, Potter, who had become almost a second father to Halstead, joined the Republican cause. When Potter decided that the *Commercial* should become an outright Republican paper, his young editor supported the decision. All of his life Halstead was an enthusiast. Whenever he gave his support to a cause, he did so wholeheartedly. Seeing the large circulation of the *Commercial* as a fertile field for Republican propaganda, he wanted to launch an all-out campaign in its columns. Potter, on the other hand, believed that Cincinnati business interests, which provided the main support of the paper, might not approve. Thus Potter insisted on moderation. Although sometimes straining within this harness of moderation, Halstead nonetheless came to recognize the wisdom of the older man's policy as the paper continued to grow and to prosper.[30]

Halstead's long career as a national political reporter and commentator originated with the first Republican national convention in June 1856 in Philadelphia. Potter attended the convention and took his assistant editor along to write firsthand reports for the

Photograph courtesy of the Cincinnati Historical Society

Murat Halstead as a graduate of Farmers' College in 1852.

Commercial. The great question before the convention, in Halstead's opinion, was the extension of slavery to the territories. In an earlier editorial, he had voiced fears that both Republican and Democratic politicians, more concerned with offices than principles, would avoid the slavery question. He feared that both parties might nom-inate weak candidates in an attempt to offend no one; he called politicians "trucklers, temporizers and compromisers."[31]

The *Commercial* supported Salmon Portland Chase, a Cincinnati attorney who helped found the Liberty and Free-Soil parties, for the presidential nomination. Chase had served as a senator from Ohio from 1849 until his election to the Ohio governorship in 1855. His opposition to the Compromise of 1850 and the Kansas-Nebraska

Act made him the no-nonsense candidate that Halstead believed the people needed for a fair test of the "Great Question." At first possessing great prestige in the new movement, and certainly an early front-runner for the nomination, Chase eventually lost. The Whig element in the party found it difficult to forget his days as a political opponent. William H. Seward, a New York senator, and another early front-runner, also ran into trouble because of the polymorphous nature of the movement. While Seward found support from ex-Whigs, his advocacy of greater rights for naturalized citizens and his courting of Catholic voters in New York made him unacceptable to the party's Know-Nothing element.[32]

Only one man combined support from all the various interests in the party. John C. Frémont captured the imagination of the country with his expeditions in the West. A figure of romance and adventure to the nation, he possessed all the elements which seemed necessary for victory. The Know-Nothing element gave him enthusiastic support; the Germans respected his interest in science; and his marriage to the daughter of Senator Thomas H. Benton made him the "spiritual heir to Jackson." Chase's defeat disappointed Halstead. He complained that Frémont, a product of availability, had been used by politicians to win office. As such, the voters had no clear trial of the issues. Nonetheless, the *Commercial* supported Frémont's candidacy for the presidency. In a letter to Congressman T. E. Day of Cincinnati, written soon after Halstead's return from Philadelphia, the editor expressed belief in Frémont's success. He predicted civil war should Buchanan win and Democratic policy toward Kansas not change. The country disagreed with Halstead; Buchanan won.[33]

Although his candidate's defeat disappointed the young editor, he had developed new interests. A few years earlier at a party he had met Mary Banks, daughter of Mrs. Hiram Banks, widow of a Cincinnati builder. Soon Cincinnati society looked upon "Mary and Murat" as partners. Potter arranged the honeymoon for the March 1, 1857, wedding. The couple traveled to Washington, at the expense of the *Commercial,* and Halstead, combining work with pleasure, sent back firsthand accounts of Buchanan's inauguration.[34]

Halstead and his bride arrived in Washington on a bright and sunny day. The sun brought out the crowds which the young editor-reporter from Cincinnati felt very poorly mannered. If the crude and boisterous crowd received his condemnation, so did the too-refined and too-cold Buchanan. "It would appear from the exquisite polish upon him, and the expression of his lips, that he must sleep between rose leaves with a little lump of fresh butter in his mouth." When the honeymooners arrived in Washington, everyone claimed the bright sun a good omen for the new administration. A partisan Halstead could happily report that when Buchanan spoke, the sun went behind a cloud and it grew cooler. Disappointed with American politics, and a little less confident in the ability of the American voter to choose a president, Halstead and his bride left for Baltimore on the first train after the ceremony.[35]

As sectional bitterness grew more intense in the following years, the *Commercial* under Potter's direction continued to steer a middle course. On January 15, 1859, Potter appointed Halstead editor-in-chief and permitted him to purchase another one-sixteenth interest in the firm. The newspaper had prospered; the second purchase cost $10,000, or double the first. The firm's capitalization also doubled, now standing at $160,000. While strongly Republican, the newspaper under Halstead nonetheless took the position that the nation's outstanding problems could be solved without disruption of the Union.[36]

On the night of October 16, 1859, an event occurred with great portent for both the nation and Halstead's career. John Brown and eighteen followers attacked and captured the federal arsenal at Harpers Ferry, Virginia. Brown planned to distribute the military stores of the arsenal to the slaves in the area. His raid electrified the South. A complete failure, the raid seemed to prove that abolitionists would go to any length in attacking southern institutions. Northern Republican papers, such as the *Commercial*, embarrassed by the raid, called it the act of a madman and declared that Brown had no northern support.[37]

A speedy trial followed, and Brown was sentenced to be executed on December 2, 1859. Many *Commercial* editorials criticized the outcry in southern journals against Brown and his alleged northern support. In one editorial, Halstead said that southern editors had become "mad as March hares—mad as Old Brown"; he singled out the editor of the conservative *Richmond Whig* as a leader in what he termed a "race of fanaticism."[38]

Halstead's first national assignment as editor-in-chief sent him to Washington to report on the opening of Congress. What might have been a routine story took on new interest when the editor routed his trip through Harpers Ferry so that he could witness Brown's execution. Although Potter and other friends warned Halstead that because of the views of the *Commercial* he might be arrested or mobbed in Virginia, he refused to listen.

Aboard the train his fellow passengers also feared for his safety. Rumors that no one could debark at Harpers Ferry circulated throughout the train. Some passengers believed Virginia authorities planned to search them when they crossed the state line. These rumors seemed justified when they received a proclamation by General William B. Taliaferro, commander of Virginia's militia in the area, stating that until after Friday, December 2, all "strangers" appearing within Jefferson County, unable to give a satisfactory account of their presence, would be "at once arrested."

Although Halstead found the proclamation discouraging, he still decided to carry out his plan. The master of transportation for the Baltimore and Ohio Railroad happened to be aboard the train. An acquaintance of the reporter, he introduced him to the railroad's agent at Harpers Ferry. Halstead received a cordial welcome and the promise of aid. The agent vouched for him to the commander of the military contingent at the terminal, who took him to a local hotel.[39]

Halstead discovered that a single newsman had the freedom to come and go with only minor restrictions. Governor Henry Wise ordered the proclamation because he believed bands of armed men had been organized in the North to rescue Brown. The governor also authorized security precautions that included the mobilization of over a thousand militia. Halstead pointed out the absurdity of these arrangements; Virginia's fears made as much practical sense as the citizens of Cincinnati believing five hundred Chinese might attack their city in an attempt to revolutionize Ohio.[40]

On the morning of the second, Halstead arose early and went out to see the gallows. The authorities scheduled the hanging to take place in the center of a thirty-acre clover field. Halstead found two companies of infantry and one of cavalry posted in the field. Flags marked the areas off limits to civilians. On returning to town he discovered that the commanding general had a list made of the reporters who could witness the hanging from a close vantage point. Halstead later found that several of the reporters responsible for compiling the list complained about adding his name. They feared the general might decide to restrict all reporters rather than allow a representative of the *Commercial* close to the gallows.[41]

Two hours before the appointed time, a military contingent escorted the reporters through the deserted streets to the execution site. Although rigid orders prevented people from coming into town during the morning hours, at the field Halstead counted between three hundred and five hundred civilian observers. Brown impressed the reporter with his great dignity. Halstead described an old man with white hair and beard, sitting very straight and riding in a small cart on his own coffin. He thought that the officers, with their plumes and highly polished sabers, and the long ranks of soldiers contrasted sharply with the simple dignity of Brown. The hanging took only a minute: "There was a moment of intense stillness, a sudden movement, a sharp twang of the rope, a creaking of the hinges of the trap door, and at fourteen and one-half minutes after eleven the old man, indomitable to the last, swung between the sky and the soil of the Old Dominion. As he dropped, he turned sharply round and faced North."[42] Halstead believed that the simplicity of Brown's death and his calm and resigned demeanor mocked the elaborate preparations of the Virginians.

Halstead reported that Brown did more for the abolitionist cause in dying than he had in all the years of his stormy career. Nonetheless, the sympathy which Halstead naturally felt for the old abolitionist did not interfere with his evaluation of the event. Although many northerners and southerners, he wrote, asserted that Brown should not have been hanged, he might have escaped imprisonment and attempted another Harpers Ferry. Moreover, Brown certainly had been guilty of a crime. Virginia could not set him free. No one could say that Brown's conviction and sentence did not conform to Virginia's laws. The reporter saw the tragedy in the situation in that Virginia, doing only what her laws demanded, assured Brown's "niche in the gallery of illustrious traitors."[43]

Many newspapers in the North reprinted Halstead's reports. The *Commercial*'s representative had been the only reporter for a Republican paper at Harpers Ferry. To his friends he complained that dispatches of the *Cincinnati Enquirer* (a Democratic newspaper) had been approved by the authorities. He immediately telegraphed back to his family in Cincinnati, but could only tell of his safe arrival. Yet he also admitted that he had received kind treatment in Virginia. His first report of the execution appeared in the *Commercial* on December 5, only three days after the event.[44]

The situation Halstead found when he reached Washington confirmed his growing fears for the nation. A serious controversy arose over the organization of the House of Representatives. Halstead supported John Sherman, a fellow Ohioan, for Speaker. Sherman, along with sixty-eight other Republican members of the House, endorsed a book by Hinton R. Helper, a native of North Carolina who had lived in the North for many years. Helper's book, *The Impending Crisis of the South, and How to Meet It,* developed the thesis of the economic superiority of the northern states. He stated that the whites in the South who did not own slaves could prosper only with the abolition of slavery. Moreover, he threatened violence against the slave owners unless they freed their slaves. Helper's economic thesis and the abusive character of his argument incensed the South. Sherman's nomination produced a resolution that denied the post of Speaker of the House to anyone having endorsed a book suggesting violence. Sherman lost, but Halstead believed a well-organized Republican party could have produced victory. Since at least ten men aspired to party leadership, united action on the part of the Republicans became impossible.[45]

Disappointed in the politicians running the Republican party and fearful that no rational settlement of the problems dividing the nation could be found, Halstead returned to Cincinnati on December 15 to spend Christmas with his family. Washington's abominable weather, its crowds of adventurers, its "loafing" lobby members, and its office seekers made him proclaim, "sotty and porky as Cincinnati is at this time, I should be desolate indeed if it did not offer more attractions than this wretched wilderness of false pretences."[46]

Halstead's first major national assignments established his reputation as a political reporter. They also set his journalistic career on a course that he followed for the rest of his life. The editor of a large urban newspaper must by necessity concern himself with many issues and problems; Halstead took as his particular interest national politics. Moreover, both his firsthand reports and editorials reflected the lessons he had mastered as an apprentice. The young reporter had been an early convert to the Republican party because he believed it could find solutions to the problems facing the nation. His attendance at the Republican convention at Philadelphia and the opening session of Congress in 1859 shook his faith in the party and, more important, in its leaders. Halstead remained a Republican. Although the *Commercial* (with only one exception) always supported Republican presidential condidates, Halstead became skeptical of politicians' promises and motives. His reports and editorials reflected this skepticism for at least the next twenty-four years.

2

The War Years

During the 1860s Murat Halstead gained national prominence as a journalist. He attained his reputation through the support of Potter, his abilities as a writer, and his dedication to hard work. The *Commercial* also prospered. The decade opened with the *Commercial* claiming the highest daily circulation in the Midwest. With an average daily circulation of 15,000, the proprietors asserted that 90,000 people read every edition, twice the number of any other Cincinnati newspaper. Through the war years circulation continued to rise.[1]

The proprietors also believed that the paper's growth depended on technical improvements and accurate reporting of the news. Potter felt that Halstead's earlier newsletters had proved his abilities to capture the interest of Cincinnati's readers. Consequently, he decided that the *Commercial* could greatly increase its reputation by sending the young editor to all the 1860 political conventions. Although Halstead drew a tight schedule for the three expected conventions, before returning to Cincinnati in late June he actually attended seven. These included the Republican and Constitutional Union conventions, two "northern" Democratic conventions, and three "southern" Democratic conventions.

Once more apprehensions arose for Halstead's safety. When the reporter traveled to Harpers Ferry he had been treated politely, but the Democrats scheduled their convention for Charleston. Friends warned him that South Carolinians hated Republicans much more than Virginians did. Nonetheless, Halstead decided to risk the dangers and, leaving Cincinnati on April 16 by train, he traveled in easy daily stages to Nashville and Atlanta and finally reached Charleston on the eighteenth.[2]

Halstead found southerners to be more sociable travelers than northerners. Everyone in his car introduced himself, and everyone tried to make the editor's journey pleasant. He found the same courtesy and friendliness in Charleston. Although convention delegates and visitors crowded the city, he rented a clean and airy room at a reasonable price.[3]

Halstead spent his time in Charleston interviewing delegates and mingling with politicians in crowded hotel lobbies and on the streets. When the convention opened on April 23, he found a seat in the reporters' gallery of Institution Hall. His preparation allowed him to report the convention in depth. He could now analyze the significance of various maneuvers and predict the strategy of the leaders.[4]

Before the end of the first day of the convention, Halstead saw a split developing in the ranks of the Democratic party. Stephen A. Douglas, the front-running candidate, found his position on slavery in the territories unpopular with southerners. Oregon and California delegates, supporters of President Buchanan, voted with those from the South to make a majority of the resolutions committee anti-Douglas. The platform, the antithesis of popular sovereignty, declared that the federal government had a duty to protect slavery in the territories. A minority report of the Douglas faction called for reaffirmation of the platform of 1856, which endorsed the Kansas-Nebraska Act, with the added proviso that the party abide by Supreme Court decisions on the right of property in the territories. The Republican reporter thought both platforms bad, although he considered the majority recommendations at least honest. He declared the minority report "a miserable and cowardly evasion." After a long and bitter debate, the Douglas platform carried in the convention. Halstead now called it the "most uncouth, disjointed, illogical, confused, mean, cowardly, and contemptible thing in the history of platforms."[5]

With the Douglas platform ratified, southern extremists seceded from the convention. Until the secession, Halstead said that the South had the preponderance of brains in the convention. Now he decided that the action of the extremists had proved him wrong.

He reported that the citizens of Charleston approved the secession, turning out enthusiastically to support the action of the seceders. In front of the courthouse a crowd of several thousand gathered, shouting for William L. Yancey, the Alabama fire-eater who led the fight for the majority report.[6]

With the southern delegates gone, and the two-thirds rule of the Democratic party applying to the total vote of the convention, Douglas did not have sufficient support for nomination. Calling for southern states to fill vacated seats with new delegates, the convention adjourned to meet on June 18 in Baltimore. The secessionists met at Military Hall and adopted the rejected platform. They also adjourned without making nominations, planning to reconvene on June 11 in Richmond.

Leaving Charleston for Washington on the last day of the conventions, Halstead felt that the sectional cleavages proved the "false pretense" of the Democratic party. He saw in the action in Charleston the party's final dissolution. Nothing could have been more fervently desired by the Republican editor, who wrote: "May it die hard."[7]

In 1860 many potential presidential candidates held seats in the United States Senate. Arriving in Washington only two days before the Constitutional Union convention met in Baltimore, Halstead hurried to the Senate reporters' gallery to observe the candidates in daily battle. He found Seward, Douglas, Jefferson Davis, and Chase on the floor, and took particular delight in describing their activities. He spared neither friend nor foe, although his partisanship showed in sketches of the Democrats. Actually, the senators seemed to be marking time until after the conventions, and so Halstead could only observe them and report their appearance.[8]

The old church in which the Baltimore convention met seemed appropriate for the Constitutional Union party. Halstead found the delegates all fine-looking and "eminently respectable" gentlemen, but he thought their convention "unanimated" and that the great issues of the day were being ignored. Fully resolved to save the country, and devotedly patriotic (the church had been decorated with a full-length painting of Washington, a carved American eagle, two great flags, and masses of smaller flags and tricolored drapery), the convention stressed fraternal feelings uniting the nation but did not attempt to resolve any of the issues dividing it.[9] According to Halstead, the only excitement of the convention occurred as delegates changed their votes to give John Bell, a Tennessee conservative, the presidential nomination. A sudden loud crash in the hall resulted in panic. The delegates, fearing the overcrowded balconies had started to collapse, rushed for the windows and doors. Actually only a bench had broken.

The convention, its candidates, and its platform drew this summary from the reporter: "The whole talk was of the Constitution, the Union and the laws, of harmony, fraternity, compromise, conciliation, peace, good will, common glory, national brotherhood, preservation of the confederacy. And of all these things it seemed to be understood the Convention had a monopoly. The Constitution, the Union, and peace between the sections would appear from the record of proceedings to be in the exclusive care of, and the peculiar institutions of, the no-party and no-platform gentlemen here assembled."[10] The conservatives had found no solution to the problems of the nation.

Halstead continued on his travels, arriving in Chicago before the May 16 opening of the Republican convention. As host to its first national party convention, Chicago had built the "Wigwam," a 10,000-seat wooden auditorium costing $7,000. Large crowds of visitors, reporters, and delegates filled the hotel lobbies and the streets.[11]

Halstead arrived in Chicago a firm supporter of William H. Seward of New York. He reported as objectively as he had for the other conventions, although he obviously supported this party and hoped for Seward's victory. Moreover, he failed to see, or at least to report, the significance of the platform. Seward's support came from the old abolitionist wing of the party; the platform rested on a broader base than the issue of slavery. The "Dutch Planks," which opposed any change in the immigration laws and demanded passage of a homestead act, and planks which supported river and harbor improvements and called for a Pacific railroad, made the platform sectional although not abolitionist.[12]

On the eve of the balloting, Halstead still predicted Seward's victory. He showed his disappointment when at the end of the third ballot a delegate from Ohio arose and gave Lincoln four additional votes and the nomination: "The fact of the Convention was the defeat of Seward rather than the nomination of Lincoln. It was the triumph of a presumption of availability over pre-eminence in intellect and unrivaled fame—a success of the ruder qualities of manhood and the more homely attributes of popularity over the arts of a consummate politician and the splendor of accomplished statesmanship."[13] Halstead believed that Lincoln's nomination proved the inability of conventions to take strong, meaningful action.

Leaving Chicago on the night train, Halstead discovered that Lincoln's choice had struck a responsive chord in Illinois and Indiana. At every station along the way tar barrels burned and cannons boomed. Although he still believed that the convention had made a mistake, he could understand the joy of these people who felt that one of their own had been nominated.[14]

When the southern Democrats, or Constitutional Democrats, as they preferred to be called, met in Richmond on June 11, Halstead was there. Few delegates attended, deciding to wait until after the regular Democrats met in Baltimore to take action. After two days of inconsequential debate, the meeting adjourned.[15] Once more Halstead stopped off in Washington, as did most of the Richmond delegates, for the latest capital gossip. From what he learned in Washington, the debates in Congress between conventions served to deepen the split within the party. The bitter personal nature of the controversy convinced him that two Democratic tickets would be nominated.[16]

The seceders, again under William L. Yancy's leadership, demanded readmission to the Democratic convention. The convention agreed, except in the cases where states had selected new delegates. This decision provoked a new secession which left only northern and border-state delegates and the southern replacements. On June 23 they nominated Stephen A. Douglas for the presidency.

The seceders met in Institute Hall on the last day of the regular Democratic convention and nominated Buchanan's vice-president, the moderate John C. Breckinridge of Kentucky, for president. When the greatly diminished Richmond group confirmed the second Baltimore nomination, Halstead returned to Cincinnati, knowing that it had no other choice.[17]

Halstead had written the most complete eyewitness accounts of all the conventions but the last Richmond meeting—a major attainment for his newspaper. Not even the larger eastern journals could boast such broad coverage. He received the great compliment of having his reports copied by many northern and midwestern newspapers, usually with full credit given to the author, although one newspaper even claimed to have its own special correspondent. This newspaper, the *Cleveland Herald,* changed a few words and then signed its articles with an "S." The *Commercial* editorially defended "On the Circuit of the Conventions," as it called the newsletters, from attacks of other newspapers. Honored by the copying and criticism, the *Commercial* seemed more amused than annoyed at the harping of jealous journals. However, criticism of Halstead's wrong guesses, without mentioning his correct predictions, annoyed the *Commercial*'s editorial writer. [18]

Nonetheless, the criticism and the copying proved that many had read the reports and had obtained their firsthand information of the conventions from the pen of Murat Halstead. The Columbus firm of Follett, Foster, and Company, publisher of the Lincoln-Douglas debates, noted the importance of these interesting and informative reports and brought out Halstead's newsletters in book form as a companion piece to William Dean Howells's 1860 campaign biography of Lincoln. [19] Halstead's often sarcastic commentary found few defenders among the politicians of 1860, but his reports remain a basic source for historians. In 1890, when Nicolay and Hay quoted him in their biography of Lincoln, Halstead received many requests for information about the book. He said that it could be found only in libraries with large collections, and had become a "curiosity." Nonetheless, this curiosity has been quoted by every major historian writing on Lincoln or the Civil War years. [20]

Although he remained disappointed that Seward failed to receive the nomination, Halstead threw the resources of the *Commercial* into the battle to secure Lincoln's election. He honestly believed Seward the stronger man. Only after Lincoln's death could Halstead appreciate the qualities which made him a great president.

The Republican victory led to ordinances in southern states dissolving the Union. At this point, Halstead began searching for a compromise solution. Cincinnati had close ties with the South. Some of her prominent citizens were of southern origin; many of her leading businessmen engaged in trade with southern states, and only a river separated her from a slave state. These close ties convinced many Cincinnatians of the impossibilitiy of compromise. Still Halstead urged that the national government take no coercive steps against the South. Instead, he proposed a national convention to end the old Union on lines satisfactory to all the states.

The firing on Sumter ended the editor's agitation for a national convention. The Union had been attacked, and he declared his loyalty to the national government. Potter did not share Halstead's apprehensions about Lincoln's abilities, and so the *Commercial* gave the president every chance to prove himself in office. While Halstead still felt Seward and Chase more able than Lincoln, he supported the administration for the good of the Union.[21]

Although the events of the day had personal meanings for the editor of the *Commercial*, Halstead's uppermost concern was how they would affect his newspaper. Although for several years Halstead had been introducing into the news-gathering practices of the *Commercial* many of the innovations that had by now become general, a revolution in journalism took place with the coming of the war. The most important of these innovations resulted from the necessity for prompt reporting and publishing of the news. A newspaper might still remain a sounding board for its editor's opinions, but without up-to-the-minute reports, its readers looked for another source of information. As armies marched off to battle, newspaper readers demanded more news. They refused to accept accounts of battles written weeks after they had happened. They demanded reporters on the spot whose stories might vicariously re-create the action, the suffering, and the bravery found on the field.[22]

For several years the *Commercial* had been receiving brief telegraphed reports of the latest New York and Washington news, which it supplemented by longer articles from the latest editions of the exchange newspapers or by reports from special correspondents. With the added emphasis on speed, Halstead looked to the telegraph.

Though the idea of reporters stationed around the country had yet to become a part of American journalism, many newspapers had special correspondents in Washington or shared one with another paper. The war changed all this. The major journals tried to have a staff of reporters with each army. To bring the reading public the complete picture of a battle meant that reporters had to be on the front lines with the men, at army headquarters with commanders, and at points of vantage to see the whole sweep of the fighting. Few newspapers could fulfill all these requirements, although many tried. Although the *Commercial* attempted to have correspondents with each of the major armies, it could not compete with the leading eastern papers. Often reporters from the

New York *Tribune* or *Times* sent articles to the *Commercial;* sometimes Halstead became a special correspondent.[23]

Halstead spent most of the month of June 1861 in and around Washington sending a daily newsletter to the *Commercial*. In his first dispatch from the capital, Halstead began to criticize the war actions of military officers and government officials. This criticism later caused journalistic rivals to give him the title "Field Marshal." Soon after Halstead arrived in Washington he visited the camps of the Ohio regiments. After passing the tents of beautifully uniformed and well-supplied volunteers from other states, he said he was mortified by the Ohio soldiers, finding them both demoralized and without proper uniforms. In one indignant newsletter, he said that these troops had been hurried out of the state unprepared. Once they had left Ohio, a dispute arose between state and federal officials over who had the responsibility to provide for them. While this argument was still in progress, Halstead reported that some uniforms had been sent, though of material comparable to paper. The seams of the trousers, he wrote, "could be pulled open with the fingers." Since Ohio had appropriated a million dollars for her troops, he asked why they had to appear as paupers by comparison with those of other states.[24]

Halstead's reports and the protests of Ohio congressmen in Washington were eventually successful. By June 10, he wrote that the troops had been given new uniforms and that they would receive a month's pay the next day. He declared that if the government granted a liberal furlough policy, the men would stay in the army until the end of the war.[25]

During the month Halstead spent in Washington hardly a day passed without his finding some bit of military strategy or civil administration that required modification or correction. Although he was critical of Secretary Gideon Welles's handling of the Navy Department (Cincinnati boatbuilders complained they had not been receiving their fair share of the contracts), the editor concluded that Simon Cameron's administration of the War Department remained the greatest problem: "No one ever suspected Cameron of honesty, but there were hopes that he had business capacity and that . . . he would make a reputation for integrity. In truth, however, he is very incompetent. . . . Cameron attends to the stealing department. . . . It would be of greater advantage to the country than to gain a battle, to have Cameron kicked out of the Cabinet." Specifically, Halstead charged that Cameron was incapable of running his department, and that General Winfield Scott and Secretary of the Treasury Salmon P. Chase did most of the work. Moreover, he said that all of Cameron's relatives either had been placed in the War Department in lucrative jobs or sold goods to the army at highly inflated prices.[26] Halstead reported that he had met a fellow Cincinnatian who had come to the capital to gain a contract for his foundry to cast cannon balls. Cameron told the foundryman that he had decided to give the contract to some Pennsylvania foundries; the cynical Halstead concluded that the Pennsylvania foundries probably belonged to Simon Cameron. The only person in the cabinet Halstead praised was Chase. Halstead said that Chase did the work of the secretary of war and asserted the whole administration would collapse without him.[27]

One recurring theme of Halstead's Washington newsletters concerned censorship. When he learned information about battles or troop movements, he had to contend with the censor in the telegraph office. Reporters from New York papers told him that censors always cut dispatches with correct intelligence and passed them when wrong. Halstead realized that the enemy might gain advantages from the reports of resourceful newsmen who learned advance army plans; he believed this information should be kept from the telegraph. He mainly criticized the way the censors applied the rules.[28]

There seemed to be no easy solution to the problem. Commanders claimed that knowledge gained from northern newspapers allowed the southern army to escape traps or prepare for action when the northern plans called for surprise. On the other hand, Halstead and other northern editors asserted that the reading public had a right to news about the army. The problem centered on the censors' inability to make intelligent decisions on what news to release and what to withhold. The controversy resulted in bad feelings between the reporters and the War Department.[29]

Some commanders even barred reporters from their camps. Halstead's most serious conflict with a northern general occurred in December 1861. Henry Villard, a German immigrant who had covered Lincoln's campaign for the *New York Herald* (and later gained control of the Northern Pacific Railroad), represented the *Commercial* and New York newspapers at General William Tecumseh Sherman's headquarters in Louisville. In November, Secretary of War

Cameron arrived for an inspection visit. For several weeks other guests at Sherman's hotel watched him pacing up and down the corridors hour after hour so preoccupied that he did not seem to notice his surroundings. This preoccupation led to gossip about Sherman's mental condition. When Cameron arrived in Louisville, Sherman asked for a private interview to discuss the military situation in the West. A reporter for the *New York Tribune* traveling with Cameron attended the meeting with Sherman. During the course of the talk the general told the secretary he needed at least two hundred thousand men to march south. The *Tribune* man later told Villard of this figure and said that he felt Sherman must be "unhinged."[30]

When this news became known in Louisville, many people, remembering the reports of Sherman's strange behavior in his hotel, concluded that he must be insane and should be removed from command. The rumor soon spread that he feared a southern invasion, and might take his army to Indiana, abandoning Louisville. Since the people of Louisville believed that any accusations they might make about Sherman would be attributed to their southern leanings, they met with Villard and asked him to report their fears to Halstead, a man of unquestioned loyalty to the northern cause. This resulted in the *Commercial* headline "General Sherman Insane."[31]

Sherman may have been overworked, but all those close to him could testify to his sanity. Asking to be relieved of his command, he returned to his Lancaster, Ohio, home briefly, then went to St. Louis, where he served temporarily in a subordinate position. Sherman's anger about the incident found an outlet in a continuing hostility to the press, and Halstead in particular. In his memoirs he said: "The newspapers kept up their game as though instigated by malice, and chief among them was the Cincinnati *Commercial,* whose editor, Halsted [*sic*] was generally believed to be an honorable man. P. B. Ewing [Sherman's brother-in-law], being in Cincinnati, saw him and asked him why he, who certainly knew better, would reiterate such a damaging slander. He answered, quite cavalierly, that it was one of the news-items of the day, and he had to keep up with the time; but he would be most happy to publish any correction I might make, as though I could deny such a malicious piece of scandal affecting myself."[32] Sherman never trusted reporters, and often lectured them on what they could and could not say about his plans and ideas. After this incident, a reporter could expect to receive scant information from Sherman's army. Sherman even ordered many from his camps. Reporters from the *Commercial* were particularly unwelcome.[33]

From the outbreak of the fighting, Halstead and the *Commercial* supported the war and the Union completely, although this did not mean blind support for party politics. Halstead's stand on these two matters brought him into conflict with many in Ohio, particularly the *Cincinnati Enquirer*, a Democratic newspaper and the *Commercial*'s closest rival, and Clement Vallandigham, a Democratic congressman from Dayton. The "Peace Democrat" position which Vallandigham and the *Enquirer* upheld conflicted with Halstead's uncompromising support of the Union. Thus, as early as July 1861, Halstead called Vallandigham and the editor of the *Enquirer* "semi-secesh," beginning a course of almost daily abuse directed against the Dayton congressman and the entire staff of the *Enquirer*.

Halstead constantly complained that the *Enquirer* did serious injury to the national cause. Its daily manifestations of sympathy with the South encouraged that section to carry on the war. Whenever politicians, "whose tongues are uttering . . . treason," made a statement, the "pitiful, whining, sneaking, snarling" *Enquirer* could be counted upon to spread their sensational exaggerations. This type of editing deceived the South with the impression that the great masses of northern people lacked loyalty for the Union. Nothing could be farther from the truth, because there existed an "inexorable resolution to wipe out in blood the insolence of the rebels."[34]

Halstead asked why the federal authorities allowed the *Enquirer*, an "organ of the traitors . . . the border guerrilla sheet, the comforter of assassins, the solace of horse thieves, the favorite of house burners," to continue to publish, since the encouragement the newspaper gave the enemy prolonged the war and caused the murders of young men fighting under the Union's flag.[35]

Part of Halstead's criticism of the *Enquirer* stemmed from its support of the Peace Democrats, and Vallandigham in particular. The Peace Democrats, or Copperheads (Halstead called them "venomous and crawling creatures . . . sticking their heads out of holes, and darting their forked tongues as if they would like to bite"), felt that a peaceful solution might be found to end the conflict.[36] The Copperheads insisted that the use of force for the preservation of the Union was both unconstitutional and futile. They argued that only a "union of hearts and hands" could endure.[37]

To Halstead the problem had become peace or the preservation of the Union; between the two he saw no possible compromise. What did Vallandigham do when the secessionists seized United States forts, robbed United States arsenals, and fired on Fort Sumter? Only when the nation assumed an attitude of self-defense and he could see the demands of justice being executed did the congressman become excited. "The blood of the innocent victim didn't disturb [him], but the hanging of the criminal was frightful."[38]

Halstead asserted that Vallandigham and the *Enquirer* had discouraged young men from volunteering for the army. They argued that a "nigger war" should not involve northern white men. Halstead insisted that the question of slavery should be secondary to that of the preservation of the Union. Although he believed the war would result in crushing the institution of slavery, its real objective should be to vindicate the laws of the nation. In many editorials he criticized "rabid antislavery agitators," stating that antislavery men often furnished the Copperheads their best material in their war against the government.[39]

As the 1862 fall elections approached, Halstead became convinced that the real danger was not "that the armies of the Union will fall in a fair fight," but that the internal dissensions raised by such demagogues as Vallandigham would shatter the confidence of the people in their government. To Halstead, the choice was simple. The nominees of the Union party pledged their support to the administration and the Union, and deserved the support of all loyal citizens. The Democratic nominees dedicated themselves to the embarrassment of the administration. Their election could only give comfort to the enemy. The *Commercial* waged its major campaign in the fall of 1862 against Vallandigham's reelection to Congress. Vallandigham's district had been gerrymandered by the state legislature to include overwhelmingly Republican Warren County. The Democrats could justly claim that this alone made his defeat possible. To stop the criticism, Halstead called for Vallandigham's defeat in the old district as well as the reorganized area. If he could not be beaten, the disgrace would be "black, burning, and infinitely shameful."[40]

Vallandigham lost, although the Union party suffered many other defeats. George Pendleton, the Democratic congressman from Cincinnati's first district, had been reelected even though Halstead editorialized that Pendleton invariably voted with Vallandigham and gave speeches "tinctured with a tender feeling towards the rebel in arms."[41]

Halstead found several reasons to explain the action of the voters. Many voters believed that Democratic victories would end the war. Others, dissatisfied with the administration's conduct of the war, voted Democratic as a protest. Some had been influenced by racial prejudice. Then too, many thousands of soldiers in the field, who supported the Union ticket, could not vote.[42]

Although Halstead still insisted that the administration remained the nation's best hope for victory, he admitted the validity of some of the criticisms. He felt the prospect of indefinite war had produced cynicism in the country. For months at a time, large segments of the army remained idle, battles produced no decisive results, and even victories resulted in no real advances. Although many factors contributed to this situation, he said that under the American political system the administration must take responsibility for defeat if it wished to receive credit for victory.[43]

Embittered by his defeat, Vallandigham became even more defiant in his antiwar speeches. He continuously urged peace between sections by conciliation, and denounced the unconstitutional measures of the Lincoln administration. Halstead believed his utterances treasonable, and General Ambrose Burnside, commander of the Department of Ohio, agreed. In General Order No. 38, Burnside announced his intention to arrest anyone who declared sympathy for the enemy. In a speech at Mt. Vernon, Vallandigham denounced the war and attacked General Order No. 38, declaring his authority "General Order No. 1—the Constitution." Burnside placed Vallandigham under arrest and tried him by a military commission, whose authority Vallandigham refused to recognize. Found guilty, the former congressman was sentenced to prison for the duration of the war. The trial and conviction made Vallandigham a martyr for the Peace Democrats' cause and immensely increased his popularity in Ohio. Lincoln realized that Burnside had blundered, and changed the sentence to exile to the Confederacy. Sent to Tennessee by the military authorities, Vallandigham traveled to the east coast, then continued to Canada by ship. The Ohio Democratic convention, which met in June of 1863, in reaction to the alleged unconstitutionality of Vallandigham's trial and sentence, nominated him as their candidate for governor.[44]

John Brough, a former Democratic state auditor who had retired from politics before the war to become president of a railroad, received the Union party nomination. Brough delivered a strong Union speech in Marietta, which convinced Halstead that the issues between the two parties had been squarely joined. The editor declared Ohio on trial. Should Vallandigham win, the victory would be hailed by southern rebels, British Tories, French interventionists, and northern traitors, "by all the enemies of America," as their victory. It would "[presage] the irretrievable downfall of the Union."[45]

Halstead first realized during the campaign that the arrest and trial of the Democratic candidate had been a mistake. Vallandigham in exile proved to be a strong candidate. Halstead said that Vallandigham would lose thousands of votes by campaigning in Ohio. Moreover, he thought that the Democrats realized this and refused to accept Lincoln's liberal pardon terms in order to keep the candidate in Canada.[46]

Brough won with over a 100,000-vote majority, allowing the relieved editor to claim that the victory proved Ohio's wholehearted support of the Union.[47] With its defeat in the election, Copperheadism no longer posed a serious threat to the Union. Vallandigham also lost much of his influence in the Democratic party, and when he returned before the end of the war, the government, rather than give him added publicity and notoriety, chose to ignore his presence.[48]

Halstead traveled to Washington for the December 1, 1862, opening of Congress. As on his earlier visits, he secured a pass and rode out to inspect the fortifications that circled the city. He found every elevation crowned with a fort. Acres of underbrush had been cleared and the fences all removed. What only two years before had been rich farm land was now a vast waste dotted by encampments and forts connected by long lines of rifle pits and occasional placements of siege guns. From what he saw, Halstead concluded that Washington was reasonably safe. He thus wondered why the government retained such large numbers of troops for defense when they could be used to better advantage elsewhere: "Why not use [them] to take Richmond?" Many northern editors urged the government to march on the Confederate capital. Halstead believed Richmond remained uncaptured because the nation did not have a man at the head of its military affairs who could promptly and competently dispatch executive business.[49]

Halstead heard rumors of approaching action, and his newspaper-man's instincts demanded that he try to get the story. After much difficulty, he secured passes to join the Army of the Potomac. When Lincoln relieved General McClellan of command of the Army of the Potomac and appointed General Ambrose Burnside as his successor, Halstead defended the president's action. Democratic newspapers complained that Lincoln had succumbed to radical antislavery pressure in his removal of the conservative McClellan; Halstead disagreed. The president wanted a man of action, and Halstead believed that he had him in Burnside. Now that the long-awaited march on Richmond might finally start, the Cincinnati editor planned to be with the new commander's army.[50]

Halstead spent two days securing his passes; they remained in his pocket from the time he left the War Department until he reached General Burnside's tent in Virginia, where he arrived on the evening of December 13. Although welcomed, he was warned that the Union army intended to cross the Rappahannock the next day. An hour before dawn, operations commenced. The troops, taking up their haversacks and cartridge boxes, marched off to the Battle of Fredericksburg.[51]

Although Halstead had no formal training as a military reporter, he quickly realized that the battle was a "blunder and disaster." Historians have agreed with his judgment. Randall called it one of the "colossal blunders of the War."[52] In a signed editorial, one of the few in all the files of the *Commercial*, Halstead declared the battle "hopeless from the beginning." The large rebel army commanded a formidable natural position and had well-placed artillery. The whole situation "was an enormous trap, and the Union army had to withdraw at once or worse would yet come."[53]

Ohio regiments suffered heavily. Halstead, who had friends among the casualties, experienced guilt for not being in the ranks with them. Potter, a semi-invalid by this time, had prevented his enlistment by insisting that an effective writer could do more for the Union with a pen than with a gun. Returning to Cincinnati after the battle, Halstead voiced his fears for the Union cause. His spirits revived with the announcement of Burnside's resignation and the appointment of General Joseph Hooker. Halstead called Hooker a fighting man who could restore the confidence of the army.[54]

The *Commercial* supported the administration from the beginning of the war. Although the evidence shows that Halstead felt Lincoln managed the war poorly, the editor's desire to present an undivided front to the South restrained his published criticisms of the president: "It did not seem to me there was any other way of going on. If the country was gone, why chaos and black night would come."[55]

Halstead received constant reports of Lincoln's administrative failures from Secretary of the Treasury Salmon P. Chase. Chase had three major complaints: that the "inadequate administration" made it impossible for him to maintain the public credit, that the unfit men appointed to high command had prolonged the war by years, and that Lincoln never listened to his advice. Chase convinced Halstead of the president's inability to cope with the problems of the war.[56]

Halstead's private opinions can best be seen in a group of letters written to Timothy E. Day, a Cincinnati congressman. In one he said: "Lincoln is simply of no account. He is a little in the way, that's all. He don't [sic] add anything to the strength of the Government—not a thing. He is very busy with trifles, and lets everybody do as they please. He is opposed to stealing, but can't see the stealing that is done. I use the mildest phrase when I say he is a weak, a miserably weak man."[57] The harsh and unrestrained manner of this letter shows Halstead's contempt for the president. Yet his private contempt rarely found its way into the columns of the *Commercial*.

Halstead directed his strongest criticism at the activities of various members of the cabinet. Since much of his information came from Chase, it can be assumed that he expressed Chase's opinions when he denounced such cabinet members as Simon Cameron and Gideon Welles.

Official and personal relations between Chase and Lincoln became severely strained by the last months of 1863. Chase used his position to scheme for the presidential nomination in 1864, forcing Lincoln to ask for his resignation from the cabinet. Nonetheless, when Chief Justice Roger Taney died in October 1864, Halstead and many other Ohioans called upon Lincoln to appoint the former secretary to the vacancy. Halstead argued that even though the president disliked Chase, the people wanted him appointed. A good politician, Lincoln realized the advantages of having Chase removed from politics. He thus yielded to the onslaught from the Ohioans and made the appointment.[58]

As the war progressed, Halstead's private criticism of the president became less frequent. He supported Lincoln's nomination for a second term and once again used the full weight of the *Commercial* to help in his reelection. Throughout the campaign he believed Lincoln would win, but he demanded more than victory; the presidential election should serve as a symbol of American loyalty to the government and its leaders, to prove to America's enemies that the people stood behind the Union.[59]

Throughout 1864, in editorials and letters, a definite softening of Halstead's personal hostility to Lincoln and his government may be seen. He termed Lincoln's post-election speeches "magnanimous in sentiment" and praised them for their conciliatory tone. The inaugural message received praise as a "sensible, quaint, brief document, expressing deep religious feeling as well as patriotic sentiments."[60]

In April 1865 Halstead wrote an editorial entitled "The Surrender of Lee!" Yet in the midst of the joy came the word of Lincoln's assassination. Halstead no longer felt the contempt for the president he had at the beginning of the war. Now he could write that in all the world no life had proved so valuable to the people as Lincoln's. He declared that the president had matured under his great responsibilities and, with his new maturity, good sense, and kindness of heart, had been the hope of the nation.[61]

Years later, speaking before the first Ohio Lincoln Day Banquet in 1888, Halstead said that his love and admiration for Chase had blinded him to the "serious greatness" of Lincoln. He now believed that many of the differences between the two men resulted from their vastly different personalities. Chase had a brilliant mind, but often acted rashly. In addition to intelligence, Lincoln also had patience. In summary, Halstead quoted Chase, "I do not know but he was wiser than all of us."[62]

By the end of the war, Murat Halstead had become one of America's leading journalists. Beginning with his widely read reports from the national party conventions of 1860, and continuing with his strong and often controversial stands on the war issues, his reputation as a forceful and independent reporter made him one of the country's best-known newsmen. His news-gathering initiatives and technical innovations demonstrated his abilities as an editor. By 1865 the *Commercial* had become Ohio's leading newspaper. Halstead had become recognized as the force behind the *Commercial*. As such, he had assured his position of power in local, state, and national affairs.

3

The Making of a Journalist

In the years immediately following the war, the *Commercial* grew and prospered. Under Halstead's leadership the newspaper expanded its news-gathering operations and continued innovations in its printing and technical facilities. Halstead's reputation as both editor and reporter rose with that of his newspaper. By 1870 he could claim friendship with the most influential leaders of American journalism, literature, business, and politics. Moreover, in the East he emerged as the chief spokesman for western journalism.

Part of Halstead's national prominence stemmed from his leadership of western publishers in a dispute with the New York Associated Press. In the years before the war the leading New York City and Brooklyn newspapers cooperated in establishing the New York association. Originally formed to share the cost of sending boats to meet incoming transatlantic ships for the latest European news, the association soon began sending telegraphic news reports from New York and Washington to newspapers across the country. The western newspapers, which received these reports from the association, had no control over their content. When the war started, western newspapers assigned their own correspondents to the field. They discovered that their men could report as well as the representatives of the New York dailies. Consequently, a movement began among western publishers to gain more control over the content of the news purchased from the New York association. [1]

Late in 1862, at a meeting in Indianapolis, representatives of newspapers of Cincinnati, Cleveland, Pittsburgh, Chicago, Detroit, Louisville, and St. Louis decided to unite to work out their differences with the New York dailies. An executive committee, chaired by Joseph Medill of the *Chicago Tribune,* negotiated the right to place an agent in the association's office to file a 1,000-word dispatch at night and a 300-word dispatch in the afternoon. This would give the western journals some control over the reports.

This agreement did not solve the conflict between the New York association and western newspapers with their differing news needs. At the western publishers' second meeting, Halstead suggested revising the contract to allow the western newspapers a choice in the length of the New York dispatches. Under this system, newspapers with large resources could purchase more news. Although they did approve adding five hundred additional words to the night telegram and doubling the dispatch for the afternoon papers, the New York newspapers refused to allow this flexibility. All newspapers continued to receive the same reports with no control over the content.[2]

Many differences existed between western journalists and the New York association. The westerners complained that they often received wordy, sensational, and unreliable dispatches containing editorial opinion from the New York newspapers rather than straight news. At their 1864 meeting in Detroit, the delegates decided that a formal organization might have more success with the New York group. Thus the Michigan legislature incorporated the Western Associated Press.[3]

For the next two years the westerners perfected their own organization by establishing rules governing news-gathering and dispatching techniques and by persuading other western newspapers to join the association. By 1866, the Western Association felt strong enough to assert its demands. The public appetite for news, whetted by the war, continued unabated. The Atlantic cable, the consolidation of telegraph lines under unified management, and the establishment of new journals made it possible to satisfy this appetite. The older newspapers of the West realized that they needed to strengthen their position in order to gain the advantages of these additional news sources.

As both president of its board of directors and a member of its executive committee, Halstead had become one of the leading figures in the Western Association by 1866. He infused life and courage into an essentially feeble organization. When a second national news service from New York began operation in November, he took the lead in formulating an ultimatum to the New York Association. Earlier, the westerners drew up a bill of particulars outlining their grievances. They objected to being forced to pay for marine reports from the Atlantic and Pacific coasts, local legislative and political intelligence, announcements of the arrival and departure of vessels at foreign ports, and news needed by the New York commercial class but of no use to their own readers. Moreover, the Western Association claimed that the expenses for gathering the news had been lumped into an account called "the original collection of news." The western press, charged on a pro-rata basis, could not examine the books. Finally, they protested that the seven-member New York Association maintained a monopoly in the city while encouraging the establishment of new journals in the rest of the country.[4]

In their ultimatum the directors of the Western Association demanded the correction of these abuses. They proposed the establishment of an exchange system allowing the Western Association to supply western news in return for news from the East. The executive committee headed by Halstead received full power to negotiate with the New York Association. On November 27 Halstead and Horace White of the *Chicago Tribune* threatened to subscribe to the second news service unless the New York Association met their demands.

The New York Association answered the challenge by declaring that any newspaper accepting news from a rival organization could no longer use its service. On receipt of this answer, Halstead and White made a contract with the United States and Europe Telegraphic News Association to supply the Western Association with east coast and European dispatches. They then informed the papers that retained the New York Associated Press service that they could no longer have the western report. Nearly all western and southwestern newspapers decided to accept the service of the new company.[5]

A special meeting of the Western Association, in Chicago on December 12, approved the executive committee's action. The westerners also decided to sever all relations with the New York Association, to inaugurate a campaign to recruit more members, and to include New York newspapers in the new organization.

The brisk rivalry between the two associations lasted only a few weeks. The key to ultimate victory lay in the action taken by the New England Association and James Gordon Bennett, whose *New York Herald* ran its own news service. The westerners gained the advantage when the New England Association agreed to a contract with the western group. Bennett, in return for concessions for his service, also agreed to cooperate with the West. In this situation, the New York papers decided to conclude peace, and Halstead negotiated a mutually acceptable arrangement. New contracts, dated January 11, 1867, agreed to a division of territory and an exchange of news. The New York Association received payment for foreign news, both associations pledged mutual respect for each other's monopoly of their self-assigned fields, and the westerners gained a most-favored-treatment clause for telegraph rates.

In a confidential letter to the members of the Western Association, Halstead said that he regarded the new contracts as a complete victory for the association: "The contract establishes the independence of the Western Associated Press, its complete control over its own affairs, the collection, compilation, and transmission of news, and over the news agents within its own lines." The complaints of the Western Association had now been eliminated.[6]

The two press associations worked in cooperation for the next sixteen years. In 1882 they decided to merge their management. This resulted in a more efficient operation which saved expenses. A joint executive committee of Charles H. Dana of the *New York Sun*, Whitelaw Reid of the *New York Tribune*, Richard Smith, now Halstead's partner on the newly formed *Commercial Gazette*, W. N. Haldeman of the *Louisville Courier-Journal*, and James Gordon Bennett of the *New York Herald* took over the management of the new "Associated Press." William Henry Smith, who had been a reporter on both the *Commercial* and the *Gazette* and general manager of the Western Associated Press, became general manager of the joint operation with headquarters in New York.[7]

Halstead also gained national prominence through his leadership of a group of editors who claimed that a newspaper should be independent of political parties and pressure groups. These editors, which included Horace Greeley of the *New York Tribune*, Horace White of the *Chicago Tribune*, and Samuel Bowles of the *Springfield Republican*, believed that their newspapers' editorial policies should be completely separated from influence by any particular interest group. Opposed to the idea that a newspaper should be the mouthpiece of a particular politician or party, they looked upon the field of journalism as a business, and attempted to run their newspapers along sound business lines. They also felt that a newspaper's income should be based on its circulation and advertising revenue. Moreover, they believed that advertising revenue should result from a newspaper's ability to transmit the advertiser's message, not its editorial policy. This philosophy of newspaper management became known as "independent journalism."[8]

Halstead led the independent journalism movement from the first. By training and temperament, he disliked the shackles imposed on the editor of a political organ; he believed that an effective newspaper had to be completely free to present the news without color or favor. The clearest statement of Halstead's philosophy of journalism can be found in an address he delivered to the Kentucky State Press Association on May 20, 1874. In this address he said that a newspaper should be an influence for good. To be such an influence, the editor had to present truth, and to Halstead truth meant news. The editor should neither color nor tamper with his report, no matter how unattractive, unwholesome, or damaging. Since American citizens had the responsibility to govern themselves, they needed facts, not instructions from editors, to be well informed. An editor must always assume his readers capable of accepting facts. Halstead also believed that American journalism should be a force for the restoration of public faith. To accomplish this, American journalism must become dissociated from political bosses and rings.[9]

Halstead said that public confidence could be regained only if newspapers refuse to print any paid matter except advertisements. This "was the essential feature of independent journalism." Moreover, an advertiser in selecting a newspaper made a purely business transaction. The businessman did not patronize the press; the press furnished him the means of reaching the public. The purchase bought only the best possible space, not the right to influence editorial policy.[10]

Halstead maintained that official advertising remained the greatest obstacle to a truly independent press. The private advertiser, to receive the greatest value for his money, patronized the paper with the largest circulation. Public advertising became an award for backing winning political candidates. The great mass of public advertising paid for political support. With official advertising as an end, many editors subverted their newspapers by giving support to unworthy men. Consequently, public advertising actually endangered the freedom of the press as it compelled support through the threat of its discontinuance. Although Halstead admitted that it was impossible to abolish official advertising, its influence might be reduced through a formula to distribute it equitably among all newspapers. The loss of liberty could come just as easily from official favoritism as from official oppression. [11]

Halstead believed newspaper owners owed it to their readers to "draw the line" between features of an entertaining, informative, and instructive nature and those for individual advancement. In other words, paid matter should never be published so as to conceal the fact. For a newspaper to have any editorial influence, its reading public must know that its editorial articles could not be purchased. [12]

Halstead's independent journalism did not mean the removal of editorial opinion from the newspaper. The editor should express opinions on almost every topic of the day, but these opinions should be placed on the editorial page, not interspersed with the news. An independent newspaper could be partisan and still be a great force for truth. When an editor accepted no money from a political party or an interest group, he could give his readers the truth. Moreover, his opinions would command respect.

Halstead stated that he always had been guided by these principles; he had never asked or received, directly or indirectly, a price for silence or for favor. He enjoyed absolute independence in journalism. "There is no influence that can affect my purpose to speak with freedom of those who are plotting forever in public affairs for their private advantage." Even near the end of a long career, he still said that he had never written an editorial for any money except his salary as a writer. [13]

The editor said there were no principles of the press greater than the privileges of the people. Although any citizen had the right to speak or write the truth, the far wider audience of the newspaper gave it a greater responsibility. On the whole, the press in the United States failed in its responsibilities. This could best be seen in the fact that a political "boss" held power in almost every city, county, and state in the country. This situation could be corrected by editors earnestly and constantly telling the truth, irrespective of considerations of personal, political, or monetary advancement. The rule of the corrupt rings could be overturned, and the strongest, thriftiest, and most honorable republican form of government firmly established.[14]

Halstead's overall philosophy of journalism can be summarized in his own words:

> . . . if we accept no favors, we may exact justice. If we can claim for ourselves only what we earn, we can deny to others that which they do not deserve.
>
> The thing needful in establishing a base of operations for the help of the people against those who are mighty in aiming to devour their substance, is integrity; and with it belong the courage of convictions and the consciousness of independence. With these we are equipped for the field, and the field is the world.[15]

For journalism to be effective, it must be independent. Moreover, an independent journalism can be a force to change the world.

One of the best examples of Halstead's independent journalism in this period can be found in his editorial treatment of the administration of President Andrew Johnson. The editor had little confidence in Johnson's ability. Yet, as a firm supporter of the Union, Halstead withheld editorial judgment and gave the president the opportunity to prove himself in office. Halstead found that he agreed with Johnson on reconstruction policy. Like the president's, Halstead's main concern through the years of the war had been the preservation of the Union. Now that the northern armies had been victorious, he wished to reestablish normal relations between sections as soon as possible. Thus, following a course markedly different from other Republican papers, such as the *Cincinnati Gazette,* the *Commercial* gave Johnson editorial support throughout 1865 and until the early summer of the next year.[16]

By the summer of 1866, the composition of the new Congress to be elected in the autumn assumed great importance to the nation's political leaders. Johnson needed to rally conservatives to his position to keep the new Congress from the complete domination of radical Republicans. Consequently, the president called a national convention of the Union party to be held in Philadelphia. The convention, a conservative gathering which included many Democrats, met in August. All the states, both North and South, sent representatives. Unfortunately, many moderates did not attend. Moreover, many moderate and conservative Republicans, whom Johnson counted on to make the convention a success, thought it represented a break with Republicanism and refused to join the movement. From the time of the convention, Halstead's ardor for Johnson's administration began to cool. While seemingly maintaining an impartial position, his editorials became more critical. [17]

Halstead's growing alienation from Johnson, brought on primarily by the president's increasing Democratic support, caused him to decide that the president had to take responsibility for reconstruction problems. The president's "inherent and perverse obstinancy" kept him from being reconciled with the majority in both houses of Congress. Thus, in less than a year, Halstead's editorial support for Johnson changed to condemnation. When the October congressional elections returned an almost unbroken line of Republicans to Washington, Halstead declared the Johnson-Democratic coalition broken, with those who had saved the country from rebellion standing firm on principles that had made them victorious in war. [18]

As Halstead received reports from Washington of the deepening struggle between president and Congress, the editorial policy of the *Commercial* once more began to shift. While he now placed the blame on the shoulders of Johnson, he could not hold the radicals blameless, since he believed it wrong to inflict vindictive punishment upon the South. Until the summer of 1867, the *Commercial*'s editorials remained hostile to the president, although without the extreme bitterness of the campaign period.

Although he did not personally support Johnson, the impeachment found Halstead strongly on the side of the presidency. He called the impeachment political, and defended the institution of the presidency. He claimed that a case of malfeasance in office had not been proved by congressional radicals. When the Senate trial began on March 13, 1868, Chase presided in his capacity as chief justice and William S. Groesbeck, a Cincinnati acquaintance of the editor's, served as a defense attorney. During the trial, Halstead asserted that because of the hatred for the man Johnson, the office of the presidency should not be violated by impeachment. He said the Republican party had backed itself into a corner on impeachment. The best course for the party "would be to show the capacity to do justice, though provoked and tempted rather to deal harshly and unjustly." Thus when the Senate returned the verdict of "not guilty," the editor called it a "triumph for sound principles in government."[19]

The *Commercial*'s editorials throughout Johnson's administration justified its masthead slogan: "An Independent, but not a Nonpartisan Newspaper." The *Commercial* continued to be independent. Though Halstead disagreed with Johnson on many points, he still supported him when he thought his position deserving. At the same time, the *Commercial* remained "not Non-partisan." Halstead believed in the Republican party. Although he could point to mistakes, he thought that these reflected on the poor leadership of the party, not the underlying principles that he supported.

Halstead also improved the technical plant of the *Commercial* during this period. The war had brought many changes in the process of news gathering and printing. The *Commercial*, which had greatly increased its circulation and advertising during the war, attempted to keep abreast of the latest technical advances in the field. With the largest Cincinnati circulation, and an advertising revenue of $55,732 for 1863, Halstead felt that the *Commercial* could well afford more modern equipment, and set about planning a radical transformation of its printing process.[20]

The primary purpose of his changes—to gain greater speed in production—meant that the newspaper might go to press later, allowing the editorial staff more time for its work. It also meant that news received later in the night could be included in next morning's edition, and, in the case of a truly important newsbreak, an extra edition could be quickly printed. His first innovation meant printing from stereotype plates instead of type forms. The stereotype process called for pressing upon the type surface layers of wet tissue paper which when dry became a mold for any number of thin metal castings. Thus, with only one setting of type, any number of presses could be used to reproduce the same material. The *Commercial* used two presses from mid-October 1864, thereby reducing the printing time by half. The *Commercial* became the first newspaper outside New York City to adopt the stereotype process.[21]

Potter had grown very wealthy through his years of ownership of the *Commercial*, and had constructed a new office building at Fourth and Race streets both for an investment and to house the *Commercial*'s operations. He had a twenty-two-foot-deep basement built to house the printing rooms. He installed the stereotype process and completely new Hoe high-speed cylinder presses when the *Commercial* moved into its new building. The new $30,000 presses had just been put into operation when the Hoe Company announced a perfecting press that printed both sides at once, cut the paper into page size, and folded it. The secret lay in using a continuous roll of newsprint running between two cylinders. Halstead convinced Potter to adopt the even newer and more advanced system. The printers had just become accustomed to the stereotype process and presses when the new machinery arrived.

On October 23, 1865, the *Commercial* became the first newspaper west of the Alleghenies to be printed on a Hoe eight-page rotary press. An increase to eight pages—it had been a folio, or four—and a reduction from nine to six columns made it less cumbersome. Larger print and topically assembled advertising put the paper on a parity in appearance with the most advanced eastern journals. Two weeks later Halstead introduced a successful Sunday edition. Relying heavily on literary features, Halstead built Sunday circulation to 10,000 during the first year.[22]

When Potter died on April 3, 1866, Halstead came into active control of the newspaper. He established the firm of M. Halstead and Company, a copartnership of active and special partners. The active partners, like Halstead, had acquired ownership under Potter and remained interested in some phase of the business. The special partners, Potter's widow and his daughter Mrs. Julia Pomeroy, held interest in the company but had no part in its operation. The *Enquirer* soon began to accuse Halstead of defrauding the Potter heirs. The attacks continued for over ten years. In 1877 Mrs. Potter published a letter in which she declared the *Enquirer*'s accusations false. She said Halstead had always acted in an honorable manner, and that her husband had told her to place her complete confidence in him.[23]

At the time of Mrs. Pomeroy's death, Halstead dissolved the partnership and purchased the shares of her estate, Mrs. Potter's shares, and those of one of the active partners. He then chartered a stock company. Far from defrauding the heirs, Halstead stated that the worth of the company at the time of Potter's death had been set at $100,000 by the appraisers, although he had insisted on $300,000 in order to include the accumulated goodwill. The new stock company had a paper value of $400,000.[24]

In these years Halstead employed several reporters who later gained national fame. Henry Villard, who became a leading railroad promoter in the 1870s and later the owner of the *New York Evening Post,* reported during the war. Donn Piatt became the *Commercial's* Washington correspondent in 1868. Piatt had an innovative style, and Halstead gave him free rein in exploiting his method. It consisted of personal comment, lightened by humor and "made attractive by a tinge of nonchalant good-nature." His efforts proved popular. Halstead, though often disagreeing with the sentiments expressed in his articles, rarely edited them. Piatt's journalism resulted in his being followed home by a president's son, bent on assassination; being beaten on the floor of the Senate chamber; and being hunted on the streets by a senator with a loaded revolver. His first association with the *Commercial* ended in 1871, when he established the *Washington Capital,* a Sunday newspaper. He became Washington correspondent for Halstead again in the late eighties. Halstead, less permissive now, edited some of his reports. In one article he said that future historians "would laugh at Sherman's 'March to the Sea' as a crazy retreat saved only by Thomas' superb campaigning." When Halstead removed this from his story, Piatt wrote an angry letter saying that he refused to submit to such petty annoyances and humiliations. Hitting directly at Halstead's pride, he said that he knew the wartime situation through means unavailable to an editor living in Cincinnati. He concluded that if Halstead did not like his views, he could end the Washington newsletters. Shortly thereafter Halstead hired a new Washington correspondent.[25]

Of all Halstead's reporters, a young man called "Big Bill," who worked as a court reporter for the newspaper while he studied at the Cincinnati Law School, gained the most prominence. According to a popular *Commercial* story, Halstead admired the young reporter's work and offered him a high salary to remain permanently with the newspaper. "Big Bill" had taken the $6-a-week job only to earn extra spending money. He thanked Halstead for the offer, although he refused the permanent job; he wanted to finish law school and settle down as a lawyer. In 1909, William "Big Bill" Howard Taft became the twenty-seventh president of the United States.[26]

Halstead's independent journalism, his often impetuous reporters and correspondents, and his own gruff style (which through assurance of his position and power sometimes led him to editorial name-calling) guaranteed the *Commercial* a constant stream of enemies. Often these enemies took action in the form of libel suits against the *Commercial* or Halstead. Halstead believed that a good newspaper invited libel suits. A newspaper had to present the facts; often a party to the facts did not want them known, and so he sued.[27]

In all of the many suits over the years, Halstead either won or the plaintiffs received only small damages. The editor felt particularly bitter about the latter cases. He believed that in awarding the negligible amount the jury actually decided for the defendant. On the other hand, even in granting small awards, the jury assessed the defendant the court costs. He thought these decisions had been made only because the *Commercial,* as a corporation, could pay the costs. Halstead lamented that the *Commercial* lost more than a thousand dollars, with lawyers' fees and court costs, in such a case.[28]

In the fall of 1873 a dispute developed between Roman Catholic Archbishop John B. Purcell of Cincinnati and Halstead that had serious consequences for the *Commercial.* The archbishop, a prominent figure in the American Church, lacked business ability, and his archdiocese suffered as a consequence. When a controversy erupted about Church influence in the public schools, the *Commercial* printed articles about the impending bankruptcy of the archdiocese. The two issues became intertwined. The Church wished to place nuns in the schools to teach the Catholic students; the *Commercial* claimed that this would violate the principle of separation of Church and state. An editorial battle ensued between the archdiocese's newspaper, the *Telegraph,* and the *Commercial.* After a month of name-calling, on October 23 the *Telegraph* printed a letter from Archbishop Purcell asking Catholics to cancel their subscriptions to the *Commercial.* In the letter, the archbishop said that since the *Commercial's* columns had been filled with malicious items against the Catholic Church, the time had come to "stop the vile sheet." Moreover, Purcell declared that the spirit of the paper had become infidel, "if not atheistic." Halstead reprinted the letter the next day under the headline "A Paper Bull against the *Commercial.*"

Halstead said that the archbishop's anger stemmed from the *Commercial's* printing of the truth. Many American newspapers did have a decided anti-Catholic bias. The *Commercial* had in the past defended the rights of Catholics to their beliefs. Nonetheless, Halstead felt called upon to answer the archbishop's letter, saying he made no war upon a man's religion, even if he "choose to believe in the miraculous efficacy of consecrated relics or any other extreme notions or dogmas." He concluded by declaring that even "prelatical fulminations" could never deter him from characterizing conduct of the Church as it deserved. Halstead did admit that the clergy had rights among its people in the realms of religion and morals, although he asserted that they should never attempt to project those rights into other fields.[29]

It is impossible to show that the archbishop's letter resulted in large numbers of Roman Catholics cancelling their subscriptions or advertisements. The *Commercial* did begin to experience declining profits in this period; Halstead's quarrel with the archbishop did not help its financial condition.

In the same year Halstead also contended with the Ohio legislature. He had long been an opponent of lotteries, feeling that their promoters swindled the poorer classes, while the promoters made large profits. More important, the *Enquirer* used a lottery promotion to enlarge its ciruclation—at the expense of the *Commercial.*

A bill to regulate lotteries had been introduced in the state senate. Halstead heard rumors that lottery operators had opened a "grocery" in a hotel across the street from the capitol to distribute bribery money. A *Commercial* editorial drew attention to these rumors with the result that the state senate decided to hold investigations, calling Halstead as its first witness.[30]

On March 31, 1873, when Halstead took the stand, he admitted being the author of the editorial, which stated: "Senators who opposed the Little Bill [the lottery bill] were dishonest in all their bones . . . if they were not too dull to know what they were about." He also acknowledged writing that Bill Smith, a lottery promoter, "had been placing some of his money where it would do the most good, and that seemed to be most effective in the Democratic Party." When he was questioned about the dollar signs following such paragraphs, the gallery broke out in laughter. On close inquiry about his exact information, Halstead said that the current lottery bill had been written after a public investigation following the defeat of an earlier bill in the house. This investigation brought forth evidence that $10,000 had been paid for suppression of the house bill. Since the usual "grocery" operated, and the earlier bill had been worth $10,000, Halstead concluded that the Little Lottery Bill had to be worth an even larger sum.[31]

After his testimony Halstead told reporters that the senate would not accept his evidence. Yet he believed the bill would pass when Bill Smith testified that he had no financial interest in the measure but only wished to defeat Halstead, whom he considered "a bad man."

The committee made its findings public four days later. It reported that Halstead had no evidence to back his allegations, stating that he had testified under oath that he made the charges for the purpose of inflaming public opinion. The report concluded that Halstead did a rank injustice to members of the senate, degraded the profession of journalism, and threatened the influence of the press as guardians of public morality and peace. Yet, Halstead could claim vindication. The day the committee reported, the senate voted twenty-seven to ten to pass the Little Lottery Bill. On April 11, the house concurred in the senate's measure.[32]

One year later, on Saturday evening, April 11, 1874, Halstead became one of the few individuals ever arrested for violating the lottery law. According to his report, an advertisement had been placed in the *Commercial* to run twenty-three times. After its first appearance he realized that it could be construed as an announcement for a lottery, and so he removed it from the paper. Several days later, Thomas Procter, a soldier stationed at the Newport Barracks with close connections to an *Enquirer* reporter named Baker, swore out a warrant for Halstead's arrest. The *Enquirer* paid Procter, a stranger in Cincinnati, to swear out the warrant. After collecting his money, Procter went to a saloon; he eventually landed in the guardhouse for drunkenness and neglect of duty. Halstead concluded that Procter should have a permanent position on the *Enquirer* staff. "Under the system of journalism announced by the proprietors of that paper, the usefulness of such a man must seem to all observers quite clear." After many delays, Halstead ultimately paid a small fine.[33]

Halstead's fame as a fighting editor also had a more violent side. Cincinnati levee hackmen did not like an item about them which appeared in the *Commercial*. One, mistaking Halstead for the author, started an argument and then called him "an offensive name." In the next instant the hackman found himself sprawled on the street with an aching jaw.[34]

In 1871 the "fighting editor" added to his reputation when a visitor to his office called him a liar. The result, a "terrible fight" in which Halstead did the punishing, made the New York newspapers. Whitelaw Reid, of the *Tribune*, telegraphed for details. The editor answered that his veracity had been questioned and that proper justice had been administered.[35]

The *Commercial* and Halstead prospered in the late sixties and early seventies. The *Commercial*'s average net income during these years amounted to $200,000; Halstead's personal annual income was over $30,000 as early as 1868. His growing income allowed him to purchase a large three-story brick house on Cincinnati's then fashionable West Fourth Street in 1871. His new residence, within walking distance of the *Commercial*'s editorial offices, typified that of the well-to-do citizen of his day. Its many well-furnished rooms had become a necessity, as his family grew with his income. Jean, born in November, 1859, was followed by John, Marshal, Clarence, Robert, Albert, Hiram, Mary, Clarissa, Griffin, Frank, and finally Willet, born in December, 1881. John died in infancy and Hiram at seven.[36]

Halstead had become socially prominent by the sixties, holding memberships in both the Literary and Queen City clubs. William Cullen Bryant, Rutherford B. Hayes, Jacob Cox, John Walter of the London *Times*, John Sherman, Benjamin Bristow, Grant's secretary of the treasury, and Matthew Arnold enjoyed his hospitality in Cincinnati. Moreover, his circle of friends included most of the celebrated names in journalism and literature in the country. Whitelaw Reid and William Dean Howells worked on Cincinnati newspapers before going east. Halstead corresponded with Reid for the rest of their lives and often met Howells in New York. He became friends with George W. Childs of the *Philadelphia Enquirer* at the 1856 Republican convention. Their correspondence also covered many years. After Potter's death, Childs offered to purchase the outstanding shares of the *Commercial* in order to give Halstead a free hand in its management. Halstead was also a close friend of Joseph Medill of the *Chicago Tribune*. After the Chicago fire in 1871, Halstead sent Medill an extra font of type by express, enabling the *Tribune* to publish an edition only a few days after the complete destruction of its plant.[37]

Henry Watterson remained Halstead's closest friend in the journalistic field. Watterson came to Cincinnati in the spring of 1865 after federal authorities closed the newspaper which he edited in Chattanooga. Both his aunt, the wife of Halstead's Literary Club associate Stanley Matthews, and his grandmother lived in the city. Watterson found employment on the *Cincinnati Evening Times* as a reporter. Soon after he took the job, the *Evening Times* editor drowned when he fell from a ferryboat crossing the Ohio River. Since no other member of the staff had had editorial experience, the publisher made him managing editor. A week later Watterson introduced several changes in the paper, which prompted the *Commercial* to print a number of humorous paragraphs about the *Chattanooga-Cincinnati-Rebel Evening Times.*

Artemus Ward, the humorist, who had visited Cincinnati days earlier, had given a dinner for his friend Watterson. Halstead had been among the guests. Ward told Watterson that the young editor should be watched as the "coming man on the *Commercial.*" The *Commercial*'s paragraphs, although amusing, called attention to Watterson's past as a "rebel" editor, which Watterson felt might cause him to lose his job. He decided to call upon Halstead to persuade him to cease the humorous attacks. Claiming to be "the merest bird of passage with my watch at the pawnbroker's," he told Halstead the personal allusions might result in his unemployment. A magnanimous Halstead replied, "They were damned mean—though I did not realize how mean. The mark was so obvious and tempting I could not resist, but—there shall be no more of them. Come, let us go have a drink." Thus, Watterson recalled the beginning of a friendship that lasted nearly half a century.[38]

Watterson, who later became the powerful editor of the *Louisville Courier-Journal,* rarely agreed with Halstead on political issues, although their personal friendship continued to grow over succeeding years. They often exchanged visits, traveled to New York and Washington together, and corresponded regularly. Their political opposition took the form of friendly rivalries and feuds carried on in the columns of their respective newspapers. During one of their feuds— Halstead ran a series of articles attacking the South in the *Commercial* —an associate of Watterson's wrote an editorial attacking the Cincinnati editor. When Watterson saw the proof, he rushed into the room where his assistants worked and said: "Look here, boys, Murat Halstead and I have been fighting literally and figuratively for many years, but we understand each other and know when to fight and when to be friends. He is my particular meat. You boys shinny on your own side and leave Murat to me."[39]

Energetic, enterprising, with a catholicity of taste and culture,

Halstead had a fun-loving nature and made friends easily. He loved to escape his work for a holiday in New York and soon came to be a familiar figure at the Fifth Avenue Hotel. In 1870 Halstead joined the Lotos Club, the most fashionable organization for journalists of the time. A small intraclub group developed, which included the actors Joseph Jefferson and Edwin Booth and a group of newspapermen and writers such as Mark Twain, Thomas Nast, Bret Harte, John Hay, Samuel Bowles, Whitelaw Reid, Henry Watterson, and Halstead. Meeting at the Lotos Club, Delmonico's, or the Fifth Avenue Hotel, they often attended plays and dined together.[40]

On one of these occasions Watterson received a card from a *World* reporter requesting an interview. Watterson, who had not finished his dinner, refused. Twain then asked for the card and left the table. He told the young and innocent reporter that Watterson could not be interviewed, although he could arrange a meeting with Murat Halstead. He then introduced Watterson as Halstead. The young reporter knew neither of the editors; Watterson gave him material for a long column that reversed Halstead's opinions on every subject. He made Halstead say: "The 'bloody shirt' is only a kind of Pickwickian battle cry. It is convenient during political campaigns and on election day. Perhaps you do not know that I am myself of dyed-in-the-wool southern and secession stock. My father and grandfather came to Ohio from South Carolina just before I was born." No one knew how the interview passed through the *World's* editorial office without the joke being discovered, but the story appeared the next day. On the day after, the *World* printed a note from Halstead repudiating the interview, although it added a one-line disclaimer that read: "When Mr. Halstead conversed with our reporter he had dined." A few days later John Hay wrote an amusing story for the *Tribune* giving all the details of the "Halstead" interview.[41]

In the summer of 1870, Halstead began a long-anticipated vacation. Since Potter's death, he had left Cincinnati for only brief periods. His passion for personal supervision of the various details of the *Commercial's* daily operations made him reluctant to trust its management to the hands of his subordinates. Yet, the strain of his long and irregular hours had begun to show. Receiving letters of introduction from several friends with European connections, he sailed for the Continent in the middle of June.[42]

Although he considered the trip to be a vacation, Halstead planned to send travel letters to the *Commercial*. A feature of American journalism of the period, travel letters allowed the writer to practice his literary style. They also gave readers a glimpse of a life most of them would never see. In proposing to write the letters, Halstead could quiet his conscience about leaving the management of his newspaper.

Halstead arrived in Paris about the first of July. He spent several weeks sightseeing, visiting historical monuments and museums. Just as he prepared to leave for Switzerland, war broke out between France and Prussia on July 19. The declaration caught him almost completely unaware, although he saw an immediate opportunity to gain prestige for the *Commercial* as a great American newspaper. In addition, he realized that the large German population of Cincinnati had intense interest in the war. In usual circumstances, the *Commercial* could have expected to receive its war news from reports of English correspondents and a few reporters of New York newspapers. With Halstead on the scene, he could send home firsthand accounts of the fighting, a major accomplishment for a western journal.[43]

Halstead applied through the American minister for authorization to become a war correspondent with the French army. With his experience in Washington during the Civil War, he realized that there might be difficulty in obtaining the proper credentials. Days passed without a word from the war ministry. On the day the emperor joined the French army at Metz, he learned that the government had refused, without exception, to give credentials to newspaper correspondents. Halstead said that the French could gain nothing from this decision, since the Germans already had detailed information about their army. In a newsletter sent to the *Commercial*, Halstead said the history of the war would now be written from the German point of view.[44]

When he left the United States, Halstead had received an impressive special passport bearing a large American eagle, tricolored ribbons, and an "immense amount of wax." With this impressive document, and a promise from the American minister to answer any telegram, no matter how trivial, Halstead decided to join the army at Metz.

Halstead's attempt to become an unofficial war correspondent with the French army resulted in a series of frustrations. At the railroad station, guards warned him that he could be arrested if he went to Metz. Determined to get to the front, he forced his way onto the train. Halstead traveled to Metz, hoping to find the French army in action and the attention of the authorities directed toward the enemy. Unfortunately, the army had not yet engaged in battle. The police followed him wherever he went, and confiscated a dispatch he had written for the *Commercial*. Remembering the threat of the guards at the Paris railroad station, he decided to take the train to Strasbourg.[45]

During Halstead's last days in Paris he had met Moncure D. Conway, a former Unitarian clergyman from Cincinnati. Conway, at that time a correspondent for the *New York World*, also wished to get to the front. They had decided to join forces if Halstead had no luck at Metz. When the two met in Strasbourg, they determined to cross over into Germany. Entering Germany by traveling from France to Switzerland, they crossed the frontier from that country, proceeding to Karlsruhe, the capital of Baden.[46]

In Karlsruhe the American minister introduced them to the grand duchy's minister of war. Although this official gave them passes for German headquarters, he warned of the difficulties involved in the trip. They also learned that the French army had suffered a defeat, and that Prussian King William I, Moltke, and Bismarck had just crossed the Rhine in preparation for the invasion of France. With the hope of finding the king's headquarters they immediately decided to follow. They found an unoccupied compartment on a westbound train, where they stayed until they reached the frontier. Here a German officer ordered them out of the car and forbade them to go any farther. A cattle train loaded with German soldiers had arrived. Halstead and Conway boarded one of the cars and passed out cigars to the soldiers. When the inspectors came along, the soldiers did not betray their generous friends.[47]

The Germans had established headquarters at the village of Saint-Avold, where the two men arrived late in the afternoon. The landlord of the Hotel de Ville de Paris, after serving them a dinner of cold meat and red wine, allowed them to sleep in his barroom. That night a messenger looking for Moltke awakened the two reporters. Halstead said that the messenger at first mistook him for the field marshal, although the landlord soon arrived and straightened out the situation. The editor later said that a distorted account of what had happened resulted in the *New York Sun* conferring upon him the rank of "field marshal."[48]

The French army had been outnumbered, outgunned, and out-maneuvered from the beginning. In the first week of August, the French suffered defeats at Wissembourg and Forbach. After these losses, the emperor surrendered command to General Bazaine, an intriguer who had disgraced himself in Mexico. Bazaine decided to withdraw from Metz and fall back toward Paris. The German army crossed Bazaine's line of retreat at the Battle of Mars-la-Tour. Neither reporter knew about the battle until its conclusion. At his hotel, Halstead fell into a conversation with a Prussian officer who spoke English. The officer sympathized with him for missing the battle. At three o'clock the next morning the officer knocked on Halstead's hotel room door and told him to proceed immediately to the village of Gorze.[49]

In a short time he and Conway arrived at the battlefield. On ascending a ridge the two men could hear the distant sound of rifle fire and could see on a hilltop in front of them a small group of men. With his glasses, Halstead made out the king's carriage, and so he and Conway decided to head in that direction. When they reached the hill, they stationed themselves some distance from the king's official party. They could see the Lorraine countryside for miles. The German troops moved toward Germany, while the French faced Paris. From their elevation the reporters could see masses of men advance and retreat. For the rest of the day the reporters watched the battle.[50]

As the sun set, they decided to seek shelter for the night. A short distance from their vantage point a German artist sat sketching. When the artist discovered that the reporters represented American newspapers, he invited them to share his room. The cannon still roared when the two Americans hastened away to find the artist's room. Since wounded German officers filled the hotel, Halstead retreated to the privacy of the room to write his report. His story of the Battle of Gravelotte appeared on the front page of the September 9 issue of the *Commercial*. The day after the battle the reporters returned to the battlefield, where they met Bismarck and his American visitor General Philip Sheridan. Sheridan, in what Halstead called "true American fashion," asked him how he came to be in such a strange and remote place. The editor replied that he had walked this way because he thought it an interesting part of the country. The exchange struck Bismarck as extremely humorous, and he shook with laughter. When Sheridan told the reporters that arrangements had been made to move headquarters to Pont-à-Mousson, they decided to leave for Brussels that same night with their firsthand reports of the battle.[51]

After Bazaine's defeat at Gravelotte, the emperor and Marshal MacMahon began gathering a new army. With almost no hope of success, they led their army back toward Metz, where the remaining portion of Bazaine's army had retreated. Bazaine remained inactive, and MacMahon and the emperor, not receiving the needed support, found their army penned in at Sedan. On September 1, Napoleon III surrendered his 84,000 men, 2,700 officers, and 39 generals. When the news reached Paris, revolutionary crowds appeared in the streets. The empress and the prince imperial, sensing the danger, fled to England. Halstead, now back in Paris, stood in the Place de la Concorde on September 4 when an enormous crowd gathered around the Tuileries to watch the fall of the emperor's flag, indicating the death of the empire.[52]

When Halstead had left Cincinnati, he had felt much respect for the French, but little for the Germans. The French had produced Lafayette, Napoleon, and of course Murat. On the other hand, he associated Germany with the Cincinnati Germans of the "over the Rhine" district—a sturdy, thrifty people, although not the kind that Halstead particularly liked or whose company he enjoyed. With some exceptions, such as the publisher Frederick Hassaurek, a few brewers, and others, the average German in Cincinnati did not move in the same circles as Halstead. The editor's ideas underwent a radical change on this first European trip. Although he returned to France several times, he always felt more at home in Germany. He thought German unification proved the superiority of her character as well as of her arms. He also found a hero in Bismarck, who had used parliaments, kings, field marshals, and armies as instruments to fashion his victory. As a result, "The figure of Bismarck, the statesman of blood and iron, who reconstructed Germany and gave her solidity and glory, will forever stand foremost in the world."[53]

Years later, in the summer of 1874, Halstead was invited by Cyrus Field, the builder of the Atlantic cable, to join him on a trip to Iceland. Field had passed south of Iceland several times while laying the cable and had always wanted to visit the island. In 1874 Iceland commemorated a thousand years of European settlement. Field decided to charter a ship, gather a party of friends, and become the unofficial American representative at the celebration.

The Edinburgh and London Shipping Company offered Field the use of the steam yacht *Albion*, which his party boarded at Aberdeen. The little steamer, flying an American flag, left harbor on July 22. At the Faeroe Islands it joined the fleet of the king of Denmark. Iceland had originally been settled by Norwegians, but in 1380 with the union of Norway and Denmark, Iceland passed into Danish hands.[54]

The citizens of Iceland received Field's steamer in state, mistaking it for the king's. On their visits to the island's geysers and volcanic relics, the American party received almost as much attention as the king, since the Icelanders believed Field planned to build a new cable by way of their island.

The party left Iceland on August 8, arriving back in Scotland five days later. After Halstead finished writing a series of travel letters entitled "Notes on a Long Journey," he sailed home with Samuel Bowles, the editor of the *Springfield* (Massachusetts) *Republican*.

Altogether, Halstead crossed the Atlantic fourteen times during his life. Travel became his great recreation, allowing him to be constantly on the go, to see new places, and still to contribute to his newspaper. He also made trips to Cuba and to the Pacific. In almost every instance, he wrote newsletters, articles, or books about the places he had visited.[55]

By the early seventies, Halstead belonged in the first rank of American journalism. Albert Shaw, writing in the *Review of Reviews* at a later period, said that he had shown the brains, character, and distinctive personality of a great journalist by this time. He also declared the son of Paddy's Run had become one of the most conspicuous representatives of America's greatest school of journalism, and placed him alongside Horace Greeley and Charles A. Dana because his work, like theirs, always showed originality, frankness, sympathy, and intense American patriotism.[56]

4

The Liberal Republican Movement

The essentially nineteenth-century liberalism that Halstead accepted as a college student found application when he became an early leader of the independent journalism movement. His belief in those principles and in independent journalism guaranteed his dissatisfaction with the stalwart politics of the Grant regime. This dissatisfaction ultimately led to his renouncing the Republican party and associating the *Commercial* with the Liberal Republican party of 1872. Halstead's decision proved costly for his newspaper.

Halstead's criticism of Grant started during the war. In the fall of 1862 he wrote to Secretary of the Treasury Chase condemning the commander of the army in the West. Grant, the editor charged, had been drinking again. According to Halstead, the general, a "poor stick sober," when drunk became "idiotic and an imbecile." "Grant will fail miserably, hopelessly, eternally. You may look for and calculate his failures, in every position in which he may be placed, as a perfect certainty." Chase forwarded this letter to Lincoln with the comment that the *Commercial* had great influence in the West. With Grant's military successes, Halstead forgot his earlier opposition.[1]

Although Halstead considered supporting Chase on either the Democratic or a third party ticket in 1868, he declared Grant particularly fitted for office when the Republicans nominated the Union hero for the presidency. Grant, the editor now asserted, proved

57

able to bear the greatest responsibilities with ease, showed executive talents, and acted in a quiet, decided manner. During the campaign, the Grant-Colfax ticket received editorial support from Halstead, who wrote after the election that the victory meant the triumph of law and order in the United States.[2]

The marriage of Halstead's independent journalism with the Grant administration lasted only through a short honeymoon and ended in a quick divorce. Halstead often found fault with radical reconstruction. He hoped Grant could exert his leadership and bring an end to its abuses. He also hoped Grant could lead the party in civil service and tariff reform. In less than a year, Halstead knew Grant had no plan to lead a reform movement; the anti-Grant faction in the Republican party could claim his support.[3]

A number of Americans during the early seventies shared Halstead's criticism of the Grant administration. As they learned of Grant's naiveté in trusting corrupt friends and relatives, a call went out for a reform movement to purge the party of the president and his appointees. Although the movement contained many differing elements, all reformers agreed on their desire to rid the country of Grant.

The movement, which took the name "Liberal Republican" to distinguish it from the "Radical Republicans," had its formal start in Missouri. Although the state remained in Union control during the war, it had been deeply divided. A radical postwar constitution disfranchised everyone who had served the Confederacy or had given it aid and support. It also disqualified such persons for public office, jury service, professions such as the law and the ministry, and officeholding in private corporations. In 1870 the Missouri Republican party split over the issue of repealing these restrictions. The reformers founded a party under the leadership of Carl Schurz and Benjamin Gratz Brown. Schurz had represented the state in the United States Senate since 1869; Brown received the reform party's nomination for governor. The movement achieved success with Brown's election.[4]

From this start in Missouri, Liberal groups soon organized in other states. The basis for these groups has been variously described as "patrician dissidents," the "American gentry," and the "best men." These men found Grant a sad disappointment as president. To them, public office should be a public trust. The officeholder had to "observe high standards of integrity, impartiality, and honesty." He should be guided in his official office by the same standards that a gentleman assumed in private life. Because of their inherited wealth, education, and social position, they saw themselves as standing above the turmoil of industry and politics. They found it impossible to believe that anyone involved in "grimy industrialism" could ever want a government "free from money-minded self-seeking." The ideal government should consist of individuals free from this self-seeking, who could impart justice for all citizens.

All Liberals agreed in their hatred of Grant. Most could also agree to the need for civil service reform and the end of radical reconstruction. They differed over the issue of the protective tariff. Many eastern Liberals believed the tariff a necessity for American industry. Other Liberals said the protective principle favored one class and penalized everyone else. They called for a revenue tariff to lower domestic taxes and prices.[5]

Halstead, by temperament and training, could easily accept the Liberal Republican standards. He used the *Commercial's* columns both to attack Grant and to support the reformers. Although he disliked much of what he saw on the national political scene, he particularly criticized Grant's distribution of patronage: Grant disregarded the Republican party in selecting the cabinet and filling important federal offices. Although most of his appointees belonged to the Republican party, according to the editor, their personal friendship with Grant, not their party leadership, had been responsible for their appointments. Moreover, he declared that these friends apparently bought their offices with gifts. As to the charges of nepotism leveled against Grant, Halstead claimed that he appointed only a small number of relatives to office, "but he has appointed personal friends, and the friends of friends, and the favorites of relatives, to a degree that is not creditable to his sagacity as a man of the people." Later his attacks on Grant's relatives, "down to the second cousins and their connections by marriage," increased. He particularly liked to point to Grant's elderly and often ill father, the postmaster of Covington (a small city in Kentucky across the Ohio River from Cincinnati), as an example of those unable to fulfill their duties.[6]

The editor moved on to attack a host of other related evils such as presidential interference of the "most obnoxious form" in the southern states. Instead of reconstruction and rehabilitation, Halstead claimed Grant's southern policy only attempted to assure his own reelection. "The power and patronage of the Executive . . . is to be used hereafter . . . for the perpetuation of an administration which politicians, and not men selected purely and simply for their integrity and capacity, are to play the conspicuous parts." To cleanse the government, he demanded civil service reform, less interference by the national government in state affairs, and the election of a new president in 1872.[7]

On many other points Halstead could agree perfectly with the opposition to the Grant regime. For several years he had been critical of a high protective tariff. As early as 1866 he wrote Rutherford B. Hayes "[not to] go the whole hog" with Morrill on the tariff. The protective principle ruins the economy for the sake of "those damned harpies of Pennsylvania and New England." He saw only high prices for American goods, a loss of foreign markets, and higher rates of internal taxes to compensate for the loss in revenue. Many middle western Republicans believed a protective tariff benefited only the East, and so Halstead's criticisms fell on fertile ground.[8]

Halstead joined a distinguished group of American editors who used their newspapers to fight the corruption of the Grant regime and to convince their readers of the need for reform. Samuel Bowles of the *Springfield Republican,* Horace White of the *Chicago Tribune,* and Horace Greeley and his editor Whitelaw Reid of the *New York Tribune* all attacked "Grantism." Although these newspapers usually supported the Republican party, radicalism and the Grant administration convinced them to experiment with an independent editorial policy.[9]

This group also included Henry Watterson, the Democratic editor of the *Louisville Courier-Journal.* As a southern Democrat, Watterson had to be extremely circumspect during the early months of the movement. If he went too far in support of the Liberals, he risked repudiation by his own party and administration charges that southern politicans controlled the reform group. Watterson believed in returning home rule to the South and reconciliation of the two sections. He concluded that this could only be done through a coalition of Liberal Republicans and Democrats. Thus, by the spring of 1872, Watterson worked closely with Halstead to insure that the Liberals nominated a candidate Democrats could support.[10]

The early leadership of the Liberal movement contained many newspapermen. The newspapers of Schurz and Brown in Missouri,

White in Chicago, Halstead and Frederick Hassaurek in Cincinnati, Godkin, Greeley, and Reid in New York, and Bowles in Springfield —all spread the Liberal message throughout the northern and northeastern United States. Since the Liberal movement depended upon popular support rather than party machinery, these men played an enormous role in assuring its success.[11]

Other dissident groups across the country soon copied the Liberal organization of the Missourians. In March 1871, over seventy leading Cincinnati citizens, all Republicans, formed the Central Republican Association of Hamilton County. This group, which included Stanley Matthews, George Hoadly, Jacob D. Cox, George R. Sage, H. L. Barnett, Frederick Hassaurek, and John Shillito, issued a statement similar to that of Missouri Liberals. The association said the continued usefulness of the Republican party could be guaranteed only by meeting the issues of the day. To accomplish this, it called for the burying of the enmities and resentments of the war, the removal of all political disabilities, a tariff for revenue purposes, and an end to the patronage system. Stanley Matthews became president of the new organization. Halstead, who did not sign the statement, nonetheless predicted the group's success, calling Matthews an excellent choice for leadership.[12]

By early 1872, the organization of such clubs, the constant opposition to Grant among independents in Congress, and the campaign by liberal newspapers had convinced most men interested in the movement of the necessity to establish a national party. Originally Bowles, Schurz, and Halstead hoped they could accomplish their aims within the framework of the old party. When Halstead believed the Democrats planned to nominate their own "reactionary" candidate, he opposed splitting the Republican party. He believed Grant the lesser of the two evils. Only when he thought the Democrats might endorse their nominee did he begin to consider a Liberal candidate.

Administration supporters scoffed at the idea of a separate party organization. They could not understand the opposition to Grant, believing that the editors plotted to gain control of the party. Moreover, the *New York Times*, a Grant newspaper, claimed that the reformers' aims had not been clearly defined. The "vague suggestions" for change, according to the *Times*, could be effected through the regular channels of the Republican party, "the party of progress."[13]

In January 1872, the Missouri Liberal Convention called a national convention to meet in Cincinnati on May 1. Schurz urged this early date because he still thought the Liberals' strength might convince the Republicans to repudiate Grant. Moreover, should the Liberals nominate candidates, this early date would forestall any action on the part of the Democrats.[14]

As long as Halstead believed that the Liberals could work within the Republican party, he supported Horace Greeley for the presidential nomination. He praised the New York editor's integrity and independence, saying that his understanding of the desires of the American people recommended him to the whole country. As late as April 1871, *Commercial* editorials boosted the *Tribune*'s editor as a candidate to bring the country peace. The Greeley boom did not end until Halstead realized that the Liberals could not work for a Republican reform nominee; instead, they needed a candidate acceptable to the Democrats. Halstead believed that Greeley had alienated too many Democrats for them to accept his nomination.[15]

The tariff reformer element among Liberals also opposed Greeley because of his stand on the protective tariff. Although Halstead hoped to gain concessions on the tariff issue, he decided after a breakfast meeting with the New York editor that Greeley's position could not be changed. Moreover, he "moved in an eccentric orbit and had been an experimenter in affairs—a character which however estimable in itself, did not commend itself to the popular instinct as one that gave an assurance of public safety in the highest executive office." Reformers could no longer consider Greeley as the nominee.[16]

Other Liberal editors mentioned Charles Francis Adams as the ideal candidate. Adams's standing as a Republican and his long service to the Union cause during the war made it impossible for regular Republicans to attack him as a southern sympathizer. He could also command many Republican votes. His dignified retirement after the war, his education, and his family background all recommended him to that section of the reform leadership who felt the candidate's only interest in the White House should be for public service. Moreover, Halstead felt Adams's dissociation from the radical program made his acceptance easier for the Democrats. Halstead had never met Adams. As no one supporting Adams's nomination at Cincinnati received promises of political preference, the conclusion can be drawn that Adams men made an entirely personal decision to support the ablest candidate.[17]

Before the decision to nominate a separate Liberal slate had been made, Halstead supported Gratz Brown for the vice-presidential nomination. Later, he said that the candidate should come from a doubtful state. Missouri's guaranteed vote against Grant eliminated Brown. Because of Illinois' greater population and doubtful status in the election, Halstead suggested either Governor J. M. Palmer or Senator Lyman Trumbull as more practical choices. He believed Trumbull to be more acceptable to Democrats. In late April, the *New York Times*, attempting to cause dissension among Liberals, said that Halstead thought Greeley, Brown, Palmer, and Trumbull "experimentalists" who should not be nominated. In reality, Halstead had decided to support Trumbull for second place on the ticket a month before the convention.[18]

Once Halstead made the decision to support Adams and Trumbull, he used the *Commercial* to secure their nominations. Hardly a day passed throughout the month of April without some comment about the good qualities of both men. On the first two days of the convention, the *Commercial* published front-page stories entitled "The Public Services of Charles Francis Adams" and "Charles Francis Adams, the Public Career of the Eminent Statesman, the Great Services to His Country in Politics, Legislation, and Diplomacy, the Qualifications Necessary for a President of the United States." As the unofficial newspaper of the convention, the *Commercial* was read by all the delegates.[19]

The Liberal editors arrived in Cincinnati several days before the convention. Bowles, one of the earliest arrivals, also supported Adams. While they awaited the other editors, he and Halstead mapped out their strategy. White also came early, and began button-holing delegates for Trumbull. Watterson, the last to arrive, recalled that the convention could have been mistaken for the annual meeting of the Associated Press. Halstead and Bowles met him at the railroad station and drove him to the St. Nicholas Hotel, where White waited. Watterson and Schurz shared a suite, with the parlor between their bedrooms becoming the "committee room" of the editor-strategists, soon to be called the "Quadrilateral"—from the four great fortified towns used by Austria to dominate northern Italy.[20]

These men, who had promoted the Liberal movement for months, now hoped to control the convention. Although they did not agree on candidates, they wished to ensure a nominee acceptable to all the elements of the opposition, whether Liberals or Democrats. Yet more important, they wished to write a platform that conformed to the ideals of the reformers. Although experienced newspapermen and political observers, they had little actual political experience.[21]

While "Quadrilateral" described Watterson, Bowles, White, and Halstead, Schurz and Reid also joined the ranks of the leaders. Schurz became the guiding hand of the movement; Whitelaw Reid sought Greeley's nomination. Since the other leaders agreed that the New York editor should not be nominated, they admitted Reid into their council reluctantly. Watterson urged his participation to assure *Tribune* support, and so the editors agreed to include Reid, feeling that they could "both eat our cake and have it." They regretted their decision.[22]

These six took seriously their self-appointed job of saving the country. They spent their time before and between sessions of the convention going over developments and laying plans. The boom among the delegates for Supreme Court Justice David Davis became the first important obstacle for the editors. They believed Davis to be a political opportunist. Although nominally a Republican, he had no strong party ties, having been mentioned as a possible Democratic candidate for president. His nomination with a Democratic running mate on the Labor party ticket in February and the support he enjoyed among Democratic congressmen did not help his cause with the reformers. Moreover, politicians with large sums of money had set up headquarters in Cincinnati. The Liberal leadership feared their influence, deciding that the time had come to "kill off" Davis. "What business had the professional politicians," Watterson asked, "with a great reform movement?" That the Davis supporters tried to wrench control of the convention from the Quadrilateral seemed to be "flat burglary."[23]

The Davis men represented those elements which the reformers believed the Liberal movement should remove from American political life. Some had been bought, some received railroad tickets to Cincinnati, and some had been given free room and board. One Davis delegate, who wrote a book about the convention for campaign purposes, supported Grant. He came to Cincinnati on a lark—and to embarrass the movement.[24]

At a dinner meeting at Halstead's home, the Quadrilateral decided to use the only weapon at their command: the power of the press. In concert they prepared editorials for their newspapers blasting Davis's candidacy. Thus, from four major cities came the word, but to ensure that the delegates saw the anti-Davis editorials, on the morning of April 30 Halstead printed them in the *Commercial*. With so much anti-Davis sentiment showing itself across the country, the "Davis boomers were paralyzed."[25]

At noon on May 1, Colonel W. M. Grosvenor, a leader of the Missouri Liberals and chairman of their executive committee, brought the convention to order. In a short speech he called on the delegates to act against the "power which has so long and injuriously controlled party organizations and political machinery." Following his brief opening remarks, Grosvenor named Stanley Matthews as temporary chairman. On taking the chair, Matthews said that the "time had come when it is the voice of an exceedingly large and influential portion of the American people that they are determined that they will not be longer dogs to wear the collar of the party." Following his speech, loud cries for "Schurz," came from all parts of the hall. Schurz symbolized the Liberal movement. He had organized the Missouri Liberals, had led the national reform group, and had received the brunt of the attack from party regulars. Conducted to the platform amid tremendous applause and cheers, he refused to make a speech. As the Quadrilateral wished a convention free of personalities, Schurz called the delegates to the business at hand, saying, "The first of May was a moving day."[26]

The Quadrilateral lost its knowledgable political leader the second day of the convention when the committee on organization named Schurz as permanent chairman. In accepting the chair, Schurz surrendered all hope of directing the work of the convention from the floor. Schurz's opening speech called upon Liberals to put aside the selfish spirit of political trade: "We want a Government which the best people of this country will be proud of. Not anybody can accomplish that, and, therefore, away with the cry, 'Anybody to beat Grant'; a cry too paltry, too unworthy of the great enterprise in which we are engaged." The party could succeed only if it found a better man than Grant.[27]

The convention's first crisis arose when the resolutions committee could not agree on the tariff plank. Adams and Trumbull delegates called for downward revision; Greeley wished to retain the protectionist principle. Unable to find a satisfactory compromise, the committee could not report. The delegates wished to start nominations immediately. As this ran counter to the Quadrilateral's demand of principle above the man, they objected, but defeated the move only with great difficulty. Watterson later said that this was a mistake. Halstead, Bowles, White, and he had concluded that Trumbull could not win nomination. Although they felt Adams could win on the first ballot, "inspired by the bravery of youth and inexperience, we let the golden opportunity slip," preferring principle above the man.[28]

The next morning Horace White, the resolutions committee chairman, reported the platform. Although in most respects it conformed to the wishes of the Quadrilateral, on the tariff the committee accepted a compromise. Greeley refused to agree to tariff reduction in any form. The compromise solution had been proposed by Halstead on May 1. To avoid intraparty rivalry over the tariff, he suggested settling the question in the congressional elections. The committee adopted this solution. White later wrote that although the committee decided tariff revision could wait, immediate action had to be taken on pacification of the South and civil service reform. The other uncontroversial planks of the platform called for removal of southern disabilities, civil service reform, a "speedy" return to specie payments, and limiting the president to one term. The Quadrilateral surrendered on the tariff, feeling that they could name the candidate.[29]

With the platform adopted, the convention began the nominations. The Quadrilateral believed Trumbull could be persuaded to accept second place on the ticket, allowing Adams a first ballot victory. Unfortunately, the Trumbull delegates refused to surrender without a test of strength. They hoped a deadlock between Greeley and Adams might allow Trumbull to emerge as the compromise candidate.[30]

Tension built in the hall as the first roll call began. Alabama divided her eighteen votes among Trumbull, Davis, Greeley, and Gratz Brown. With the Wisconsin vote, those keeping a private tally knew that Adams had shown the greatest strength, with a total of 203, but was over 100 votes short of the 308 needed for nomination. Greeley received 147, Trumbull 108, Davis 92½, and Brown 92. At the conclusion of the ballot, Gratz Brown asked for recognition. After thanking his supporters, he recommended that they switch to Greeley. Although New Jersey attempted to change her vote (it had given seven votes to Brown), Schurz refused to recognize the delegation and called for the first ballot totals.[31]

Brown arrived in Cincinnati the night before the balloting, determined to stop Adams's nomination. He and Schurz had quarreled over the Liberal leadership in Missouri. Although Schurz had not announced for any candidate, Brown believed he supported Adams. On arrival, Brown took a room at the St. James Hotel and began conferences with Greeley men. In return for the vice-presidential nomination, he promised to support Greeley's candidacy. The members of the Quadrilateral had been informed of Brown's arrival. Grosvenor ran up and down the corridors of the Burnet House knocking loudly on doors shouting, "Get up! Blair and Brown are here from St. Louis." Although they heard rumors of a deal, they did not know how to stop Brown. Only Halstead took action. He inserted an editorial in the *Commercial* warning that a deal had been made.[32]

In the hope of stemming a Greeley stampede, Schurz gave the chair to George Julian of Indiana and left the hall with the Missouri delegation. Missouri had voted for Brown; it now had to decide if it should switch to Greeley on the second ballot. Schurz used his influence to keep Missouri out of the Greeley column. On the second roll call, Greeley led by two votes, 245 to Adams's 243, and Trumbull trailed with 148. Although Greeley gained almost one hundred votes over the first ballot, he did not receive the nomination as a result of Brown's withdrawal. Alabama, Arkansas, California, Georgia, Nevada, New Jersey, and Oregon transferred their support from Brown to Greeley; Kentucky and Missouri divided their Brown votes between the two front-runners. Iowa gave her Brown vote to Adams, while Tennessee gave hers to Trumbull. The Quadrilateral felt that the crisis had passed when the Brown-Greeley deal did not throw the convention onto a Greeley bandwagon. They now looked for Trumbull supporters to give Adams the nomination on the third or fourth ballot. Yet on both ballots only slight variations occurred in the vote. Although Adams regained his lead, he still needed almost a hundred more votes for victory.[33]

The fifth roll call brought the Quadrilateral new hope. Keeping careful count as the balloting progressed, Halstead saw a stampede begin for Adams. With the announcement that Adams's vote had gone over 300, "a thousand handkerchiefs waved, a thousand hats were flung in the air, and the scene, honestly, for once, really justified the much abused phrase and tired reporter's resource, 'It beggared description.' " The added votes came from the Trumbull and Davis delegates, and so Halstead believed that the long-awaited break had come.[34]

Hoping to press the advantage, Schurz immediately began the sixth ballot. Halstead reported that as the ballot started, Greeley men in the New York delegation began cheering and shouting each time their candidate received a vote. Taken up by other delegates, a continuing demonstration started. Halstead said that it did not help Greeley's cause. Nonetheless, more and more votes changed from the other candidates to the *Tribune*'s editor. When Pennsylvania cast its 50 votes, Greeley received his victory. The vote totaled 482 for Greeley, 187 for Adams. The Quadrilateral discovered the difference between the professional and the amateur in politics. They had foreseen an Adams stampede; instead, they met one for Greeley. The results left the Adams supporters so angry that they rejected a move to make the vote unanimous.[35]

The Quadrilateral blamed the results of the balloting almost entirely on Brown's withdrawal; however, Brown's decision to support Greeley did not give him the nomination. Had the Quadrilateral convinced the Trumbull men to support Adams, the nomination could have been kept from Greeley. The Quadrilateral had not made a concentrated anti-Greeley attack for fear of losing *Tribune* support. In not eliminating him early, they had let his strength grow. Greeley's managers worked with the professional politicians, and the Halstead group attempted to hold themselves aloof. Thus many of the politicians who might not have voted for Greeley felt him the lesser of two evils; at least Greeley recognized their importance. Many reformers, particularly in the Middle West, also voted for Greeley. They refused to support Adams because of his extremely cold and aloof personality and his opposition in the 1850s to the Free Soil–Democratic coalition. Westerners also believed he lacked the personal popularity to carry the election.[36]

After the presidential nomination, interest in the proceedings lagged. Because the delegates wanted to leave, an immediate roll call began for vice-president. On the first ballot Brown lacked a majority, although he had almost a hundred more votes than his nearest competitor. Halstead declared that this proved "The Brown Party [had] handed over the goods, and were ready to receive their pay." Brown won on the second roll call, receiving a unanimous ballot.[37]

Halstead's editorial the next morning called the nomination of Greeley and Brown "unfortunate." Repeating his support for the Adams and Trumbull ticket, he refused to endorse the Liberals' choice. All of the editors but Reid found themselves in an awkward position. Having claimed Greeley an impossible choice, now they had to decide which of the two presidential candidates represented the lesser evil. Should they accept four more years of Grant, or risk the country to Greeley's "experimentalism"? One of the *New York Times* reporters at Cincinnati pointed up the problems the editors faced. When he asked Bowles for his comments, Bowles replied "[I'm] going to think about it." Halstead, "the Murat of 'Independent Journalism, ' " only "swore with an emphatic oath," while Watterson surveyed his wrecked hopes with a "sickening sensation."[38]

Of the Quadrilateral members, only Reid could boast of success. The other editors took him into their group because they needed the *Tribune,* and now Greeley needed the other editors' support. Consequently, Reid insisted that they be his dinner guests. Watterson received the task of bringing them together. He succeeded in this "uphill work" only by a combination of coaxing and bullying. He characterized the atmosphere of the dinner as "frosty conviviality," saying that he and Halstead failed when they attempted to enliven the festivities "through sheer bravado." "Horace White looked more than ever like an iceberg; Sam Bowles was diplomatic, but ineffusive; Schurz was as a death's head at the board." Although the dinner party broke up early, the guests ultimately accepted the decision of the convention. Although they agreed to united action, they decided to withhold their immediate support. Bowles sent his often-quoted telegram to the *Republican* with instructions to support Greeley "but not to gush." Schurz waited several weeks to announce his decision. In a May 6 editorial, Halstead said Greeley was "worthy of the office," citing his honesty, sincerity, experience, and executive abilities. Yet should the Democrats nominate a true reformer, he might support him.[39]

Some leading Liberals refused to accept Greeley. Although few renounced the movement, many did not endorse its ticket. Adams sat out the Greeley campaign. The failure of the platform plank calling for a reduction in the tariff and then the nomination of Greeley, a protectionist, caused Stanley Matthews to return to the

Republican party. Godkin also returned to the Republican party, saying that he had "a burning desire to help train up a generation of young men to hate Greeley."[40]

Party leadership realized that the defections had to be stopped. They knew that the Democrats could not accept a candidate who had little reformer support. In early June, Halstead received a "confidential and strictly personal" invitation to meet on June 20 with gentlemen "belonging to the different branches of the opposition" at the Fifth Avenue Hotel in New York. As Halstead had decided to support Greeley, he accepted the invitation to convince other Liberals to make the same decision. Some Liberals hoped the meeting could persuade Greeley to withdraw, allowing the leadership to nominate a new ticket. About one hundred Liberals attended the conference, which Jacob Cox chaired. Few wished to choose a new ticket. An early poll of the conferees showed that the majority had decided to accept Greeley. The meeting did give Schurz and Trumbull a chance to announce their support for the nominee.[41]

The conference adjourned with the majority agreeing to work for Greeley's election. A rump session of free traders met the next day and nominated their own candidates, although William S. Groesbeck, the Ohio Independent Democrat, and Frederick Law Olmsted, the New York landscape architect, both declined. Thus, Greeley could claim that the conference had been a success.

After the conference, Halstead believed that the Democrats had to accept the Liberal nominee. Democrats from both South and West, with only minor exceptions, did support Greeley's nomination. The South had lost its confidence in the Democratic party to win; its hatred of the *Tribune's* editor had been diminished by his sympathetic and conciliatory postwar attitude. In the West, Watterson convinced party leaders that Greeley had a greater chance for victory than either Adams or Trumbull. The only real opposition to Greeley came in the large mid-Atlantic states of New Jersey, New York, and Pennsylvania. Democratic leaders of these states maintained that Greeley's nomination meant the trading of one set of Republicans for another. By the time of the Baltimore convention, the pro-Greeley forces prevailed. The party endorsed the Cincinnati platform and accepted the Liberal candidates. A group of "true Democrats" held another convention in Louisville. Although the candidates they named refused to accept, their names appeared on ballots in twenty-three states.[42]

Throughout the campaign, Halstead and the other Quadrilateral editors gave their promised support. Halstead, still believing that Brown had made a corrupt bargain, found it easier to support Greeley. Brown went east to campaign in July; at a Yale class reunion he criticized all things eastern. "Gratz Brown must have been drunk as a damned fool can get at New Haven," Halstead wrote Reid. He said he knew men who wished to vote for Greeley but refused to do so because of Brown.[43]

Greeley proved to be a good campaigner. In August he toured some of the New England states, and in September the "October States"—those, like Ohio, that held elections in October. By the September tour, Halstead had lost confidence in a Liberal victory, although Greeley had gained new stature in his eyes. Greeley's speeches surprised both friends and enemies by their high tone, good temper, and vigor. He emphasized the need for restoration of peace and brotherhood to the still divided nation.[44]

Realizing that the election had been lost, Halstead justified his support for Greeley because the campaign had exposed the evils of Grant and Grantism. Moreover, the Democrats could never repudiate the principles they endorsed in their 1872 platform. There could be no further opposition to the constitutional amendments or the result of the war. "Look at it as we may . . . the Liberal movement is one which ought to gratify every patriotic soul."[45]

Prepared for defeat, Halstead still found the Ohio returns disheartening. Although the Liberals did well in the larger cities, they lost heavily in the smaller towns and rural areas. The Republicans also made important gains in the central and northern parts of the state. Even the Liberal-Democratic success in Cincinnati did not entirely pleae Halstead. Rutherford B. Hayes had been defeated in his bid for Congress from Hamilton County's Second District. Halstead said that this defeat did no damage to Hayes's "sterling reputation" but resulted from a loss of public confidence in the county Republican organization.[46]

By national election day Halstead had decided that Grant's luck, "in politics as in war," had secured his reelection. Consequently, his usual election day editorial tried to justify the reformers' opposition to the president. Repeating that the Cincinnati convention could have nominated a better candidate, he also declared Grant "a safe sort of president." Under him the nation could stand firm. Moreover, Greeley's defeat did not mean the failure of the Liberal movement. The success of the movement could be measured "in the removal of the asperities of party differences, and in harmonizing the antagonists of other days over the questions of this day, toward the homogeneity of the American people—a work of inestimable benefice." The reformers had accomplished the liberation of both parties, thus justifying the time, money, and hard work. Although Halstead thought that many Democrats had refused to vote, allowing Grant to win by default, and he also concluded that the president's personal popularity remained high among the voters.[47]

Halstead believed the Liberals' defeat was sealed at the convention; had the Quadrilateral controlled the platform and candidates, the movement could have succeeded against Grant. However, there is no evidence that Adams could have won in 1872. The "motley collection" of often self-appointed delegates, which included disappointed office seekers, free traders, protectionists, and reformers, never had the cohesion of a true opposition. Moreover, Grant's personal popularity could not be disputed. His victory, even against a well-organized opposition, seemed assured.

Although Halstead wished to believe that the Liberal movement had changed American politics, it had actually contributed little of lasting significance. Grant had received four more years in the White House, and reform had been soundly defeated. In fact, John G. Sproat has suggested that the party's real importance lay in demonstrating the futility of reform and emphasizing the power of the new Republican alliance of politicians and industrialists.[48]

Although Halstead had enjoyed the importance and public recognition that leadership in the movement had given him, he said that he had no interest in political power. In later years he regretted his participation in the Liberal cause. His support of Greeley remained the costliest experience of his life, resulting in large circulation and advertising losses for the *Commercial*. Finally, the struggle convinced him that success in reform meant working within the regular party organization. He never again played the role of a political independent.[49]

5

Return to Orthodoxy

The failure of the Liberal Republican party in 1872 and the depression that hit the country the following year had serious consequences for the *Commercial*. Although Halstead remained personally committed to independent journalism and the principles of reform, this commitment resulted in falling revenues for his newspaper. Long-time Republican subscribers turned to the loyal *Cincinnati Gazette* for news, and official advertising was channeled to other newspapers. As Halstead's basic political philosophy remained Republican, his financial condition dictated an early return to the party. The state gubernatorial election of 1875 began the process of reunion. The Democrats renominated Governor William Allen, and adopted a platform favoring inconvertible paper currency. The Republicans nominated ex-Governor Rutherford B. Hayes and demanded that greenbacks be redeemed for their face value in gold.[1]

Halstead believed that the currency question had implications for the forthcoming presidential contest. A Republican victory in Ohio could force the Democrats to abandon the Greenback contest on the national level, nominate conservative candidates, and write a sound platform. Consequently, the Republicans could be forced to nominate equally sound reform candidates, assuring the cleansing of the national administration. Calling for detachment from both parties, Halstead and the Liberals declared interest only in sound policies and reform. In July, Halstead wrote Schurz urging him to campaign in Ohio. Letters from other Liberals persuaded Schurz to spend part of September in the state. His popularity among German-Americans, and the impression of sincerity he had made on the hundreds of others who heard him, caused the chairman of the Republican state committee to give him credit for Hayes's victory. However, Samuel Bowles gave the credit to Halstead, who "did it" through his intelligent and informed editorials on the issue of resumption.[2]

Although a few Liberals wished to keep their party organization intact, most thought they saw strong reform elements within both the Republican and Democratic parties. While their prime enemies remained Grant and his associates, most Liberals saw their best chance for reform working within the Republican party. The capture of the United States House of Representatives by the Democrats in 1874 frightened many of the reformers, who claimed "Jeff Davis and Company" were responsible for the Democratic congressional program.[3]

Although Halstead had returned to the Republican party, he decided that the Liberals should retain an informal organization to have influence in the party. The rumor that Grant might try for a third term frightened him, although he declared that not "three Republicans in any Ohio school district" supported the move. He and Bowles promoted Adams as the best candidate for the Republicans in 1876.[4]

Near the end of April 1875, a group of Liberals gathered in New York to plan for the national campaign. While in New York, a reporter for the *Sun* interviewed Halstead, who declared himself an Adams man, although he mentioned Benjamin Bristow, Grant's reforming secretary of the treasury, as a possible Liberal nominee. When asked about the Democratic nominee, he answered, "not Governor Tilden . . . [because] he is positively an honest man." A year later in May 1876, the Liberals held a second New York meeting of about two hundred leaders at the Fifth Avenue Hotel. This gathering proposed to "prevent the national election of the centennial year from becoming a choice of evils." The leaders called upon both of the major parties to nominate reform candidates. Halstead, and the Liberal leadership who had returned to the Republican party, decided that party regulars could not accept Adams. They now turned to Bristow as their best candidate.[5]

Bristow, a Kentuckian, had an enviable record both as a soldier and an administrator. He had served as a lieutenant colonel of infantry under Grant, who appointed him solicitor general in 1870, and in 1874 secretary of the treasury. Although his activity in the prosecution of the whiskey frauds made him popular with reformers, it angered the president. The reformers saw him as the one uncorruptible and courageous man in the administration.[6]

Although Bristow had the support of the Liberals, James G. Blaine had greater backing with the party rank and file. A congressional amnesty debate, in which he defended "the boys in blue" and condemned the "rebel chieftain," made him a hero to millions in the North. In a letter to Halstead, Blaine stated that he had justified "that Credit Mobilier matter." However, since early spring the Cincinnati editor had known of the Mulligan letters, making it impossible for him to accept Blaine's pleas of innocence. Since Halstead wanted a reform nominee, he vowed to fight Blaine. While he wished to expose the Mulligan letters, he feared Blaine's reaction. Blaine might retaliate, throwing his support to a third candidate. Dana's *New York Sun* published the letters in late May. As Halstead had feared, Blaine believed the Bristow men responsible, resolving to block Bristow's nomination.[7]

While many candidates vied for the nomination, only Governor Hayes stirred widespread public support. An organization captained by William Henry Smith, the general agent for the Western Associated Press, secretly worked with the Bristow men to defeat Blaine and at the same time build second-choice support for Hayes.[8]

The Republicans met on June 14 in the Cincinnati hall used by the ill-fated Liberals. Many commentators mentioned that the "Spirit of '72" hovered over the building as the delegates "paid tributes to honest government." Pious sentiments to honesty in government notwithstanding, Blaine remained the most popular candidate. The short "plumed knight" speech of Colonel Robert G. Ingersoll sent the crowded galleries into wave after wave of cheering. He might have carried the delegates along with him had there been an immediate roll call. When the voting began on June 16, Blaine led for five ballots with opposition votes scattered between Oliver P. Morton, Roscoe Conkling, Bristow, and Hayes. On the sixth ballot, the Blaine strength began to increase, forcing stalwarts to choose between Bristow and Hayes or see Blaine nominated. Since the Bristow supporters had offended many old-guard Republicans, they naturally turned to Hayes.[9]

Most of the reformers echoed Halstead's opinion that while the party had "lost a great opportunity," it had "escaped a great disaster." Hayes had an unblemished record of faithful public service. Moreover, he proved his popular appeal as the first Ohio governor to gain a third term. His Civil War record and soundness in financial matters added to his stature. Halstead found him a satisfactory choice, "not a giant, but of good dimensions for reasonable service."[10]

After the convention, Halstead told Hayes that the pre-convention campaign had not expressed his personal feelings. He added that his public statements did not give a true estimate of the candidate. "It has not seemed to me becoming to be in haste to be expressive." Pledging to "keep step to the music and follow the flag of the Union," Halstead volunteered his services in the contest. Halstead believed that the convention had made a wise choice when his Washington correspondent wrote that "the original Hayes men, the Bristow men, a few of the Morton men, and very few of the Conkling men, in brief, the real reform element" constituted the "Hayes Party." Moreover, Schurz and other reform leaders felt that Hayes supported civil service reform.[11]

The Democratic convention, which met in St. Louis, nominated Samuel J. Tilden, the Democrat Halstead called "positively an honest man." As both parties nominated reform candidates, the Liberals had a hard choice. Most of them, believing their best chance for lasting reforms lay with the Republicans, supported Hayes.[12]

Halstead's endorsement of the Republican nominee caused some Democratic newspapers to point out his inconsistencies. How could he be unsparing in condemnation of Grant, while still damning the Democratic candidate and party? Halstead replied that he had not criticized the Republican party; he had fought Grant, who wasted and squandered the "glory of the party," making "the triumph of the Confederate Democrats possible." Though he conceded the "many and inexcusable" sins of the Republican administration, he called it folly and "national suicide" to turn the government over to a set of men whose "devoted adherence to constructions of constitutional dogmas . . . led logically to disunion."[13]

Halstead took a deep interest in the campaign, freely offering advice to the candidate. He told Hayes that the issue of southern war claims would decide the election. The war claims issue resulted from fear that a Democratic president and Congress might submit to southern demands for payment of Confederate debts. "The lately rebel elements will virtually dictate the measures . . . which the Democrats will carry out in Congress." The Democratic party gave abundant evidence of its subservience to southern influences.[14]

In September, Halstead began a campaign against war claims. Writing to Hayes, he said: "The Confederacy is attempting now what the idiots missed doing when they preferred war." Unsatisfied with his newspaper contributions to the campaign, Halstead suggested that he publish a newspaper supplement on the war claims issue for distribution in the doubtful states of New York, Ohio, and Indiana. He also promised to speak on the same issue in New York.[15]

Hayes agreed to the war claims speech in New York: "It touches the two vital things, first the whole Rebel menace; second it reaches Men's pockets—it is an answer to 'hard times.' " He also agreed that a New York speech and a newspaper supplement by the Cincinnati editor would be a great help to the campaign. Halstead spoke at Cooper Institute on October 25; he distributed the speech in the principal northern states as a newspaper supplement. Halstead considered this effort important. In the habit of dashing off editorials and long articles in minutes, he spent three days and nights on its composition.[16]

The New York speech brought out a large and fashionably dressed crowd. As Hayes had suggested, Halstead emphasized the unpatriotic character of the South and pointed out the danger to the American economy of granting southern claims. Speaking to an audience with a greater immediate interest in financial concerns than his Cincinnati readers, he carefully emphasized economic problems and pointed to continued horrors that the nation might expect from a once again powerful South: "It is the flagrant intention that these claims shall ultimately include the slaves emancipated by the sword, and that there shall be added to them the value, according to the estimates of the owners, of the cotton destroyed, and the corn, green and dry, in the fields, and cribs, that was consumed by men and beast in the national service. Then we see coming, like a cloud of grasshoppers, myriads of thousand dollar mules and pianos, and an endless array of velvet parlor furniture and rosewood fence-rails." Tilden's election, he asserted, would mean financial ruin for the country.[17]

When Halstead heard reports of Democratic frauds in southern states, he cautioned Hayes about a disputed election. He predicted that should the Democrats use intimidation and fraud to win, the Republicans would vigorously contest the election. Election day brought Tilden a popular majority, although South Carolina, Florida, and Louisiana produced disputed returns. The Democratic candidate carried the large northern states of New York, Indiana, Connecticut, and New Jersey for 184 undisputed votes, one short of election. Hayes needed all of the disputed votes to win. In the face of these overwhelming odds, the Republican national chairman decided to concede, but John Reid, a *New York Times* editor who had spent time in Libby Prison (one of the worst of the Confederate prison camps) during the war, persuaded him to claim the disputed states and the election for Hayes.[18]

In the three southern states, the Republican party controlled the election machinery. The party counted upon this control, along with the masses of black voters, to carry the election. The Democrats practiced intimidation and violence to keep blacks from the polls. Where possible, both parties resorted to fraud. In Florida and South Carolina, Republican election boards quickly certified Republican electors. As Democrats also claimed victory, they too sent returns to Washington.

In Louisiana, although Tilden received a comfortable majority, the Republicans controlled the election board. Even President Grant conceded Tilden a majority of some 6,000 to 8,000. For Hayes to claim Louisiana, the board needed to throw out thousands of Tilden's votes. "Observers" from both parties went south when they learned that the election depended on the vote of these three states. The Republicans asked Halstead to go to Louisiana since Watterson was to be a Democratic observer. He refused, saying he could not be of any use to the party.[19]

Without question, Halstead's career as an independent journalist ended in November 1876. His philosophy dictated telling his readers the complete story of the Louisiana canvassing board. Instead, he followed the straight Republican party line, stating that Tilden had found nothing "objectionable in his being raised to the Presidency by illegality, violence." Believing the blood of Union soldiers had been shed in vain if a "Democratic Confederacy" returned to national power, he allowed partisanship to blind him to the facts.[20]

Congress had found no solution to the problem of disputed returns when it met in December, although extremist threats from both sides frightened moderates, who forced a compromise plan. Congress formed a fifteen-man electoral commission that included five senators, five congressmen, and five supreme court justices. Because the Republicans controlled the Senate, and the Democrats the House, the legislation called for three members of each house to be from the majority party and two from the minority, making five Democrats and five Republicans. Two justices from each party chose the fifth—presumably David Davis, who had no strong party loyalties. The commission had final authority except when over-ridden by both houses of Congress. The Democrats believed Justice Davis would decide at least one electoral vote for Tilden. Unfortunately, on the day that the bill passed, the Illinois legislature elected Davis to the Senate, making him ineligible for the commission. All the remaining justices had Republican ties. Joseph P. Bradley, the most independent of the remaining justices, received the post. His colleagues hoped the gravity of the situation and not partisanship would determine his course.[21]

Abram S. Hewitt, the Democratic national chairman, also caused one vote from Oregon to be in dispute. Although Hayes clearly won a majority in Oregon, one of his electors, a local postmaster, violated the constitutional provision against electors holding positions of trust under the federal government. The Democratic governor refused his commission and certified a Democratic elector. The uncertified Republican resigned as postmaster, allowing the Republican electors to name him to the vacancy. Thus, Oregon also sent two sets of returns to Washington. Republicans maintained that the electoral commission had no right to investigate the canvassing boards' decisions. Hewitt reasoned that Oregon's case assured an investigation. Nonetheless, the commission voted to accept the Republican returns without investigation. In every case, it voted on strictly party lines for Hayes.[22]

The northern Democrats, angered by the partisan vote, found a solution to this new problem. They proposed a filibuster to keep the House in separate session, preventing the completion of the count before Grant's term ended. They felt the possibility of the country without a president might force the Electoral Commission to reconsider its decision. Surprisingly, when they proposed this plan in the Democratic caucus, the southerners lined up almost solidly in opposition. Since Halstead claimed the South would do anything to regain power for the Democratic party, he should have been surprised by the southern decision. Actually, he actively worked to produce the vote.[23]

During the preceding session of Congress, Hayes supporters noticed a division between the northern and southern members of the Democratic party. The southerners, their homeland suffering from the effects of reconstruction and depression, wanted federal grants for internal improvements. They argued that they deserved a share of the hundreds of millions already spent in the North. By 1876, northern Democrats had become spokesmen for reform and retrenchment, refusing to support additional subsidies. The Hayes men looked to this split in Democratic ranks as the key to Hayes's victory.[24]

As early as November, Halstead attempted to arrange a meeting between Senator L. Q. C. Lamar of Mississippi and Hayes. Lamar, a leading southern Democrat, visited Halstead in Cincinnati, although he refused to see Hayes in Columbus. Following Lamar's visit, Halstead arranged for Colonel W. H. Roberts, a close personal friend of Lamar and the managing editor of the *New Orleans Times*, to meet with Hayes. The *Enquirer* saw sinister implications in the meeting, although Halstead explained that "a gentleman of the press" had just paid a courtesy visit to Ohio's governor. Halstead said Roberts telegraphed reports to the *Commercial* from Louisiana; when he stopped in Cincinnati on his way to Washington, Halstead gave the New Orleans editor a letter of introduction to the governor. Roberts and his friend James M. Comly, editor of the *Ohio State Journal*, called upon the governor to give him a firsthand report on conditions in Louisiana.[25]

Though an opening had been made, the meeting did not produce a compromise. Roberts stated he had no authority from southern Democrats to make any "proposition looking to a compromise." Although Halstead thought the Hayes-Roberts conference promising, he did not know how to proceed. With Hayes's visitors closely watched by the press, additional meetings needed to be in less conspicuous places, between men on more intimate terms.[26]

An organization which could provide these conditions already existed. The Western Associated Press, which Halstead served as president, had on its board of directors leading publishers of the western press, both north and south. Colonel A. J. Kellar of the *Memphis Avalanche* commanded the respect of southern political leaders. He hated the northern Democratic party, calling Tilden "the most contemptible and dangerous politician this country has ever seen." He willingly agreed to help Hayes gain the presidency in exchange for concessions to the South.[27]

William Henry Smith, Western Associated Press general agent, and others of the Hayes faction proposed a Republican–southern Democratic alliance. Smith privately discussed the possibilities of a union between the Republican party and the Whig and Douglas Democratic elements of the South. He believed that many of the political leaders of the South had more in common with the Republican party than with northern Democrats. Many had been Whigs before the slavery controversy drove them into the Democratic party, and many retained their Whig economic orientation. Hayes's advisers thought that promises of federal aid for river and harbor improvements, a federal subsidy for the Texas and Pacific Railroad project, and closer economic ties with the North could sever their shaky alliance with northern Democrats.[28]

Halstead saw no reason why some former Whigs who supported the southern Democrats during the war "should not, now that those issues are out of the way, seek party relations that are more congenial on other questions." Smith arranged for General Henry Boynton, the Washington correspondent for the *Cincinnati Gazette*, to negotiate with Kellar. In accepting the Republican nomination, Hayes promised noninterference in the internal affairs of the South. This became the point emphasized by Boynton and Kellar in their negotiations. As a Tennessee newspaperman, Kellar could talk to southern Congressmen without arousing suspicion. Kellar spent December in Washington sounding out southern representatives. On his return to Memphis he stopped in Cincinnati to tell Halstead of "the death of the Solid South."[29]

As a result of the talks, Hayes agreed to end carpetbag rule in the South, appoint a conservative southerner to his cabinet, support federal grants for southern internal improvements and education, and favor a subsidy for the Texas and Pacific Railroad. In return, southerners promised fair treatment for blacks and cooperation on the electoral count.[30]

Halstead also had an active role in helping Hayes choose his cabinet. One of his sons later claimed that "Sam Bowles, Horace White, Carl Schurtz [sic] and my father selected the cabinet . . . in our parlor"—an exaggeration, although Hayes did have a conference on the cabinet in Halstead's parlor on February 11, 1877.

Hayes asked Halstead for a meeting "to talk over the situation."
The editor replied that he felt "highly the honor and the responsibility of the privilege." He suggested the Halstead home to avoid
"any newspaper nonsense about seeing you." Years later Halstead
commmented that Hayes asked his advice on the cabinet because
he had a large circle of distinguished friends and could answer
questions about them.[31]

Halstead urged Hayes to appoint Carl Schurz to the cabinet. He
believed that Hayes could reward the aid he received from the
Liberal wing of the party by this appointment. Moreover, he felt
the Missourian had administrative abilities. When Schurz suggested that the reform element might be better represented by Bristow
in the Treasury Department, Halstead replied, "You suggest I go to
Columbus to meet Hayes and talk Bristow. I saw him here and
talked Schurz." He believed Schurz best suited for Interior because
of the possibility of civil service reform in that department. On
February 25, Hayes announced his intention to appoint Schurz
secretary of the interior. William Henry Smith did not want any
prominent reform figure in the cabinet; he declared Schurz's choice
"was Halstead's work after I left."[32]

For the rest of the cabinet, Halstead urged Hayes to appoint
William M. Evarts as secretary of state; John Sherman as secretary
of the treasury; John M. Harlan, Bristow's campaign manager and
law partner, as attorney general; Eugene Hale, Zach Chandler's
son-in-law, as postmaster general; and General Joseph R. Hawley, of
Connecticut, as secretary of the navy. This slate, Halstead claimed,
satisfied everyone and left the War Department open for further
maneuvering. Halstead believed that Harlan, a Kentucky Union
man, fulfilled the promise to appoint a southerner. Hayes did not
think the South would accept Harlan. He suggested Thomas Settle, a North Carolina politician for the Navy Department, with
Hawley going to the War Office. Settle remained in the revised
cabinet plans only a short time. On February 19 Halstead wrote
Hayes, "He is said to be a very hard drinker—habits spoiling him
for business—and a fraud in other respects, shaky as to integrity,
etc." Moreover, southern congressmen wanted more than the Navy
post. Hayes gave in to their demands and appointed David M. Key
of Tennessee postmaster general. Key, Kellar's friend, had been
the choice of the arbitrators.[33]

Halstead advised Hayes to include no one in the cabinet from

Indiana. Hayes showed "practical political sagacity" in not heeding his advice as Morton had worked hard for Hayes's election. Moreover, after Thaddeus Stevens's death, Morton led the radicals in the Senate. Hayes needed Morton's support for a new southern policy. Consequently, he named Richard W. Thompson secretary of the navy. The appointment of Thompson, a Morton "puppet," appeased the powerful Indiana senator.[34]

Hayes decided two other appointments on practical political grounds. He named Charles A. Devens, a Massachusetts judge and law partner of Senator George F. Hoar, attorney general. Iowa Congressman George W. McCrary, who sponsored the electoral commission bill, became secretary of war. A friend of General Grenville M. Dodge, the chief engineer of the Texas and Pacific Railroad, McCrary could act to fulfill arbitration commitments for the railroad subsidy.[35]

Of the original group discussed in Halstead's parlor, three—Evarts, Sherman, and Schurz—sat in the most important seats in the cabinet. Hale declined the postmaster general's office. Hayes filled the other four positions at the end of February. Although his son's account of the parlor conference may be inaccurate, it demonstrates the important role Halstead did play in advising Hayes. In 1872 Halstead denounced the Republican party and all of its policies; in 1877, as a close friend and trusted adviser of a Republican president, he helped choose the cabinet.

The phrase from Hayes's inaugural, "He serves his party best who serves his country best," vindicated Halstead's course in returning to the Republican party. This one phrase also served to sum up Halstead's political philosophy. He never again pursued an independent course in politics, arguing that he could serve his country best by serving the Republican party.

During the Hayes administration, the warm relationship between president and editor continued. Both Halstead and his daughter Jenny frequently visited at the White House. The relationship between the two men remained intimate, with press reports saying that Hayes planned to appoint his friend to a diplomatic post. Halstead always denied these rumors. Soon after the inaugural, several newspapers mentioned the French post; Halstead said it "has never been seriously thought of." Later many newspapers carried the story of Halstead's impending appointment as minister to England. The editor said he could not accept a foreign appointment because of his newspaper affairs. Having recently gone into debt to increase his interest in the *Commercial,* he told Hayes that he "must make money."[36]

Early in his administration, Hayes said he did not plan to seek reelection. Halstead editorially decried Hayes's announcement disavowing a second term. Hayes declared his intention not to run "under any circumstances," and requested Halstead to stop mentioning his name. He said that such talk weakened his efforts to "improve and purify things." Halstead regretted Hayes's decision, because he thought Grant had support for a third term in 1880. If Grant received the nomination, Halstead said he "wouldn't fool away time on a third party but go for the Democrat."[37]

As Grant's stalwart support became evident, Halstead began an editorial campaign against the former president. Grant's partisans, Halstead declared, had interest only in "the weaknesses, the stupidities and the corruption of his administration." Later the editor said that they wished for a dynasty. "Imperialism means facilities, without limitation of time or fear of investigation, for robbing the people. If Grant is demanded for a third term . . . and . . elected, the demand for him for a fourth term, if he should live so long would be redoubled." Privately Halstead expressed the same opinions. He told Whitelaw Reid that Grant "would utterly disgrace the nation." He could be beaten in Ohio, "and I will help to do it—no matter about the opposing man." Although Halstead supported John Sherman for the nomination, he could accept Blaine in preference to Grant.[38]

Halstead proposed that the anti-Grant forces first defeat the third-term movement, then work for their own candidates. He told Reid "that the Republican leader who fights Grant first and hardest will win." Halstead also said that should the Republican convention meet in Cincinnati he could assure Grant's defeat. Holding the convention in the Queen City "would take the bloom off the Grant boom at once." The strong Sherman forces in the city, his own newspaper, and Richard Smith's *Gazette,* all actively worked against the third term. Moreover, Halstead pledged to forgo anti-Blaine *Commercial* editorials. "I will not only not abuse Blaine, but I will give him in every way fair play, and I will cultivate a local sentiment friendly to him by crediting him with bringing the convention." Halstead realized that a Cincinnati convention gave Sherman the advantage of home ground. The Blaine forces also saw this advantage to Sherman; they chose Chicago for the convention.[39]

The Blaine supporters did not trust Halstead's promises. In March 1878, Blaine had attacked Carl Schurz on the Senate floor for a decision he had made as secretary of the interior. The senator sarcastically alluded to Schurz's German ancestry. Halstead called the Maine senator "an ignorant, rude, and malicious man, and a disappointed speculator in the Presidency." He declared that the speech showed Blaine in his true light, "a coarse, sneering Know-Nothing, catering to rascalities and indulging malice."[40]

When Halstead realized the possibility of Grant's success in the 1880 convention, he put aside animosity toward Blaine. He believed that Blaine could rally the party and prevent a third-term nomination. In February 1880, Halstead even stated editorially his new-found respect for Blaine, declaring him preferable to Grant because he could win. Moreover, despite many faults, Blaine could give the country good administration and the party strong leadership.[41]

Blaine did not wish to stop Grant only to prepare the ground for another candidate. In April he wrote Halstead complaining that although everyone wished him to fight Grant, the favorite sons refused to withdraw in his favor. The Maine senator stated that he could have defeated Grant in Ohio, although he never had the chance, since Sherman refused to withdraw. If Grant should win, Blaine told the editor, it could be blamed on "local jealousy and state pride!"[42]

The opposition to Grant formed "No Third Term" clubs to fight the former president. Halstead supported this movement, although Blaine believed that it could also hurt his candidacy. When the clubs held a convention in St. Louis, Blaine feared a "Bowles-Adams, 'Young Republican,' sentimental-civil service-jackass concern," that might condemn him along with Grant."[43]

When the Republican convention met in June, James A. Garfield, newly elected senator from Ohio and Sherman's floor leader, led the anti-Grant forces. By adroit management, Garfield kept the convention from stampeding to Grant. His organizing abilities impressed many of the delegates. Later in the convention he enhanced his reputation by an eloquent nominating speech for Sherman. When the convention became deadlocked between the Grant forces and the splinter groups of the opposition, Garfield became the compromise candidate of the Blaine and Sherman supporters. He won the nomination on the thirty-sixth ballot.[44]

Although Halstead knew Garfield, he had never been a personal friend. In the past, the *Commercial* had carried editorials critical of the nominee. One had suggested that Garfield had "not kept himself in the attitude that should have distinguished an honest man in his relations to the robbers of the District of Columbia." Although the paper had also mentioned Garfield in connection with the Credit Mobilier scandal, it accepted his denial of any involvement. Halstead had also criticized him as a senatorial candidate, saying that he lacked power, "self-assertion, executive aptitude" and the qualities of "large leadership." On his election as senator, Halstead said the Ohio Republicans had made a mistake because the next Republican House of Representatives would have elected Garfield Speaker. Nonetheless, Halstead willingly wrote off "Garfield's mistakes," stating he "needed a good deal of admonition" because of a tendency to "dwell upon a mountain. . . . He was still boyish about some things and the speculative men in public life sought to beguile him." Yet Halstead found the congressman always growing. He had the ability to laugh at critical articles, "even if they had stings in them." Moreover, since Garfield's "little faults" had been publicized, he could not be accused of any wrong intent.[45]

Halstead missed seeing the developing Garfield strength at the convention. When *Commercial* reporters told him that Garfield might be the nominee, he refused to accept their judgments. After the nomination, the editor pledged his support, calling the nomination a happy solution to the difficulties of the party. While Halstead reiterated his preference for Sherman, he said the country accepted Garfield as the next president.[46]

After the convention, Halstead went to New York for a meeting of the National Republican Committee. He found the stalwart wing of the party angered and demanding special guarantees. Senator Conkling had apprehensions about "another Ohio man," and felt that Garfield should come to New York to ask for his support. Halstead advised against such a trip. The public might see it as going "to Canosa [sic]."[47]

While in New York, Halstead met Conkling for the first time. Ohio's Governor Charles Foster told the story that after the editor's introduction to Conkling, the senator had asked, "Who was that man?" Given the name again, he had said: "Halstead, Halstead, isn't he an editor somewhere? Oh, I remember, he's editor of the *Cincinnati Gazette.*" Whitelaw Reid wrote that if Foster had irritated the editor with the story, Halstead could report that Conkling, when asked to make campaign speeches for Foster in Ohio, had said: "Foster, Foster, is he a Republican then?"[48]

Garfield did not take Halstead's advice. Without New York he could lose the election. Although Conkling did not attend the New York meeting of party and candidate, he did invite Garfield to his home. Garfield told Halstead that the invitation meant, "I may have a pocket interview with my Lord Roscoe; but if the Presidency is to turn on that I do not want the office badly enough to go." Instead, he returned to Ohio.[49]

Halstead rode to Ohio with Garfield's party. Several newspapers criticized him for using his position as president of the Western Associated Press to gain news coverage of Garfield's trip for the *Commercial.* Halstead feared that he had made a mistake traveling with the candidate. To men like Conkling, Halstead represented the reform wing of the party. They distrusted his close association with Garfield.[50]

Never a close friend of the candidate, Halstead had little actual connection with the 1880 campaign. Yet he actively supported Garfield, using all the resources of the *Commercial* to gain his election. In September the editor began publishing a campaign edition of the *Commercial,* which he called "the best Republican document for universal distribution of which we have knowledge." He wrote every editorial in these campaign editions, basing them almost entirely on the "bloody shirt." The solid South, he declared, had become "the reorganized Southern Confederacy": "They do not seem to understand that they got the worst of the war. . . . The magnanimity with which they have been treated, and which all the rest of the world recognized as remarkable they do not appreciate. . . . Under all these circumstances it seems to us of infinite consequence that the Republicans should make their victories in the free States—the phrase is as good and true as it ever was—overwhelming from ocean to ocean." The editor had forgotten his earlier calls for understanding between the two sections. The country must not allow these southern "Confederate" Democratic leaders to reestablish their rule over the whole nation.[51]

The *Commercial* celebrated Garfield's victory by running a front-page engraving of the president-elect that covered five of the newspaper's eight columns. Under the engraving an American eagle sat on a draped United States flag with a Democratic cock in its beak. The cock's feathers flew in all directions. The remaining columns bore such headlines as "ALL SAFE!" "Old Man Secesh Will Smile No More." "The Stars in Their Course Fight with Us."[52]

Soon after the election, Halstead received a letter from John Sherman. Sherman had been a successful secretary of the treasury, as his strong candidacy for the presidency had shown. Although several newspapers reported that Garfield planned to retain him in that post, the new president had not communicated with the secretary. Sherman had strong support in Ohio for election to Garfield's Senate seat. Although Sherman indicated his willingness to continue in the cabinet, he preferred the Senate. Halstead wrote Garfield that Sherman had felt embarrassed because the president-elect had not talked to him about remaining in the cabinet. Halstead suggested that Garfield appoint another Ohioan to the cabinet, and save the Senate for Sherman. Garfield made no commitment, but Sherman ultimately went to the Senate.[53]

In early January, Halstead sent Garfield a newspaper clipping which stated that the editor had chosen the new cabinet. Although Halstead had given Garfield advice on cabinet appointments, he had had little influence on final choices. Blaine, the editor's choice, became secretary of state, though this had been expected. Garfield did not heed Halstead's advice to include Governor Foster in the cabinet. Some Republican leaders felt that the breach in the party could be healed with Conkling in the cabinet. Halstead wrote to argue against Conkling, suggesting Senator Morton as a possible stalwart candidate for the Treasury. However, he warned that Morton might promote his own interests. He also suggested Benjamin Harrison as a good choice for an Indiana man in the cabinet. The final Garfield cabinet bore little resemblance to Halstead's proposals. Nonetheless, Garfield said that he valued Halstead's advice.[54]

Halstead supported Garfield's efforts to strengthen his own party organization at the expense of the stalwarts. When the new president appointed William H. Robertson, a New York Blaine supporter and Conkling's archenemy, collector of the Port of New York, one of the most important patronage positions in the country, Halstead applauded, saying: "The boys are all yelling about it and the old folks are really glad." Although Conkling tried to block confirmation, Garfield stood firm. Halstead wired, "Compromises impossible, victory certain"; the appointment went through. Conkling and fellow New York Senator Thomas Platt resigned from their seats. Although they sought vindication by reelection, the New York legislature named two moderate Republicans in their place.[55]

Halstead stopped in Washington on June 30 to pay his respects to the president. Finding Garfield out, he strolled through Lafayette Square. The editor later learned that Charles J. Guiteau had also been in the park that evening. When he later returned to the White House, he found Garfield in high spirits. The president had planned a trip to Williams College for commencement in two days, thus escaping patronage problems and Washington's summer heat. He invited Halstead to join the party, which included several cabinet officers, to see "the sweetest old place in the world." Halstead declined because of business. On July 2, as Garfield's party boarded the train, Guiteau fired the shots that claimed the president's life on September 19.[56]

Soon after the shooting, a Newark, Ohio, man said he hoped that Garfield died. Captain C. A. Cook slapped the man's face. The police arrested Cook, and he received a small fine. The *Commercial* asked subscribers to send pennies to pay the fine. At first everyone sending a penny had his name printed. By August 10, 50,000 people had contributed and Halstead discontinued the lists when they threatened to take over the entire newspaper. The collection ended on September 23 when 98,838 people had sent pennies.[57]

Although Halstead had known President Chester Arthur for ten years, they had had no intimate connections. When Arthur became president, Halstead editorialized that Arthur had a "deeper and more intelligent sense of the responsibilities of the office than the people generally give him credit for." The editor asked that the new president "at least be given a fair show." Although Halstead called upon Arthur in October 1881, he remained only a political observer of the new administration.[58]

In less than ten years, Halstead's independent journalism had been cast aside and the *Commercial* had become a Republican party organ. Halstead never disagreed with the basic policies of the party. He supported tariff reform, because he believed the protective tariff hurt Ohio business interests. When Ohio businessmen accepted the tariff, so did Halstead. Although financial necessity dictated giving up his independent course, Hayes's nomination for the presidency remained the single greatest reason for Halstead's return to party regularity. Few men could resist the attraction of having a personal friend in the White House.

6

National Politics

A momentous change in Halstead's life occurred in 1884. The *Commercial,* which Halstead had controlled since Potter's death in 1867, merged with Richard Smith's *Cincinnati Gazette.* Both newspapers faced financial difficulties. Although the merger tried to reverse the decline, it also meant the complete end of any attempt to retain the concept of independent journalism. The new *Commercial Gazette* announced its support of the Republican party, and Halstead played an active role in Blaine's election campaign.

The *Commercial* had experienced financial difficulties even before the 1879 reorganization of M. Halstead and Company into a joint stock company. Halstead's support of the Liberal Republican party lost his newspaper Republican patronage and subscribers. His controversy with Archbishop Purcell further added to his problems. As the seventies advanced, new journalistic technology increased expenses more rapidly than profits. Telegraph costs mounted yearly as Cincinnati readers demanded more national and international news. The charge for composition also rose as cheap newsprint encouraged Halstead and other publishers to expand the number of pages in their newspapers. Although newspaper competition in Cincinnati had always been great, the *Commercial* retained its position through Halstead's policy of immediately adopting innovations in news gathering and printing. This process of constant technical improvement ultimately caused profits to decline. In the sixties the *Commercial* could easily absorb the increasing costs of

The Cincinnati office building of the *Commercial,* completed in 1864.

innovation, because Cincinnati was growing rapidly. The circulation and advertising market of the newspaper grew with it. By the
seventies the percentage growth of many other western cities out-
stripped that of Cincinnati. The railroad undermined river shipping and, with it, Cincinnati's position as the Queen City of the
West. Consequently, the *Commercial* competed in a closed market
with competitors as determined to gain circulation and advertisers
as Halstead. Halstead now made technical changes in the *Commercial's* plant to keep abreast of the competition, not to keep ahead of
it. Increased revenues had paid for earlier innovations, but now
Halstead was forced to turn to long-term loans.[1]

In 1883 Edward Wyllis Scripps purchased the *Cincinnati Post*, bringing to the city the experience that he and his family had gained in Detroit, Buffalo, St. Louis, and Cleveland. The *Post* became a two-cent evening publication. Both well-written and forceful, it emphasized coverage of the local scene. Above all, the *Post* distinguished itself in its devotion to the interests of the workingman.

Competition from the *Enquirer*, with its unlimited resources and its emphasis on sensation, had hurt both the *Commercial* and the *Gazette*. At a price three cents less than either the *Commercial* or the *Gazette*, the competition from an enlivened and vigorous *Post* became disastrous. The *Post* soon gained circulation leadership in the city. Since circulation determined advertising rates, the two older publications became victims of both falling circulation and reduced advertising revenues.[2]

Added to its appeal as a less-expensive paper, the *Post* also published in the evening. In the 1880s a revolution occurred in the reading habits of urban Americans. The evening newspaper could be read at leisure after the day's work. Moreover, housewives, to whom retailers directed their advertising, seemed to prefer an evening newspaper. Improved communication and new high-speed means of production also meant that an evening paper could publish the news of the current day. By the end of the decade, two of every three daily newspapers in the United States published evening editions. The *Commercial* and the *Gazette* remained morning newspapers.

Workers and their families made up the largest single element of the Cincinnati reading public. Neither the *Commercial* nor the *Gazette* had been known for its devotion to the workingman or, more particularly, to his rights. Halstead never supported the rights of workers to organize in unions. He particularly criticized any government intervention between employee and employers. As early as 1866 he denounced the concept of the state-imposed eight-hour day, stating that the next step would be government-imposed minimum wages. "What insurance is there that it will not next undertake to prescribe, not only how long, but for how much, the laborer shall be entitled to work?"[3]

Although the *Commercial* probably lost readers among the working class because of these views, more serious losses to its circulation resulted from strikes and boycotts in 1870 and 1881. The *Enquirer* and *Post* endorsed the union movement and employed union workers. Halstead claimed his problems stemmed from the unions being under McLean's control. Halstead refused to make his printing plants closed shops. In 1870 and 1881, workers walked off the job, only to be immediately replaced by nonunion printers and composers. The strikers then attempted a boycott as their only recourse. Although Halstead claimed their boycotts ineffectual, the *Commercial* lost circulation in both cases. Thus, just as the rate of increase in Cincinnati's population began to slow, the large working-class population found its champion in the *Post*.[4]

It became evident that Cincinnati could not support two competing Republican morning newspapers. Although "Deacon" Smith and Halstead had long been rivals, their agreement on party issues since 1876 had made this rivalry increasingly friendly. Smith's *Gazette*, the city's oldest newspaper, claiming origin in 1793, suffered the same financial problems as the *Commercial*. Halstead had long been recognized as a brilliant editor; Smith had organizing and executive talents. Consequently, negotiations during the fall of 1883 produced an agreement to consolidate the two newspapers, with Halstead as president and editor-in-chief and Smith as vice-president and business manager of the new company.[5]

Former President Hayes expressed the sentiment of many when he wrote to ensure his subscription to the new paper. Although declaring that the combination produced one of the greatest, "perhaps the greatest," newspaper on earth, he nonetheless felt a "certain regret and gloom that . . . the old *Gazette* and the old *Commercial* are to be seen no more." Both editors agreed with Hayes. Nonetheless, they recognized that the merger had given them a chance to save their newspapers from bankruptcy. The new combination also gave the Republican party a strong voice in Cincinnati to compete with the powerful Democratic *Enquirer*.[6]

The new *Commercial Gazette* pledged support for the Republican presidential nominee in 1884. Once again, Halstead favored the candidacy of John Sherman, although half of the Ohio delegation supported Blaine, making the Ohio senator's chances even more remote than in 1880. Moreover, by 1884 Halstead had no strong objections to Blaine's nomination, since he and the former Maine senator had established an intimate friendship, which had begun in 1880 when both men had worked to prevent Grant's nomination for a third term. By 1882 the two men exchanged visits, and Blaine sent Halstead items for the *Commercial's* editorial columns.[7]

In an article published in 1896, Halstead told of his participation in the 1884 preconvention maneuvering. A week before the Chicago meeting, Halstead received a telegram from Blaine requesting him to come to Washington. At their meeting Blaine told the editor that the political situation alarmed him. Halstead asked: "You surely are not afraid you are not going to be nominated?" To which Blaine responded, "Oh, no; I am afraid I shall be nominated, and have sent for you for that reason, and want you to assist in preventing my nomination." Blaine told the editor that he had come to his decision after weighing all the factors involved. Everything, he said, pointed to his inability to win the election. He believed that he could not win without New York and that he could not carry that state. Nonetheless, Blaine proposed a winning ticket: William T. Sherman and Robert T. Lincoln. Halstead replied that General Sherman would decline the nomination. Moreover, the general had refused to oppose his brother at the Chicago convention. The editor asked, why "not try the other Sherman?" Blaine replied that since John Sherman had had no military experience, he too could not carry New York. Although Blaine had written promising the general his support, Sherman replied that "he could not consent to be President." Nonetheless, Blaine declared, "If General Sherman had the question put to him—whether to be President himself or turn the office over to the Democratic party, with the Solid South dominant—he would see his duty and do it."[8]

After leaving Blaine in Washington, Halstead hurried to Chicago for the convention. He found the galleries packed with Blaine supporters. One delegate later called the situation impossible for a deliberative body; "I saw women jumping up and down, disheveled and hysterical, and some men acting in much the same way. It was absolutely unworthy of a convention of any party, a disgrace to decency, and a blot upon the reputation of our country." On the fourth ballot the "shrieking galleries" had their way—Blaine received the nomination.[9]

A *Commercial Gazette* editorial stated that although Blaine had worked for the nomination in 1876 and 1880, in 1884 it had come "literally without his seeking . . . the free gift of the plain Republicans of the United States, whose enthusiasm for the Maine statesman . . . defeated all attempts at a combination to defeat him. If ever there was a nomination by the voice of the people Blaine's certainly is such a nomination." Although the nomination may have been a "free gift" from the people of the party, some party leaders did not believe that the convention had made a wise choice. These men, many of them of the Liberal reform wing of the party, disbelieved Blaine's explanation of the Mulligan letters. This group, christened "Mugwumps" by the regular Republicans, announced their support for Grover Cleveland, the Democratic candidate. Some of the country's most influential magazines and newspapers, including *Harper's Weekly,* the *Nation, Puck,* the *New York Herald, Times, Evening Post,* and *Telegram,* the *Boston Transcript, Herald,* and *Advertiser,* the *Springfield Republican,* the *Philadelphia Record,* and the *Times* and *News* of Chicago, also bolted the Republican party.[10]

In a signed editorial, Halstead and Smith pledged the support of the *Commercial Gazette* to the Blaine ticket. They supported the Republicans, the newspaper's owners declared, because the southern Confederacy backed the Democrats. Halstead scoffed at the Mugwumps even though some, such as Carl Schurz, had previously been close friends and political associates. True, he declared, "Blaine was not the kind of candidate that people sprung from six generations of Harvard graduates would promote for the presidency," yet these same "particular people" took a long time discovering Abraham Lincoln's merits as president. The Mugwumps, because they disliked Blaine, planned to turn the government over to the Democrats to plunder the country.[11]

Halstead originally planned to base his newspaper campaign on the "bloody shirt." He soon enlarged this scheme to include attacks on the Democratic nominee's personal character. In the early seventies, Maria Halpin, a Buffalo department store clerk, had sexual relations with Cleveland and several other men. She named Cleveland as the father of her illegitimate son. He accepted paternity. Cleveland's supporters claimed that as a bachelor he had admitted responsibility to protect the reputations of the married men involved.[12] The scandal seemed made to order for Halstead's pen: ". . . it is our opinion that the President of the United States should be the honored head of a family. . . . it is best that the first lady of the land should be the wife of the President, and that the beauties of a virtuous home should be present in the Executive Mansion and not the perfumes of a brothel."[13] And later: "For Grover Cleveland's offenses there is no excuse. He may repent and he may reform— but the stool of repentance should not be carried to the White House by the ballot of the American people, whose government rests upon virtue, and which virtue has its abiding in the family."[14] Thus Maria Halpin supplied the Republicans an issue to help answer the Mulligan letters.

Blaine believed that the state of New York would decide the election. The strategists of the Republican National Committee agreed, finding New York City the key to the state. Consequently, Republican planners worried about the many defections from party regularity among the New York City press. Of the newspapers supporting Blaine, only the *Tribune* had a wide circulation. Moreover, a boycott of the *Tribune* by the typographical union hurt the party's cause among workers. The Republican National Committee decided to establish a lively and unrestrained "penny" campaign newspaper with mass appeal. For their editor the committee chose the "stalwart and irrepressible" Halstead. Halstead's duties on the newspaper, the *New York Extra*, allowed him to continue his editorial work for the *Commercial Gazette*. He rented a private telegraph wire to send his daily editorials to Cincinnati. Telling Cincinnati readers of the political importance of New York, Halstead said that his personal views from the scene made the *Commercial Gazette*'s political coverage equal to the best in the country.[15]

Publication of the *Extra* started in mid-August and continued until the election. In both of his newspapers Halstead conducted a campaign attacking Cleveland's moral fiber and warning that southern Democrats would dominate the country with Cleveland's election. The Democrats struck back with their own attacks against an equally vulnerable Blaine. Blaine, as Speaker of the House of Representatives, had ruled favorably on renewal of a land grant for an Arkansas railroad. Later he and Warren Fisher, a Boston broker, sold the bonds of this Arkansas railroad to their friends. When the bonds proved nearly worthless, Blaine returned the investors' money by reselling the bonds to the Union Pacific Railroad at a greatly inflated price. These very suspicious manipulations came to light when James Mulligan, an employee of Fisher's, furnished a House investigating committee copies of the Blaine-Fisher correspondence. Blaine secured the letters before their publication, and read extracts from them to the House. He combined this reading with a brilliant speech in which he claimed to have done nothing unethical. His speech and the publication of the letters before the 1876 Republican convention had caused him to lose the nomination. Though his supporters either believed his explanation or accepted his financial dealings as a product of the era, many Republicans believed that the letters proved Blaine's corruption. Soon after his nomination in 1884, further Blaine-Fisher correspondence came to light, including a draft of a letter in Blaine's handwriting exonerating himself from all wrongdoing. He requested Fisher to copy the letter, sign his own name, and send it back to him. Blaine also instructed Fisher to "burn this letter." Fisher neither copied nor burned the letter; the anti-Blaine forces had political ammunition to match the Maria Halpin story.[16]

The Mugwumps saw the additional letters as further proof of their reasons for deserting the Republican nominee. The letters particularly embarrassed Halstead because of his violent attacks on the honesty of Blaine in 1876. The editorials Halstead had written then now came out in circulars distributed by the Democratic party. Many people sent Halstead copies of the circulars "with lots of illiterate scribbling on the margins," asking him about his current opinion of Blaine.

Halstead argued that he had been unfair to Blaine in 1876. As for the new letters, they left no "shadow of a doubt upon the proposition that injustice was done Blaine in 1876, for the gravest form of accusation against him then was that he had suppressed a portion of the letters taken from Mulligan. His enemies have furnished the proof on his head." Obviously, Halstead worked hard for this argument. He utterly ignored the contents of the letters, making the issue one of suppression. Now that the letters were no longer suppressed, there could be no issue.[17]

In another editorial, Halstead defended Blaine on the content of the Mulligan letters. He argued that the letters showed a friendship between Blaine and Fisher. Even though Blaine made a ruling favoring Fisher's interest, because the ruling was correct it could not be questioned. Finally, Blaine made reference to it in a letter to his old friend—"that was not at all a surprising thing to do." After making this ruling, Blaine naturally became interested in the outcome of the enterprise and decided to participate in the undertaking. "Where was the harm in this?" The Mugwumps saw the harm in that Blaine, in his official capacity, had made decisions involving his personal financial interests. Moreover, Halstead left one critical question unanswered: would the Union Pacific have bought the bonds if it did not expect favors in return?[18]

Halstead found the New York political scene extremely complex.

In addition to the Democratic and Republican candidates, John P. St. John, a former Republican governor of Kansas, headed the Prohibition ticket with strong support from Frances Willard's Women's Christian Temperance Union; and General Benjamin Butler appeared on an Anti-Monopoly–Greenback ticket. St. John expected to draw Republican votes from Blaine. The Republican National Committee secretly financed Butler's campaign, hoping to take Democratic votes from Cleveland. The Irish further complicated the picture. Although nominally the Irish voted for Democratic candidates, Blaine could claim Irish descent. With a Roman Catholic mother and a cousin in a convent, he made a strong appeal to the Irish voter. To emphasize the point, the Republican press called Cleveland a "free trader" and the "British candidate."[19]

Many Republicans believed that Blaine's presence could guarantee the election and urged him to come to New York City. Over the opposition of Halstead, Blaine went to New York to speak during the last week of the campaign. As it turned out, Halstead had advised him correctly, since the New York tour proved disastrous for the candidate. Blaine spoke on the morning of October 29 to a group of Protestant ministers. Samuel D. Burchard, a Presbyterian clergyman introduced him by proclaiming: "We are Republicans, and don't propose to leave our party and identify ourselves with the party whose antecedents have been rum, Romanism, and rebellion." Blaine, engaged in conversation during the introduction, did not hear Burchard's unfortunate alliteration, and so made no comment on it in his speech. A reporter in the crowd did hear the remark. Within hours handbills and Democratic newspapers carried the story. Blaine had seemingly accepted an insult to the very group he courted, losing thousands of Irish votes.[20]

Adding to the morning's fiasco, Blaine attended a dinner that evening at Delmonico's given by some of the wealthiest men in the city and the party's top financial supporters. The next day the *New York World* in a front-page cartoon showed "the Royal Feast of Belshazzar Blaine," with the diners feasting on "Monopoly Soup," "Lobby Pudding," "Navy Contract," and "Gould Pie," while a starving and ragged workingman and his wife looked on through a window. The high rate of unemployment in New York meant that Blaine lost many more votes.[21]

Election day found Halstead back in Cincinnati anxiously awaiting the New York vote. Although the first returns left the outcome in doubt, they did not favor Blaine. Halstead refused to accept Blaine's defeat, claiming a Republican victory for three days after the election. Finally on November 17, the editor admitted that Cleveland had won, carrying the story without a headline. The canvass in New York had been extremely close; the official returns gave Cleveland only a 1,149 plurality in a contest in which over 365,000 cast votes. With the question of the election now decided, Halstead changed tactics and claimed fraud, declaring that in many cases Cleveland received General Butler's ballots.[22]

In an often-quoted letter to Halstead, Blaine asserted that he felt "quite serene" over the results. "As the Lord sent upon us an ass in the shape of a preacher, and a rainstorm, to lessen our vote in New York, I am disposed to feel resigned to the dispensation of defeat, which flowed directly from these agencies." There is no evidence that Blaine believed that he had won in New York. However, other Republicans besides Halstead made fraud charges; an investigation by a committee of lawyers found no fraud. "It was a lack of votes, not a theft of votes, that lost the state to Blaine." It was a year before Halstead could agree. In an editorial he found several reasons for the defeat. He listed the indifference of President Arthur and his cabinet, the "malignant conspiracy" of Roscoe Conkling, now a New York attorney, who when asked to campaign for Blaine replied, "I do not engage in criminal practice," and "the idiotic alliteration of the unhappy and absurd Burchard. . . . the rain storm that swept the state. . . . the unparallelled economy of Republican rich men, and the generosity of Democratic millionaires. . . . the magnificent dinner at Delmonico, against which Blaine in vain protested, and which was not redeemed by his splendid speech on the occasion. . . . the hostility to the Republican candidate of half a dozen newspapers that had been Republican and flew the track on personal pretense, and the unexpected faithfulness of Tammany. . . ."[23] Though unmentioned by Halstead, two other important factors helped account for Blaine's defeat. First, the election came in a year of hard times; second, the Mugwump bolt claimed many Republican votes. Both factors moved many normally Republican voters into the Democratic camp.

Halstead's reluctance to admit defeat in New York stemmed from his editing of the campaign newspaper. Obviously the Republican National Committee had wasted its money in publishing the *Extra*. In fact, one of Halstead's critics called the *Extra* as valuable to

Blaine's cause as wrapping paper with the legend "Vote for James G. Blaine of Maine." This same critic stated that although Halstead had received $43,000 from the national committee, he spent only $11,200. The remaining sum of $31,800 "has never been accounted for except as salary for Mr. Halstead's services as editor-in-chief." These charges, made by the editor of the *Cincinnati Evening Telegram* and Halstead's bitter enemy, cannot be verified. They are based on estimates, since the National Committee never announced actual costs of publication. Halstead did find the election profitable: the *Commercial Gazette's* circulation greatly increased, approaching 90,000 copies on the day after the election.[24]

The 1884 election marked a turning point in Halstead's career. He began spending more time away from Cincinnati and writing less for his newspaper. In expanding his field of activity, Halstead wrote several dozen magazine articles and books in the next couple of decades. These changes in his career also had a less discernible aspect. Halstead, always a man of strong passions, had attempted to write reasoned and balanced editorials in his newspaper. Although he had been a Republican all his adult life and, with the exception of 1872, always supported Republican candidates, not until 1884 could he be called completely partisan. Just four years earlier he had refused to make an issue of a candidate's religion. In 1884 his anti-Cleveland editorials often went beyond the bounds of good taste. At the same time, he defended actions of Blaine that only eight years earlier had brought his most severe censure.

Part of this change in attitude came about because Halstead no longer practiced "independent journalism." When he and Smith combined their newspapers, they agreed to make the new journal Republican. Moreover, even though Halstead remained editor-in-chief, he consulted Smith's wishes on editorial policy. This meant that the *Commercial Gazette's* editorial position became a compromise between two strong forces. Then, too, Halstead by 1884 had become a close personal friend of the Republican candidate. Thus, since Halstead believed Blaine the best man for the presidency, he could go to almost any extreme in the campaign.

His age also explained the changes in Halstead's journalism. For years he had practiced his freewheeling style for which he often received high praise. Although one of the nation's best-known editors, by 1884 he was fifty-five, and his newspaper had suffered so much financially that its only salvation came in combining with the *Gazette*. As the head of a large family with expensive tastes, and with his years of active work growing shorter and shorter, Halstead became more conservative, less freewheeling, and more interested in doing those things expected of him by his party, his friends, and his readers.

7

The Payne Affair

Although Halstead had made national politics his special interest since first reporting the 1856 Republican convention in Philadelphia, he always supported strong *Commercial* coverage of Ohio politics. Ohio's national importance during the years of his active editorship often allowed him to combine these two interests. Even when he could not link the two, Ohio political issues always received the editor's personal attention. Two incidents occurred on the state scene during the 1880s that caused Halstead to lose a greatly desired diplomatic appointment and much of his reputation as a thoughtful and discerning journalist.

In the Ohio elections of 1883 the Democrats swept the state, electing the governor and a majority in both houses of the General Assembly. Victory allowed the Democrats to select the successor to United States Senator George Pendleton in January 1884. Pendleton, although a Democrat with a distinguished record, no longer had majority support within his party. Henry B. Payne, a seventy-four-year-old former congressman and father of the treasurer of the Standard Oil Company, became his strongest competitor for the post. John McLean, publisher of the *Cincinnati Enquirer* and the city's Democratic boss, promoted Payne's candidacy because he felt Pendleton discriminated against Cincinnati Democrats in senatorial patronage.[1]

In December 1883, Halstead said in an editorial that Standard Oil planned to buy Payne a Senate seat. He declared that if just "one/one hundred part" of the stories circulating around the state capitol proved correct, the Standard's money flowed on a grand scale. He demanded that the legislature investigate the corruption charges because "the honor of the great State of Ohio is involved." Payne's eventual election caused Halstead to lament that the state's honor had been seriously injured. Halstead, although calling Payne personally innocent of corruption, said his friends disgraced the closing years of the "old gentleman's life by branding his Senate seat in advance with the dollar mark." To save his reputation, Payne should decline the seat.[2]

When Payne accepted the election, Halstead declared that a "cyclone of indignation" arose among both Democrats and Republicans throughout the state. The editor alleged that everyone knew that the new senator's son spent his Standard Oil money for the seat. With millions to spend, the Standard Oil Company could make Payne its nominee for president at the Democratic convention. "How long would the Southern representatives hesitate to swing on the hinges of gold that will be provided?" Although Halstead occasionally mentioned election fraud over the next two years, no official action occurred until 1886, when the Republicans gained control of the Ohio house. They undertook an investigation of the 1884 senatorial election after a *Commercial Gazette* article implicated several house members in the fraud. Although testimony taken by an investigating committee produced no legal proof of bribery, the inability of witnesses to remember events of just two years earlier, and the many attempts to dodge subpoenas—all convinced the committee to send its findings to the United States Senate. Halstead charged that although Standard Oil spent $265,000 to secure Payne's election, the Senate might refuse to investigate. Many senators realized an inquiry could produce a scandal that might affect the whole Democratic party. The editor said that Payne's friends, now working to prevent an investigation, seemed "to raise a strong probability of guilt. . . . If Payne and his friends were . . . innocent they would . . . demand" an investigation.[3]

As predicted, the Senate's Committee on Privileges and Elections, by a seven-to-two vote, decided against an investigation. Three Republican senators, William M. Evarts of New York, John A. Logan of Illinois, and Henry M. Teller of Colorado, joined with the four Democrats on the committee in this decision. The report of the majority cited lack of evidence as the reason for its action. Senator

Logan admitted that although some money might have been used in the Ohio Democratic caucus to secure Payne's nomination, he saw no evidence of money used in the election itself. The committee reasoned that the Senate had no power to investigate the party caucus.[4]

A minority report, issued by Republican Senators William P. Frye of Maine and George F. Hoar of Massachusetts, demanded that the Senate reject the majority's decision. Senator Hoar argued that the failure to investigate suggested that Senate seats were "subject to bargain and sale, or may be presented by a few millionaires as a compliment to a friend." Both senators defended their report in the Senate and attacked the power of the Standard Oil Company. Halstead reported rumors of Standard Oil lawyers "hanging around . . . doing dirty work." He even intimated that Evarts, Logan, and Teller received pay for their committee vote. This "rottenness in high places" should follow the three senators to "the end of the days of their life as public men."[5]

Most critics took the position that the Senate should reject the committee report to dispel the corruption rumors. The *New York Times* asserted, "If the Senate were in the least sensitive to imputations upon its honor it would not permit the Committee's decision to be final." Senator John Sherman stressed that the people of his state requested an investigation because they believed there had been "gross corruption." If the Senate refused to investigate, Ohioans would remain suspicious. Nonetheless, on July 23, 1886, the Republican-controlled Senate voted 44 to 17, with 15 Republicans answering yes, to accept the committee's report.[6]

Halstead answered the upper chamber's decision by publishing a "Black List" of Republicans who voted for the majority report. These he characterized as "millionaires, servants of corporations, Logan men, and corruptionists." He stated that they had no "regard for the honor of the Senate or of purity of politics." His list included: Jonathan Chace of Rhode Island, Shelby Cullom and John Logan of Illinois, William Evarts and Warner Miller of New York, John Ingalls and Preston B. Plumb of Kansas, John P. Jones of Nevada, Harrison H. Riddleberger of Virginia, Philetus Sawyer of Wisconsin, William Sewell of New Jersey, Henry Teller of Colorado, and Charles H. Van Wyck of Nebraska.[7]

Many newspapers, both Democratic and Republican, denounced the Senate's action and questioned the ethics of the three Republican senators of the committee. Senators Evarts and Logan defended themselves on the Senate floor. Evarts likened the combined voices of the editors to a "crow carnival," saying that "they all speak at the same time, and they all say the same thing. They have a greater power of assertion, but great poverty of argument." According to Halstead, the senator proved he could be "solemn and dreary for a couple of hours and say as little that anyone cares about as anybody in the world." As one of the most persistent critics of Payne's election, Halstead had helped persuade the Ohio legislature to begin the investigation. He had also harangued the Republican senators more than other editors did. Thus, when Logan spoke he vented his anger against the Cincinnati editor. The Illinois senator said friends had warned him of being "ground to dust" if he attacked the *Commercial Gazette.* Thus he decided not to attack it, only to read from it. He then read some of Halstead's most intemperate editorials. The Senate heard that the editor once thought General Sherman insane, General Grant a drunkard, Lincoln a no-account, and James G. Blaine a "sort of broker" in railroad stocks. Logan provoked much laughter by saying he deemed it an honor and a compliment to be placed in such illustrious company.[8]

A *Commercial Gazette* editorial, "The Shame of the Senate and the Lamentable Logan," declared that the "Boodlers' " success in stopping the investigation did not end the matter. Ohio Republican editors had decided to conduct an investigation to prove their assertions. As for Logan, the editorial concluded: "It was, we are afraid we must say, simply a vulgarity in the Senator to be so loud and furious about what Mr. Halstead of the *Commercial Gazette* had done, and to follow the beaten track of the boodle blackguards who have been yelling for years precisely the maliciousness that the Senator roared." General H. V. Boynton, Halstead's Washington correspondent, stated that former Ohio Governor Charles R. Foster, the Standard Oil Company, and Logan had organized an oil and natural gas company in Fostoria. Boynton believed that publication of the list of stockholders in the company might force a Senate inquiry. Halstead never published the list. Three years later, Foster told him that although he had business dealings with Standard Oil, he never acted for the company in the Payne matter.[9]

Although Halstead tried to keep the issue of Payne's election alive over the next few years, public opinion accepted the Senate's action as signaling the end of the matter. Halstead and other Ohio

Republican editors, looking ahead to the presidential election of 1888, found President Cleveland a better target for their assaults than Senator Payne. Thus, the incident seemed to have been forgotten. Unfortunately, the senators criticized in the *Commercial Gazette* proved to have long memories. [10]

In 1888 Halstead again supported John Sherman for the Republican nomination. In the summer of 1887, Halstead met Blaine in Germany. When the two discussed the 1888 election, Blaine said that although his health made it impossible for him to run, he might accept appointment as secretary of state in Sherman's cabinet. Halstead believed that Sherman could win the nomination in 1888. In April he asserted that the senator had the complete support of Ohio, almost the entire vote of southern Republicans, and many delegates from middle and eastern states. Although Halstead realized the dangers of the front-runner position in a presidential race, he predicted Sherman's ability to stay ahead of the competition. Halstead met with Blaine supporters in New York before the Republican convention. Although Sherman promised to withdraw in Blaine's favor, the former candidate declared that he did not intend to run. Blaine refused to endorse Sherman; yet Halstead said he spoke in "terms of cordial approval." [11]

Halstead arrived several days early for the Republican convention in Chicago. When questioned by other reporters about Blaine's chances, Halstead said that Blaine's refusal to accept the nomination meant a Sherman victory. Unfortunately, Halstead let his preferences outweigh his political judgment. Although Sherman led on the first ballots, a Sunday recess allowed for backroom manipulations that gave the nomination to Indiana's Benjamin Harrison. Levi Morton of New York received second place on the ticket. Many in the Ohio delegation criticized Governor Foraker for deserting Sherman, although Halstead defended his decision, stating that when Sherman's strength declined among southern delegates without rising in any other quarter, everyone knew he had lost. [12]

The choice of the convention pleased Halstead. Harrison, his old college friend, had received the editor's support in his Indiana campaigns. *Commercial Gazette* editorials during the preconvention period also pointed out Harrison's availability and praised his public record. Upon his nomination, Halstead promised immediate support. He telegraphed personal congratulations and editorially wrote of the candidate's "genial dignity," "unfailing courtesy," and "marked ability." He praised Harrison as one of the men who has saved the Union and thus "transmitted the glorious heritage which the HARRISON family helped create, to generations yet to come." Halstead also volunteered his personal services to the candidate. He suggested acting as a "frozen barrier against the heated affections of the people," declaring that his "vast experience" could make him of "some slight assistance" in the campaign.[13]

As in earlier campaigns, the *Commercial Gazette's* editorials waved the "bloody shirt." When Cleveland's partisans asserted that he produced a new spirit in the South, Halstead scoffed that "the Leopard cannot change his spots, and the narrow-minded, tyrannical, vote-suppressing Bourbonism of Dixie crops out once in a while." The editor also compared Harrison's war record with Cleveland's use of a substitute. Cleveland investigated private pension bills for veterans, often vetoing bills he deemed fraudulent. Halstead said Cleveland's lack of a war record made these vetoes particularly brutal: they "ought to arouse such a whirlwind of public indignation as would sweep him from public office."[14]

However much Halstead tried, he could not make the solid South or Cleveland's war record the issues of 1888; Cleveland created the real issue in his annual message to Congress in 1887. He attacked the high protective traiff and demanded reductions. When a bill passed the Democratic House of Representatives offering moderate reforms, the Republican Senate refused to concur. Halstead's own position on the tariff left him extremely vulnerable. He had allied himself with the tariff reform wing of the Liberal Republican party; now many Democratic newspapers reprinted his earlier *Commercial* editorials damning the protective system. Moreover, in 1874 he had become an honorary member of the Cobden Club, an English free-trade group, at its annual banquet at Greenwich. At that time he made a speech praising the principles of free trade. With the publication of this speech, Halstead asserted his belief in "tariff reform," although he said that Democratic ignorance on matters of money and commerce had convinced him that reform must come from the Republican party. Smith had always supported a system of protection. Consequently, with only mild embarrassment, the *Commercial Gazette* told its readers that the Democratic low tariff policy meant European competition and closed factories across the nation.

The count of the votes gave Harrison an easy electoral college victory (he carried every northern state but Connecticut and New Jersey), although Cleveland won a popular plurality of around 100,000 votes. The distinction of such a victory might be questioned; nonetheless, Halstead telegraphed: "Victory worthily won, responsibility greater than since Lincoln's time. Honor and fame and glory and the confidence and congratulations of millions are yours, count me one of the millions who delivered and are glad." Shortly after the election, Halstead began offering the president-elect advice on the composition of his cabinet. He told Harrison that Blaine desired the secretary of state's post and that the former candidate should be in the cabinet. He defended Blaine's handling of the Conkling affair while secretary of state under Garfield. He recalled that both Blaine and Garfield had consulted him on the New York appointments and Blaine's advice "was that which any man would have given him, who did not desire that the Garfield Administration should be engaged in blacking Senator Conkling's boots." Although the editor advised no one from Ohio, Indiana, or Illinois be appointed to the cabinet, he facetiously suggested an alternate cabinet composed of all Ohio men: State, Sherman; War, Foraker; Navy, Grosvenor; Interior, Hanna; Treasury, McKinley; postmaster general, Foster; attorney general, Butterworth. Halstead proposed this highly unorthodox cabinet because Garfield, driven to distraction choosing his own, had told him, "Confound it, if I could make a Cabinet entirely of Ohio men I could get up a right good one, and I believe I would in that way beat anything I could do by going outside." Although many politicians suggested John Sherman for secretary of state, the editor declared it an anti-Blaine plot. According to Halstead, Sherman preferred to remain in the Senate.[15]

Halstead wrote that he feared his long letters of advice might bore Harrison. The president-elect answered that he could not "consent on any terms to be without your occasional letters . . . which throw a gleam of sunshine across a sky that is otherwise dark." Besides, he occasionally discovered in the letters "a vein of thought and valuable suggestions." Moreover, Harrison mentioned his inability to write an inaugural address, hinting that a "well equipped newspaper man" might help. Halstead answered that every president had to write his own inaugural address so that it might "be inspired in every sentence by your own sense of lonesome responsibility."[16]

Early in the new year, Halstead delivered a speech in Madison,

Wisconsin. On his return to Cincinnati, he stopped in Indianapolis to urge Whitelaw Reid's candidacy for a diplomatic post. After the meeting with Harrison, Halstead talked to reporters. The next day the Associated Press carried the report of Blaine's appointment to the cabinet. The editor told Harrison that although he had given his opinion to the reporters, he insisted that he did not speak for the president-elect. Many people asked Halstead to use his friendship with Harrison to gain them government appointments. B. W. Chidlaw, Halstead's old teacher, wished to become a visitor to West Point. The editor replied that he felt Harrison could grant such a "modest ambition." When another man requested his aid in securing the post of minister to Belgium, Halstead sent a copy of his reply to Harrison. He had answered that "the habit of the administrations has been to reserve Belgium for millionaires."[17]

Halstead went to Washington for the inaugural, sending reports back to his newspaper. When Harrison announced his cabinet, Halstead's advice had been taken in several cases. Blaine led the list as secretary of state, but no Ohioan received an appointment. Soon after the inaugural, the new president sent to the Senate his nominations for first-class foreign missions. As Halstead recommended, it included Whitelaw Reid's name as minister to France. Never mentioned in the Halstead-Harrison correspondence, although rumored in the press, for the post of minister to Germany the president nominated Murat Halstead.[18]

Although Harrison had paid a campaign debt by this nomination, Halstead had also eagerly sought the German appointment. In poor health, he believed a few years in Europe might act as a restorative. Moreover, the *Commercial Gazette*'s financial difficulties had worsened, and both his associates and creditors had attacked the editor's policies. Halstead's antisouthern editorials, which he started after Blaine's defeat in 1884 and continued through the 1888 election, angered Cincinnati businessmen who had recently completed the $20 million Cincinnnati Southern Railroad to regain some of the southern trade lost since the war. Critics claimed salesmen from St. Louis, Louisville, and Chicago carried issues of the *Commercial Gazette* to show southern businessmen in order to take their trade away from Cincinnati houses. Thus Halstead could make a graceful exit from a generally unpleasant situation by accepting the German post.[19]

On March 28 the Senate, in executive session, received the report of the Foreign Relations Committee on the first-class diplomatic nominations. Although the committee reported all of the nominations favorably, on a motion to confirm, six Republicans voted with the Democrats to reject Halstead. Sherman, acting both as a majority leader of the Senate and as a friend, realized that a number of his Republican colleagues had planned to vote against Halstead. With the announcement of the vote, Sherman immediately moved for reconsideration, beginning a series of delaying tactics designed to give Halstead's Democratic friends, such as Henry Watterson of the *Louisville Courier-Journal*, time to change votes among the senators of their party.[20]

The objections to the editor's nomination came out during the debate that followed Sherman's motion. Almost all stemmed from the *Commercial Gazette*'s attacks on the Senate, especially on the Republican senators who had voted against the Payne inquiry. The Senate adjourned for the day before taking the vote to reconsider.[21]

The next day the upper chamber devoted almost three hours of executive session to Halstead's case. Two speeches favored his confirmation, while Senators Stewart, Teller, Evarts, and Payne spoke in opposition. Both Evarts and Stewart argued that Halstead's temperament unsuited him for a sensitive diplomatic post. Evarts characterized him as "hasty, intolerant, hot-tempered," while Stewart asserted, "Our relations with Germany should be peaceful, and it would not be safe to entrust them to a minister so aggressive and impulsively warlike." Payne said, "If the nomination had been to Russia, with a proviso that the nominee should go on to Siberia, and never return, he would gladly vote for confirmation." Senator John C. Spooner of Wisconsin, in speaking for confirmation, argued that no journalist should be held accountable for everything his newspaper published during the heat of a campaign. Otherwise, only a "few could hope to pass unscathed into the golden realm of office-holding." In an effort to gain further time, Sherman asked to reply to the critics before the vote, and so the Senate again adjourned.[22]

On the third day of executive session, three Republicans, including Sherman, spoke in the editor's behalf. At the close of their remarks, the Senate refused to reconsider by a vote of twenty-five to nineteen. Six Republicans voted with the Democrats against the motion; only two Democrats, Senator Joseph Blackburn of Kentucky and Wilkinson Call of Florida, joined the majority of the

Republicans. Of the thirteen senators who appeared on Halstead's 1886 "Black List" of "millionaires, servants of corporations, Logan men, and corruptionists," only seven still held office in 1889. Four of these, Teller, Evarts, Plumb, and Ingalls, voted against reconsideration. Of the other three, Shelby Cullom and Philetus Sawyer paired with other senators, although announcing their opposition to reconsideration. John P. Jones did not vote. Senator Stewart, Jones's colleague from Nevada, spoke against confirmation, although he too did not vote. Republicans Henry L. Dawes of Massachusetts and Matthew Quay of Pennsylvania also voted against the motion. The plan to pick up enough Democratic votes to put the nomination across had not succeeded. The Democrats enjoyed watching "the trouble in Republican ranks."[23]

Writing from Washington, General Boynton said that the six Republicans had sunk to the "level of their characters." In an article covering three and a half columns of the *Commercial Gazette's* front page, Boynton vindictively sketched the careers of the senators. He accused Evarts of lobbying for acts before Congress involving large amounts of money, of forcing the Díaz government of Mexico to confirm railroad grants for his New York friends, and of purchasing his election as senator from the New York Republican caucus. He charged Preston B. Plumb of Kansas with stealing the property of A. L. H. Crenshaw of Jackson, Missouri, while a major in the Union Army. "For many years Senator Plumb has been building his political edifice upon this foundation." He denounced John J. Ingalls, also of Kansas, as another senator elected under a cloud of "bribery and corruption." He reproached Henry M. Teller for granting patents for large amounts of unearned land to the railroads and of "defrauding widows and orphans" while he was Arthur's secretary of the interior. Finally, he accused Henry L. Dawes of Massachusetts of involvement in the Credit Mobilier scandal: "Of course Senator Dawes would have no sympathy with a man who had been in the habit of telling the truth in a blunt way about Senators."[24]

Richard Smith published a signed editorial declaring that Halstead's rejection had been based on his criticism of the Senate's refusal to investigate Payne's election. "What the *Commercial Gazette* said in the whole controversy was the truth. . . . The issue for next fall has been made in Ohio by Mr. PAYNE. It can not be avoided. The defeat of HALSTEAD was the result of revenge. Now let the people of Ohio demonstrate the folly of revenge." In another letter from Washington, Boynton asserted that the move against Halstead originated with Senator Payne, who demanded the editor's defeat for "vindication." Boynton accused the Republican senators of rallying "to the coal-oil standard," making the Senate a "star chamber" at Payne's command. Boynton declared his employer qualified for the appointment because of his long acquaintance with Germany and German affairs. Authorities on international affairs at home and abroad praised the editor's qualifications. Boynton said that the six Republicans could excuse their action if questions had arisen about Halstead's fitness for the post. Since no question of fitness arose, he concluded they had acted from spite.[25]

When confirmation failed, public opinion, in general, favored Halstead. Many editorials echoed one written by Richard Smith, who declared, "The tainted Republican Senators did the editor a great service." He predicted a newspaperman would be unsatisfied with the dull order of diplomatic life, and that Whitelaw Reid's service in France might last less than a year. Moreover, he declared that the six Republican senators had raised Halstead to the highest rank within American journalism. The *New York Sun* believed that if confirmed, Halstead might have just passed into the ranks of "gentlemen sent abroad to occupy fancy places." The action of the Senate elevated him to "the category of our most attractive and most discussed citizen."[26]

Several newspapers saw Halstead as a martyr to journalistic freedom. The *New York World* said the Senate must realize that it "can not muzzle the press by withholding offices from editors. And it will invite a plainer speech than its members may relish [if it tries]." Henry Watterson also mentioned the freedom of the press in his editorial condemning the Senate's action. He declared that the Senate warned newspapers to be careful when dealing "with that body or any of its members." On the other hand, the *Nation* thought it absurd to say that the Senate's action "muzzles a newspaper." The *Nation* pointed out that although Reid's *Tribune* said nothing about Halstead's case, the *Commercial Gazette* "is expressing its opinions on all questions of the day with a freedom and emphasis not surpassed by any other member of the press."[27]

Several newspapers suggested that Halstead had become an attractive candidate for the Senate by that body's action on his nomination. The *Boston Evening Traveller* discussed other nominees rejected by the Senate. Isaac Hill of New Hampshire, appointed second comptroller of the treasury by Andrew Jackson, failed to gain Senate confirmation. Eighteen months later, New Hampshire sent him to the Senate. The editorial concluded by saying that Payne's term expired in 1891, "and stranger things have happened than that Murat Halstead should be his successor." Many of the editor's friends immediately took up the idea of his candidacy for the Senate. Former President Hayes said that the campaign should be fought on the issue of buying and selling Senate seats, and told Halstead, "Don't decline." The editor answered that although he had declined nothing, he had heard rumors that some friends had planned to nominate him for governor. Hayes told him to make "a fight . . . which has a bone in it," adding that Halstead could do well in either race. Charles Foster, the former governor, suggested Halstead run for governor. Foster saw Halstead's candidacy as timely because "it possesses 'dramatic' elements." As for the rumors that Halstead wanted Payne's Senate seat, the former governor said, "You are treading on my toes." Although others agreed to the "dramatic elements" of a Halstead candidacy, they insisted that he must "succeed Boodle Payne."[28]

While the Senate debated his nomination, the editor lay seriously ill in Cincinnati. On March 20, he had suffered an acute attack of rheumatism, complicated by erysipelas. When Halstead learned of the Senate's action, he wrote to Harrison suggesting Governor Foraker for the German post. Instead of Foraker, Harrison named William W. Phelps, whom the Senate promptly accepted. In the middle of April, when Halstead returned to his editorial duties, he suffered a relapse which affected his heart. Even with these difficulties, the first week of May found a convalescing Halstead making plans to join his wife and four of his children in Germany. Carl Schurz arranged passage for him on the maiden voyage of the Hamburg-American Company's *Augusta Victoria* at a special rate.[29]

During Halstead's European tour, his friends and the *Commercial Gazette* kept the idea of his candidacy alive. Upon his return to Cincinnati, these friends, who included Governor Foraker, Frederick Hassaurek, and Richard Smith, arranged for a public welcoming reception at the Music Hall. When he arrived in the city on Friday evening, August 2, the mayor and a party of dignitaries escorted him to his home. On the next evening, in the Music Hall, he heard speeches of welcome delivered on behalf of the blacks of the city, the press, and the people of Ohio. The First Regiment Band played, and the Blaine Glee Club, the Tenth Ward Glee Club, and the Eleventh Ward Glee Club sang.[30]

Halstead returned to an extremely complex Ohio political scene. Although Foraker received the Republican nomination for governor, the state party remained divided. The Sherman-Hanna-McKinley wing felt that Foraker discriminated against it in patronage matters, and that he favored his own political ambitions to the detriment of the party as a whole. Consequently, Foraker received only lukewarm support from this group. The Democrats, stressing the slogan "The Campbells Are Coming," nominated James E. Campbell, an extremely popular former Republican. The League for the Preservation of Citizens' Rights, formed to combat legislation increasing saloonkeepers' taxes and prohibiting Sunday liquor sales, added further complication to the campaign. The league, a Cincinnati group, found its support among the German element of the city. The German-Americans traditionally spent Sunday afternoons and evenings in their favorite beer gardens. They believed that the legislature's action represented an infringement to their personal freedom. When a "Saloonkeepers' Rebellion" threatened to keep the beer gardens open on Sunday in defiance of the law, Foraker declared stable government demanded enforcement, and promised Cincinnati's mayor state aid. Foraker made thousands of Republicans forget the other issues of the campaign; they decided "personal liberty" was more important than "stable government."[31]

Although Foraker's support of stable government lost him votes, the "ballot-box forgery" incident of the campaign proved more damaging to both his and Halstead's reputations. On June 27, the morning following his nomination, Foraker received a call from Louis M. Hadden, a Cincinnati lawyer formerly associated with the law office of Tom C. Campbell, a prominent criminal lawyer and former Republican boss of the city. At the time, Hadden combined the jobs of assistant city solicitor and president of the board of education. Hadden told the governor that James Campbell had the secret backing of many prominent Republicans. Hadden said that he had seen a contract in Tom Campbell's office, signed by James Campbell, William McKinley, Benjamin Butterworth (a Cincinnati congressman), and other leading Republicans, giving them an interest in a patented ballot box invented by Richard G. Wood of Cincinnati. Hadden asserted that James Campbell had introduced a bill into Congress requiring the use of this ballot box in all federal elections. If successful, the bill could have made the owners of the ballot box monopoly a fortune. Hadden added that when the bill failed, a disagreement arose between the principals, and that Wood might show Foraker a copy of the contract. Foraker later said that he believed the story because of Hadden's prominence in Cincinnati politics.[32]

A few days later Wood reluctantly agreed to furnish Foraker a certificate showing the names of Campbell, McKinley, Butterworth, and others. On August 6, Wood telegraphed Foraker asking for a recommendation for the position of Cincinnati smoke inspector. The governor claimed that he had investigated Wood's qualifications for the job, finding him a deserving man with "a genius for invention." He agreed to recommend Wood in return for the certificate. In September, Wood said he had to go to Washington for the certificate. Foraker gave him a letter of introduction to President Harrison and $200 for expenses.[33]

After some delay, Wood gave the governor a subscription certificate containing the signatures of Campbell, McKinley, Butterworth, S. S. Cox, and Senator Sherman. The certificate did not detail the involvement of the signers in the ballot box company. It purported to be only a subscription list to "Contract No. 1000" which contained full information in respect to the details of the operation. Foraker knew the signatures of the Republicans and believed them genuine. A friend verified Campbell's signature. Consequently, Foraker accepted the document as genuine.[34]

Halstead first became involved when he accidentally ran into Foraker on the train from Columbus to Cincinnati. Halstead expressed great astonishment when the governor told him the ballot box story. The editor strongly advised publishing the paper, declaring it a "public duty" to defeat Campbell. Halstead also suggested that because of the importance of the document, it should be photographed and additional copies made.[35]

On the evening of September 28, Foraker implicated Campbell in a ballot box monopoly during a speech in Cincinnati. He did not mention the secret contract. Later the same evening, Foraker gave Halstead a photographic copy of the certificate. On October 2, Halstead published a front-page article entitled "The Ballot-Box Fraud" which included an engraving of the certificate. He also published a copy of Campbell's bill, which directed the attorney general to buy a ballot box exactly like the one Wood patented. The editor commented that the bill looked forward to the establishment of a million-dollar trust. Halstead did not publish the list of signatures attached to the certificate. On the same evening, Campbell spoke in Cincinnati's Music Hall. Calling Halstead a "common scold" who criticized "every public man in every party that has existed since I was old enough to read," Campbell declared himself "honored when he scolds me." Although Campbell said he did not mind being scolded, he did mind being lied about. "I do object when a man of that character descends from the place of a common scold to that of a common liar." He concluded that Halstead must prove his charges. If they could be proved, Campbell asserted he would "go off the ticket." In the same speech he read a letter written by George R. Topp, a member of the Cincinnati Board of Public Affairs and a Foraker appointee, demanding a kickback on all the gravel which a contractor sold to the city[36]

The Topp letter dropped like a bombshell into the campaign. Campbell charged Foraker with appointing a corrupt governmental board and with bossism. Realizing the damage, Republicans gathered sworn statements from Mrs. Topp and several doctors, certifying Topp's insanity at the time he had written the letter. The morning after Campbell's speech, Halstead addressed a signed open letter to the Democratic candidate in which he accused Campbell of using "language becoming the representatives of the Gangsters who are the masters of your party, towards me, . . . and a crazy man's letter, hoping to reflect upon the integrity of the Board of Public Affairs." The editor added that he had had proof of Campbell's financial interest in the ballot box contract before he had introduced the bill into Congress. The evidence showed "that you subscribed to secure an interest July 3, 1888."[37]

On the following day, Halstead published a reproduction showing the certificate with Campbell's signature. No other name appeared on the list. As Campbell made no comment, both Foraker and the editor believed his silence proved his guilt. On October 8, Halstead answered reports that Republicans also appeared on the list by declaring: "a Republican did not introduce the bill, and no Republican's name appears in the 'Contract No. 1000.' " Since Halstead never saw the contract, only the subscription list, and since he believed no names appeared on the contract, the honesty of his defense may be questioned. On the following day, Campbell declared he only waited for Halstead to make a direct charge to take legal action. Halstead retorted that Campbell's "monkeying with words" could not be too reassuring to his friends.[38]

Campbell engaged several leading Cincinnati attorneys to investigate the Hall and Wood Company. They discovered that the contract signatures had been traced from frank-bearing mail. On October 10, the lawyers brought their findings to Halstead and demanded a retraction. Although the editor admitted that the evidence seemed conclusive, he asked for time to make his own inquiry. While they agreed, they forced Halstead to promise not to attack Campbell in the *Commercial Gazette* the next day. The editor talked to Hadden, Frank D. Davis, and Frank L. Milward, the men who committed the forgery, later that day and believed their story. Since he concluded his investigation very late in the evening he wrote, "A Personal Statement to the Public" for publication the following morning without consulting Campbell's lawyers. In his statement he admitted seeing proof of the fraud. He refused to go any further. "The papers that seemed to show the business behind the bill, are as published, but the signatures . . . are fabricated." Campbell, the editor asserted, remained "where the Governor left him with the ballot-box bill in his Music Hall speech." Although Halstead admitted to the forgery, he still believed that the contract actually existed. At the same time Halstead wrote his retraction, he telegraphed Foraker to alert him about the forgery. Foraker replied that he feared Halstead had been duped, declaring that Wood told him the Campbell interests had tried to make him sign such an affidavit earlier. He ordered the editor to fix the time of the forgery so that there could be no mistake.[39]

Generally the press reacted critically to Halstead's handling of the ballot box paper. The editor of the *Columbus Dispatch* commented typically in declaring the error "inexcusable." According to the *Dispatch*, Halstead owed it to the people of Ohio to tell the whole story of the forgery, so that the men involved might receive their deserved punishment. Halstead refused to publish their names, because he believed the young men had been duped. Since they had come to him with their story and explained how the forgery took place, he promised to protect them as long as possible.[40]

Benjamin Butterworth wrote Halstead that he had no "knowledge of . . . or connection with . . . or interest in" the ballot box scheme. The congressman asserted that the handling of the affair hurt him deeply. He stated that people in Cincinnati believed the story, feeling that Halstead had agreed to the forgery claims only to save his Republican friends. Nonetheless, he told the editor to handle the subject as he saw fit for the "cause of the Republican party."[41]

Halstead compared his involvement in publishing the forgery to a man accepting a counterfeit banknote. Although he accepted it as genuine, when he found it counterfeit, he did not pass it on. He declared that he published both the charge and the retraction because of a sense of obligation to give the public the complete truth. Moreover, he claimed entire responsibility, adding that he had no intention "to shirk it." Nonetheless, he said Campbell's association with the ballot box bill did help justify his mistake.[42]

A few days before the election, Campbell again brought up the case, charging Foraker with holding a financial interest in the box company and with writing to the governor of Michigan urging the adoption of the ballot box. Moreover, he claimed that the whole affair centered in a plot to elect Foraker governor and Halstead senator. Finally, Campbell also revealed the other forged names on the subscription list. The attorneys and Halstead agreed that since all the signatures had been forged, no purpose could be served in revealing the additional names. In a newspaper interview, Foraker answered that he had written the governor of Michigan only a letter of introduction. As to the ballot box forgeries, Foraker said: "the whole affair was intended to trip [me] so as to break the effect of exposure of Campbell's bill."[43]

As Halstead feared, no amount of explaining could save Foraker. The Ohio voters elected Campbell governor and returned a Democratic General Assembly. This also meant the election of a Democratic senator to replace Payne. In an editorial after the election, Halstead declared that Ohio had vindicated "the Honorable Henry Boodle Payne" and announced to the world a Senate seat for sale to the highest bidder. Since Calvin Brice had given $25,000 in election contributions, Halstead said he probably had first claim on the seat. Since Brice lived in New York, the editor added that the General Assembly might be wiser to allow *Enquirer* publisher John McLean to purchase the seat; he already lived in Washington.[44]

Foraker believed the ballot box fiasco contributed greatly to his defeat. Moreover, he declared himself a victim of Halstead's decision to publish the certificate. Although Halstead too believed the incident had cost Foraker votes, he stated that other issues helped defeat the Republicans. First, the continuing split within the G.O.P. meant that Foraker had received only partial support from the Sherman-Hanna-McKinley wing of the party. Second, Foraker had had to counteract a prejudice against third-term governors. Finally, the enforcement of Sunday closing and the higher taxes on saloons convinced many normally Republican voters that their personal liberty demanded a Democratic vote in this election. Halstead, who wished to minimize the ballot box affair, declared "personal liberty" the most important factor in the election, and that "all other un-favorable influences were insignificant in comparison." Moreover, unlike other Republicans, he refused to blame the saloonkeepers, brewers, and liquor interests for the defeat. Instead, he said that the rural Republicans in attempting this "experiment" had driven the liberal Germans to the Democrats.[45]

Several of the men mentioned by Campbell as also subscribing to the certificate demanded Halstead print the full story of the forgery. One of Senator Sherman's friends wrote that Foraker and Halstead "brought forth" the document with the ultimate intention of using it against the Republicans. A letter from Sherman reflected this suspicion. Sherman asked why, since his name appeared on the paper, Halstead did not doubt its authenticity. Moreover, he questioned the editor's not discussing the matter with him personally. Sherman added that once he had tangible evidence of the forgery, he planned to prosecute all those involved.[46]

With this pressure, Halstead used the entire front page of the November 13 issue of the *Commercial Gazette* to detail the story of the forgery. He reproduced the complete certificate including all the signatures, a letter from Foraker, and statements from the young men who had actually committed the forgery. Also, in a final paragraph, the editor tendered his apologies to all he had hurt by his use of the story:

> I am aware of the imperfections of all human testimony, and alive to the fact of many mistakes of my own—and for such mischief as I may have done to good men and a good cause I am sincerely sorry, and more than willing to accept my full share of responsiblity for the error that, so far as it affected me, I was glad to acknowledge, for the truth while it struck hard was wholesome, and I welcomed it as a relief. The sting that remains is that I could have believed of old friends what

seemed to be written in letters of fire. It is all plain now . . . and I tender my regrets and apologies. It may be that I shall be next time wiser, but as I retain self-respect through an abiding opinion that I meant to be true and have been fair, I shall be able to endure with equanimity the calumnies of those so constituted, as to find in the story of the forgery only opportunity for the perverse interpretations of a sinister hostility.[47]

Nonetheless, rumors continued to circulate that Halstead accepted the forgery story to protect his Republican friends. McKinley and Butterworth became concerned, and demanded an investigation by the House of Representatives. In December, Butterworth secured passage of an inquiry resolution. On January 16, 1890, a committee headed by William Mason began hearing testimony on the ballot box contract. Before its report on April 30, the committee had heard 54 witnesses. Halstead's testimony on February 6 lasted most of the day. Earlier, General Boynton wrote Halstead from Washington that he had nothing to fear from the committee. Although Boynton stated that several senators thought Sherman deserved better treatment than he got in the *Commercial Gazette,* most congressmen accepted Halstead's apologies.

Boynton believed that Foraker might have a more difficult time before the committee. James Campbell, according to rumor, possessed letters from the ex-governor to Wood expressing his desire to "have something on Butterworth." Moreover, Foraker also said that Wood's job as Cincinnati smoke inspector could be guaranteed "because he [Foraker] had the 'dots' on [Cincinnati mayor] Moseby." Although saying that he did not suggest that Halstead turn his back on Foraker, Boynton declared that if the rumors should prove true, it might be best for the editor if his part in the hearings remained separated from Foraker's. Henry Probasco, the assistant United States attorney for the southern district of Ohio, seemed to verify Boynton's report. He stated that Wood had confessed that Foraker incited him "to commit the deed." Moreover, Foraker had said he wished "he had some means by a similar paper, of preventing Major Butterworth from 'knifing' him in a quiet way."[48]

If Campbell possessed these letters, he did not refer to them in his testimony before the committee. In fact, Campbell placed more blame on Halstead than on Foraker. The new governor said that Halstead had known of the forgery. Since the documents implicated his friends, Campbell said they would not have been used if the editor had believed them genuine. To Campbell, it looked as though Halstead held back publication, hoping it would be too late to prove forgery.[49]

When Halstead appeared before the committee, its members and Charles Grosvenor, an Ohio politician representing McKinley and Butterworth in the investigation, questioned him. Although Foraker had appointed Grosvenor a trustee of the Soldiers' and Sailors' Home at Xenia, as a Sherman supporter he had made offensive statements about Foraker's handling of Sherman's candidacy in Chicago in 1888, and the governor had asked him to resign. Grosvenor took great pride in the institution, and consequently became even more hostile to Foraker. Foraker said that Grosvenor, as the representative of McKinley and Butterworth, conducted himself like a prosecuting attorney, "whose main purpose was to have the committee find me guilty of the crime that had been committed." Nonetheless, Foraker declared Grosvenor's attacks to be "so manifestly unjust and so unsupported by evidence that they had no weight either with the committee or anybody else." Although Grosvenor questioned Halstead less harshly than he had Foraker, the editor had a rough time on the stand. One of the first questions asked by the committee concerned the original publication of the papers: if Halstead thought them genuine, why had he printed only James Campbell's signature? Halstead could have answered that he supported Foraker and wanted to defeat Campbell. If he published the Republican names, he weakened the effect of the sensation. Although he said, "I did not want to destroy the Republican campaign," in his complete answer, Halstead proved himself a politician if not an honest witness. He stated that he had published only Campbell's name for two reasons. First, Campbell had introduced the bill to establish the ballot box trust. Halstead thought this gave him "especial responsibility" in the matter. Second, the funeral of Samuel S. Cox, another subscriber to the company, took place on the day he published the papers. Since he believed that all the other names had to be printed if he revealed any of them, good taste impelled him not to publish the Republican names.[50]

Foraker testified that he intended to publish the documents after the election. He gave them to Halstead, as a friend of the Republicans mentioned, to hold. He maintained he planned to contact Sherman and the other signatories before publication to allow them an opportunity to explain. This placed the burden of publication on

Halstead. While the editor never denied his responsibility for publication, Foraker also dodged the truth. Foraker never gave Halstead
the documents to hold; he gave him only photographic copies.
Moreover, Halstead said he planned to use the certificate in the
Commercial Gazette. In giving the editor a copy of the document,
Foraker realized that they could appear in print during the campaign. Although Halstead took full responsibility for publication of
the paper, he left no doubt that Foraker knew of his plans. No one
questioned their publication, only when it should be done. The
editor explained that Campbell promised to leave the Democratic
ticket if the charges against him could be proved. Consequently,
Halstead decided to wait until two or three weeks before the election to publish the documents, leaving the Democrats too little
time to find a new candidate. "I thought that about two or three
weeks before the end of the campaign I would let this thing fly, for
that would be long enough to put it through all the country newspapers on both sides, and it would be too late to repair damages in
the campaign."[51]

Halstead swore under oath that he had never discussed suppressing the Republican names with Foraker, although he told the
governor that "Mr. Campbell's distinction in the matter" might
make it possible to use his name during the campaign and "reserve
the rest for further consideration." Grosvenor's attempt to force
Halstead to admit he acted completely from political motives produced the following interchange:

Q: And really your motive in entering into the matter was
rather more political or moral, than patriotic, was it? A: I do
not dissociate politics entirely from morals and patriotism.
(Laughter)

Q: But the public considerations did not apply to the other
gentlemen? A: I thought they did.

Q: The other gentlemen? A: Yes, sir, eminently so; I thought
public considerations applied. But if I believed a man was a
candidate for the governorship of Ohio who had gone into a
business like that, that shell should be cracked over his head.

Q: And the other gentlemen should come in for their punishment later? A: Yes, sir; Later.

Q: You did not want confusion in the campaign at that time?
A: No, sir; not absolute rout. (Laughter)[52]

Then the editor asserted that Campbell, in his Music Hall speech of October 2, had raised the question of "personal veracity" and introduced the Topp letter. Halstead declared that many Cincinnati Republicans felt sorry for Topp's family. They knew Topp was an honest man who had been insane when he wrote the letter. The editor added that Topp had died in an insane asylum. Nonetheless, the sensation produced by the letter made it impossible to present the true facts. Halstead maintained he felt sorry for Campbell, since he possessed copies of the ballot box documents and believed it possible to ruin his candidacy at any time. Consequently, the editor published a small paragraph in the *Commercial Gazette* of the next morning, hinting of proof of Campbell's connection with the ballot box company. Halstead thought he could scare Campbell off the ticket with this article. Instead, Campbell again attacked the editor and demanded proof. Thus Halstead could not hold the certificate until the latter weeks of the campaign. Although Halstead also stated that he intended to communicate with Sherman and the other men whose names appeared on the certificate before publication, he had not had enough time. This he presented as an additional reason for not giving the Republican signatures.[53]

When Foraker denied any plan to use the documents until after the election, he forgot that he first made the ballot box issue public in his September 28 speech at the Music Hall. Although he did not mention that he held the certificate, he hinted of Campbell's greater involvement than the introduction of the bill. Before the committee, Halstead said that he had advised Foraker against mentioning the ballot box in his speech. He had wished to spring the whole sensation on Campbell at once.[54]

Many of the committee members asked how both Halstead and Foraker could have been fooled by the forged names. Both men declared their familiarity with some of the signatures and their consultation with people familiar with the others. Halstead asserted that "the young man who performed his work was a [sic] artist in his way." Moreover, the internal evidence of the document helped convince him of its genuineness. "There was in this paper, the work of a lawyer," a good lawyer, according to Halstead. He thought the device of separating the subscription certificate form "Contract No. 1000," which meant subscribers actually never signed the contract, the work of a genius. "With this artistic work and this lawyer work in the matter, I did not see any room for questioning the

genuineness of this paper." When asked why he did not communicate directly with Sherman, Halstead repeated that "circumstances
over which I had no control" forced the use of the paper before he
could write to any of the principals. The editor added that he
hesitated to write immediately because of the delicate nature of the
matter. He recalled that Benjamin Butler once said you could get a
member of Congress to sign a petition to have himself hanged. He
believed it possible that through some "hocus-pocus" the men had
been deceived into signing, never realizing the character or purpose of the document. This explained his reluctance to put a "finger
on a sore place like that and inquire."[55]

Grosvenor asked Halstead why he did not expect Campbell to
reveal that Sherman, McKinley, Butterworth, and the others had
also signed the paper. Halstead replied, "I had that in mind a bit. I
thought perhaps that Mr. Campbell would not care to undertake to
shelter himself among a lot of lambs in that way." The questioner
commented that he thought it strange that Halstead allowed a man
like Wood, whom the editor had been unwilling to see made smoke
inspector of Cincinnati, overthrow his confidence in a group of
friends. Halstead answered that although his opinion of Wood
remained unchanged, he felt the documents beyond Wood's capacity to devise.[56]

The committee also wished to know if Halstead's candidacy for
the Senate helped prompt the publication of the ballot box certificate. Halstead answered that he would "not flinch from the honor"
if the people of Ohio wanted to elect him to the Senate. When
asked if in the event the Republicans carried the Ohio legislature, a
rivalry might have arisen between McKinley, Butterworth, and
himself for the Senate seat, Halstead answered that he had never
thought of this possibility.[57]

Foraker believed that the forgery had been deliberately planted
to trick him and to gain sympathy for Campbell. Halstead also
developed this argument. Although he stated that Wood became
involved to secure the job of smoke inspector of Cincinnati, he said
that the forgers and the lawyers who drew up the certificate could
not have given their time merely to secure Wood a job. Moreover,
considering how many people knew of the forgery, it seemed aston-
ishing that no one had come forward for over a week. Shortly after
the election, Halstead published an account of an interview given
by a Democratic official stating that Campbell "knew of the ballot-

box boomerang Halstead was going to throw at him three weeks before the matter became known to the public." Campbell merely "waited until the proper time came and he was ready." The editor declared that he had had no knowledge of the document three weeks before publication. If this was a true story, it proved Foraker's contention that Wood had acted as Campbell's tool and committed the forgery in his interest. Halstead expressed amazement that when Campbell's attorneys found the evidence for the forgery, they did not have him arrested. All of these factors, Halstead thought, seemed to leave some suspicions about the ballot box papers. One of Campbell's lawyers testified that Halstead had not been arrested because of a promise to the young men who committed the forgeries that the lawyers would make their affidavits public only if they had to force the editor's retraction. Then also, the lawyers all felt that a free retraction carried more weight than one forced through law.[58]

The committee accepted the assurances of Campbell's lawyers that their client had nothing to do with the forgery. In its report, the committee found that "Richard Wood, Frank Milward, and Frank Davis were the only persons directly or indirectly aiding, abetting, assisting or knowingly consenting to the preparation of said forgery with knowledge of its character." Halstead and Foraker, however, "Aided in uttering said forgery, Mr. Foraker by exhibiting the paper to several persons and thereafter delivering it to Mr. Halstead, and Mr. Halstead aiding in uttering said forgery by publishing the forged paper on October 4, 1889, in the *Cincinnati Commercial Gazette*, but we find that neither of the parties . . . in uttering said paper, knew the same was a forgery." All of the committee but Mason, the chairman, also found that "The publication of the false paper in the *Commercial Gazette*, showing Mr. Campbell's name and suppressing all other signatures, was also as bad as the original fabrication of the paper. . . . The entire incident the committee have been instructed to investigate is an example of political methods, deserving the condemnation of all parties and all good citizens." Mason added to the committee's findings the statement "If our unanimous finding is correct that Messrs. Halstead and Foraker did not know the paper was forged when they uttered it then they were deceived by someone, for we have found it was a forgery. Being deceived, then, is their only offense."[59]

Halstead received a relatively mild censure from the committee.

It seemed only right to grant to the editor, as the committee did, that he believed the documents genuine. While many suggested the possibility of Foraker's involvement in the forgery, only Probasco, among the Republicans, ever implied that Halstead shared this guilt. Moreover, Foraker's letters to Halstead in no way suggested a conspiracy between the two men. On the contrary, Foraker indignantly defended his actions and stated that his entire correspondence with Wood had been examined by several people, who agreed it showed no "complicity on my part." Although it might be argued that a guilty Foraker had no reason to confess his part in the matter to Halstead, had Halstead been a co-conspirator, Foraker had no reason to try to convince the editor of his innocence.[60]

The real question is not Halstead's guilt in the plot. Rather, it is a question of his integrity as a journalist. When his earlier views about the duties of the press are considered, in this instance the editor violated every principle which he claimed to support. If Halstead believed the documents genuine, then it must follow that he willingly detailed the corruption of his political enemies while hiding the corruption of his political friends.

8

The Twilight of a Journalist

The last years of Halstead's life found him without a newspaper and without a regular source of income. As his friends continued their work, or retired with assured financial security, Halstead struggled to support himself. In February 1890, the *Commercial Gazette* announced that Halstead would write a monthly current events column for *Cosmopolitan Magazine*. He planned to continue writing for the *Commercial Gazette* by telegraphing editorials to Cincinnati from New York. The *Cosmopolitan* editor said that although Halstead had long been the magazine's choice for such a column, because of his "familiarity with public events . . . and entire fearlessness," his Cincinnati obligations had only recently allowed him to accept the position.[1]

Halstead's move to New York led to rumors that he had lost control of his newspaper. These rumors prompted William Berri, owner of the *Brooklyn Standard-Union*, to ask Halstead to become his editor at $20,000 a year. On April 20, 1890, Halstead accepted the editorship of the Brooklyn newspaper. Berri sought to build a strong Republican newspaper in Brooklyn. He believed Halstead's "experience, ability, earnestness, and force would materially aid such an undertaking."[2]

The *Standard-Union* had never been a successful newspaper. In Brooklyn alone it competed with the Republican *Times* and the Democratic *Eagle* and *Citizen*, while New York newspapers always found a large circulation in the city's largest bedroom suburb. Since

128

its founding by Congressman S. B. Chittenden, the *Standard-Union* had steadily lost money for a long series of owner-publishers. Berri, a carpet merchant, had been no more successful than earlier owners in making the newspaper profitable. Berri hoped Halstead could reverse this trend. As one editor commented, "If an able editor is what is required to bring the *Standard-Union* up to the level of a paying and influential newspaper, Mr. Halstead can do it." Yet he thought the "importance of the editorial writer was on the wane."[3]

Halstead confidently asserted that he could make the *Standard-Union* into one of the leading eastern dailies. Nonetheless, he took great pains to announce his continuing connection with the *Commercial Gazette*. Although Richard Smith became editor-in-chief in Cincinnati, Halstead continued to send editorials. Moreover, he emphasized that the two "labored together in harmony."[4]

Several times Halstead attempted to correct the "inaccurate and impertinent reports" of his forced departure from the *Commercial Gazette*'s management. He said that a reorganization of the board of directors of the Commercial Gazette Company brought his son Marshal into active participation in the company and signaled greater action on the part of the board as a whole in the day-to-day activities of the newspaper. Halstead asserted that he had voluntarily accepted the reorganization and had resigned as editor-in-chief to accept the New York offer. He did this to promote his own business interests and "to enlarge my usefulness as an editor."[5]

Halstead may have left the editorship of the *Commercial Gazette* voluntarily, but he did not leave to increase his usefulness as an editor. While no extensive evidence exists to explain the problems of the *Commercial Gazette*, by 1890 the newspaper's financial condition had suffered from three decades of business and editorial warfare with the McLeans and their *Enquirer*. Halstead felt that the McLeans had acted dishonestly, and he set out to expose them. In doing so, he goaded them into reprisals. As a result, Cincinnati saw one of the longest, most savage, and most spectacular newspaper wars in American history.[6]

Washington McLean purchased the *Enquirer* after a successful career as a manufacturer. Thus, he and his son John, who managed the newspaper after his graduation from Harvard, never worried about journalistic profits. In fact, their money ultimately resulted in Halstead's downfall. Halstead's financial problems could not all be linked to the McLeans. He lost party support in 1872 as a result of his venture in Liberal Republicanism, Catholic patronage as a result of his fight with the archbishop, and circulation from competition of the other city newspapers. The McLeans turned Halstead's problems to their advantage, and created additional ones for the harassed editor of the *Commercial*.

The bitter hatred which grew between Halstead and the McLeans started during the Civil War. Halstead believed the *Enquirer's* support of the Democratic party substantially aided the Confederate cause. The McLeans resented these charges, and began a series of personal attacks against Halstead that lasted for over a quarter of a century.

In the seventies, the *Enquirer* challenged the *Commercial* for supremacy in classified advertisements, the *Commercial's* greatest single source of revenue. With the McLean fortune behind it, the *Enquirer* could open its columns to classified advertisers free of charge. Moreover, the *Enquirer* also published the "want advertisements" that appeared in the *Commercial*. Although Halstead fought long and hard against these tactics, most of the *Commercial's* classified business went to the *Enquirer*. [7]

In the war for circulation, the *Enquirer's* greater financial resources also gave it other advantages over the *Commercial*. In 1885 Halstead charged that *Enquirer* agents approached newsstand dealers offering them bribes not to sell the *Commercial Gazette*. Moreover, by the eighties, sensationalism had come into vogue. Readers wanted stories of racy scandals and violent crimes. The *Enquirer*, with its unlimited funds for news gathering, could satisfy this whim and even whet the reading public's appetite for more. What at first began as a business rivalry between the two newspapers quickly produced name-calling and then a threat of violence. As early as 1877, Halstead told President Hayes he had considered "exchanging the pen for the pistol."[8]

The personal bitterness between Halstead and John McLean reached its peak in 1886 during the Senate's investigation into Payne's election. For several weeks the *Enquirer* published an article every day attacking Halstead. Typical of the language was: "Your reputation in this community is a carcass upon which crawling worms find little to feed. No one is capable of eating it save yourself. . . . it occurs to us that it is now time either to put him in an asylum or to treat him like any other mad dog." To justify its attack, the *Enquirer* once again declared that Halstead gained con-

trol of the *Commercial* by defrauding Potter's heirs, and coupled
this with the assertion that he had forced the 1884 merger with a
reluctant Smith to save his newspaper. According to the *Enquirer*,
Halstead did this because of a "maniacal" desire to crush John
McLean. When Senator Logan attacked Halstead, he answered the
charges in a long article on the *Commercial* editorial page. The *Enquirer*
mentioned that his answer appeared next to a brief paragraph on
gas. Calling the article Halstead's "farewell address to sanity," the
Enquirer asserted that in his two thousand words, the editor used
"the personal pronoun 'I' something less than one thousand times."[9]

During the preceding year the *Cincinnati Evening Telegram* also
started a campaign of vilification against Halstead. Halstead believed
that McLean controlled the *Telegram*. Since Halstead called McLean
"little beast," "Blear-eyed John," and a "political prostitute," and
in turn received "crazy horse," "small bills," and "old idiot," he
took little notice of the *Telegram*'s new attack. On August 7, the
Telegram printed another article labeling Halstead insane, suggesting
a hereditary condition, and calling Halstead's sister, Mrs. John M.
Scott, insane. The writer concluded that John McLean would answer for this statement. Although Halstead could accept the suggestion of his insanity as part of the game, he found the allusion to
his sister unpardonably offensive and resolved to gain satisfaction.[10]

Further arousing Halstead's anger, *Enquirer* articles asked if he
still had his "killing pistol," and stated that even if he did, he
lacked the courage to "shoot with anything but his mouth." Halstead concluded that the young publisher had challenged his honor.
He decided to act. On August 14, Halstead dispatched Colonel W.
G. Terrell, an old friend from Kentucky, to McLean's house at
Saratoga, New York, to arrange a duel. McLean asked General
Roger A. Pryor, a New York attorney and former southern editor,
to represent him in the negotiations. Terrell said Halstead had no
complaint about the *Enquirer*'s articles since he had replied in kind:
he demanded only satisfaction for the attacks in the *Telegram* that
"wantonly, gratuitously and falsely" affected his family. The sec-
onds satisfactorily concluded their work on August 18. Halstead
accepted McLean's statement dissociating himself from all connections with the *Telegram* and disclaiming all responsibility for the
offending article.[11]

Just when the controversy seemed closed, Tom C. Campbell
stepped forward and announced that he owned the newspaper,

that he had written the articles, and that he wished to meet Halstead. Actually Campbell and Halstead had feuded almost as long as McLean and Halstead had. Campbell had entered "an unholy partnership" with McLean to control Cincinnati politics. McLean, the Democratic leader, and Campbell, the Republican, effectively divided city patronage. Their joint rule made Cincinnati one of the worst-governed cities in the country. The *Commercial* had long complained about this alliance. The more immediate antagonism between the two men stemmed from *Commercial* articles written at the time Campbell defended a man accused of a particularly brutal murder. Campbell, known for his phenomenal success in murder trials, attained a manslaughter verdict for the defendant against overwhelming evidence of guilt. Both the judge and the *Commercial* roundly condemned Campbell's handling of the trial. Partially as a result of the *Commercial*'s articles, a mob formed before the Hamilton County jail to take justice into its own hands. Although the sheriff removed the prisoner to safety, four days of rioting, with the loss of forty-five lives, resulted. The riot discredited Campbell completely, forcing him to move to New York. He never regained his political power in Cincinnati, and never forgave Halstead for the *Commercial*'s part in his troubles.[12]

In the final settlement of the duel controversy, Halstead acted wisely. He refused to meet Campbell on the field of honor. Instead, he claimed, Campbell should challenge McLean. The *Telegram* had asserted McLean would answer to Halstead for the offending article. McLean called "this statement concerning himself . . . an infamous lie." Consequently, Halstead said the question of veracity lay between McLean and Campbell. "Mr. McLean is in Saratoga and the statement is that these parties whom he accuses of this infamous lie are on their way thither. I hope they won't injure Mr. McLean, but it is none of my business."[13]

Many newspapers commented on the threatened duel. Most echoed the position of the *Columbus Dispatch*, which declared that should Pryor and Terrell continue the negotiations and settle all differences between the two, "they would confer an everlasting favor on a suffering people." While the duel incident brought no credit to any of the principals, McLean used the unfavorable publicity to make Halstead look ridiculous as a newspaperman. He republished a story Halstead wrote as a student called "The Legend of the Wilderness." Changing the name to "The Red Headed Maiden of

Photograph courtesy of the Ohio Historical Society

Halstead, about 1890.

the Blue Miami" and introducing it as a long buried and forgotten masterpiece, McLean succeeded in making it appear "amateurish and sophomoric, and so ludicrous." A columnist for the *Chicago Tribune* saw the republication in the *Enquirer*. He wrote a series of parodies, representing them as other early Halstead stories. These stories—"Betrayed by a Butterdish," "Airy Fairy Lillian," "Knee Sprung for Love," and "The Siren and the Sucker"—ultimately found their way around the country's newspapers. Halstead lost stature by the incident, although most of the republications and jests which they inspired were in good humor.[14]

Such incidents as these all goaded Halstead into further competition with the *Enquirer*. Halstead had borrowed heavily to buy control of the *Commercial* in 1866. His generosity toward the Potter heirs, his purchase of the Fourth Street house, his decision to buy the ancestral farm at Paddy's Run, and his endorsement of family notes which he later had to assume, made it impossible for the editor to pay his debts. As Halstead said, his problems centered on "the changes in newspaper business; the enormous increase of expenditures; the decline in receipts for legitimate newspaper business; and my own expensive habits." By the time he combined his newspaper with Richard Smith's his outstanding debts totaled over $155,000. While the income from the *Commercial* allowed him a very high standard of living, he could not pay off his debts.[15]

Faced with growing personal and newspaper expenses, Halstead borrowed money on his stock in the *Commercial Gazette*. One author stated that the bank holding his notes became uneasy after receiving more and more requests for money, and decided to stop his credit when John McLean intervened, personally underwriting Halstead's loans. McLean wished the balance to reach a level that he knew Halstead could never repay. Consequently, by 1890, the bank held a majority of Halstead's stock. McLean then purchased it and took control of the *Commercial Gazette*.[16]

This explanation actually tells only part of the story. Although Halstead used some of his stock as collateral for loans, he also sold many shares. In fact, by January 1890, the *Commercial Gazette* had forty, mostly inactive, owners. These new owners, including McLean, demanded the changes in the newspaper resulting in Halstead's removal to New York. While Halstead remained the single largest stockholder, at least throughout 1890 and 1891, he no longer had a place in the management of the newspaper. At first, the reorganized company limped along under the direction of Richard Smith, who became editor-in-chief. Smith, as manager of the newspaper, proved unable to make it profitable. Consequently, the stockholders demanded further reforms in October 1891. They named as publisher Henry Blackburn Morehead, long-time Cincinnati investment broker. Morehead, following a distinguished career in banking and investments, sat on the boards of Procter and Gamble and the Ohio Valley National Bank. In 1896, having failed to respond to his ministrations, the *Commercial Gazette* fell under McLean's control. As the *Commercial Tribune*, the McLean morning journal, the *Commercial* continued its existence until the depression in the 1930s.[17]

Although Halstead sent editorials and other articles to his old Cincinnati newspaper after it fell into McLean's hands, his major interest throughout the decade of the nineties was making money. The editor's only source of income had been his ownership of the *Commercial Gazette*. When he lost it, apparently realizing nothing for his stock, he found himself with heavy and ever-increasing expenses.

Although Halstead asserted that he had left the *Commercial Gazette* to better his financial position, the remaining years of his life found him constantly struggling to meet his many obligations. He remained editor of the *Standard-Union* for only one year. Although he contributed to the *Cosmopolitan* throughout the decade, he conducted the "Current Events" column only until June 1892. With no assured income, Halstead became a free-lance writer, reporter, and lecturer. During the nineties, the old editor published over thirty articles, concerning his personal experiences with the political leaders of his day or with his travels, in the *Cosmopolitan, Criterion, Forum, Independent, Lippincott's, McClure's, Men and Women, Outlook, North American Review, Review of Reviews*, and *Youth's Companion*.

Halstead's first interest remained politics. He attended the conventions of 1892, 1896, and 1900 as a correspondent for various magazines and newspapers. For several months in late 1895, he wrote a nationally syndicated weekly column on politics. During the 1900 campaign he and Willis J. Abbott, a Democrat, produced the syndicated "Campaign Forum," a debate that appeared in parallel columns and discussed the issues and men of the year.[18]

Halstead's interest in imperialism became an important factor in keeping his name before the public during this decade. In January 1896, William Randolph Hearst sent him to report on the Cuban rebellion. Halstead stated that the Spanish authorities could not hold the island. He believed that Cuba should become an American state, substantiating "her freedom forever by consolidation in our imperishable system."[19]

For Halstead, Congress's declaration of war against Spain became a great opportunity: "It is a war of aggression to vindicate a human and otherwise wholesome ambition for the country. There is no loud cry for personal sacrifice, unless a fellow wants to get on the track to be President of the United States someday." For Halstead personally, the war represented the opportunity to become a war correspondent. With the congressional declaration, he applied to McKinley for permission to go to the Philippines as an "historian."[20]

During the Spanish-American War, more reporters applied for permission to accompany various commanders than the number who reported throughout the four years of the Civil War. Although places were hard to gain, Halstead traveled to Washington and received the president's approval to accompany General Wesley Merritt to the Philippines. On board ship, Halstead contracted typhoid fever, which confined him in a Honolulu hospital for four weeks. Nonetheless, he recovered and continued to the Philippines. He remained in the islands for most of the month of August 1898, writing stories and dispatches and visiting the rebel leader Emilio Aguinaldo. In September he returned to the United States by way of Hong Kong and Japan.[21]

Halstead went to the Philippines a convinced imperialist. As early as 1896, he delivered a Lyceum lecture entitled "Cuba and Iceland" describing his visits to the two "great American islands" and giving "reasons why they should belong to the United States." He returned from the Philippines a crusader for additional American expansion.[22]

Andrew Carnegie and other anti-imperialists argued against annexation of the Philippines, asserting that the United States should never own territory not contiguous to the rest of the nation, nor areas occupied by people of the "Mongolian and Malayan races." Carnegie also contended that a member of the Caucasian race could not grow from infancy to maturity in the Philippine climate.[23]

Halstead lectured on the Philippines in Pittsburgh in order to counter Carnegie's influence. He declared that the steelmaker knew nothing about statesmanship. All the great American leaders had been "expansionists." George Washington, Andrew Jackson, James K. Polk, Andrew Johnson, William Seward, and Charles Sumner all desired to extend the territory of the United States. If the fathers of our country had followed the policies of Andrew Carnegie, the United States might still be a "small, snug, neat republic on the Atlantic slope, leaving the Cotton States, the Ohio country, the whole continent from the Alleghenies to the Pacific, to the British, French and Spaniards." To Halstead our entire history demanded the possession of the Philippines. As for the argument that people taken by force could never be loyal, the editor asserted, "There is no better title than the sword drawn in a just war."[24]

During the next few years, Halstead gave lectures on the Philippines in many cities across the nation. Before the Economics Club in Chicago, he declared that Aguinaldo's decision to transfer his rebellion against Spain to one against the United States that of a "traitor." When a member of the audience called out that he wished Aguinaldo success, Halstead said "that the man who would utter such sentiments was a traitor." A "lively row" ensued between Halstead's supporters and detractors. Finally, the editor had to leave by a rear entrance.[25]

Speaking before the Commercial Travellers' Sound Money League in New York during the 1900 campaign, Halstead condemned the Democratic candidate because of his stand on imperialism and the Philippines. According to Halstead, Bryan proposed to extend the Monroe Doctrine to the Philippines. Although Bryan wished to grant the islands complete independence, he also desired to protect them from outside interference. To Halstead, this proposal proved that Bryan knew no history and "ought to be whipped. I think Mr. Bryan is whipped as a presidential candidate, so he will get his punishment."[26]

In a letter to Whitelaw Reid, Halstead declared that Aguinaldo revolted to help Bryan win the election. The Filipinos believed that Bryan had promised to grant them their independence. Thus the Republican victory in the fall meant both the reelection of a president who had granted Halstead many favors and also the reelection of one who had declared his determination to keep the Philippines.[27]

At the end of 1899, Halstead severed all connection with the failing *Standard-Union* and returned to Cincinnati. His financial difficulties followed him home. Shortly after his arrival, he announced the establishment of a "College of Journalism." "Professor" Halstead anxiously solicited help from his journalist friends to make it a success. The college, actually a correspondence school, had profit as its goal. Halstead asked help from Whitelaw Reid, who he thought might be amused or "even interested . . . seriously" in dictating a lesson.[28]

Of all of Halstead's activities during his later years, his many books brought him the most satisfaction and income. In the last decade of the nineteenth century and the first few years of the twentieth, he published over twenty books. In 1892, the editor wrote two biographies. The first, a campaign biography of Benjamin Harrison and Whitelaw Reid, he coauthored with Lew Wallace, author of *Ben Hur;* the second, a life of Jay Gould, he wrote with J. Frank Beale, Jr. Following the biographies came a series of books on American differences with Spain. They included such titles as *The Story of Cuba, The Story of the Philippines, Our Country in War and Relations with All Nations, Our New Possessions, Pictorial History of America's New Possessions, Life and Achievements of Admiral Dewey from Montpelier to Manila, Full Official History of the War with Spain,* and *Aguinaldo and His Captor.* Many of his books also dealt with current affairs, such as *Briton and Boer in South Africa, Galveston: The Horrors of a Stricken City, Pictorial History of the Louisiana Purchase,* and *The All World's Fair at St. Louis.*[29]

Halstead's later books shared one trait in common; he used scissors and paste more than the typewriter. He wrote very little, usually just adding introductory and transitional sentences to passages gathered from newspapers, magazines, and government documents. At times, he feared his books might transgress the copyright laws. He usually completed a book in a few weeks. This habit inspired a Boston newspaper to call him "the long-distance writer" who introduced "newspaper methods in book manufacture." As can be imagined, these works had little lasting value. His books, usually sold door-to-door by subscription, tried to capitalize on immediate interests. He published his best seller, a biography of McKinley, just days after the president's death. In 1896 and 1900, Halstead wrote campaign biographies of McKinley. Later he completed several chapters dealing with the Ohioan's administration for a projected history of the Republican party. With the president's assassination, he had a head start in producing a new biography. From the day of the assassination, he believed that the president's wounds might be mortal and began immediately to write a "memorial life of the third martyred president." He sent his completed manuscript to the publisher the day McKinley died.[30]

Over 700,000 copies of *The Illustrious Life of William McKinley, Our Martyred President* sold the first year. Unfortunately, these sales, which should have provided Halstead a comfortable income, only created additional difficulties. Although H. L. Barber of the Dominion Company, who held the copyright to the earlier biographies, urged Halstead to revise his old books on McKinley and republish immediately, Halstead had finished the new biography. Since he believed he could gain more from royalties than from a set revision fee for a book owned outright by Barber, he refused the proposal, calling it "unfair to the public." Nonetheless, the Monarch Company, which published his new biography, refused to pay Halstead a standard royalty fearing competition from Barber and the old biography—a justifiable fear since Barber republished Halstead's old book as *Life and Distinguished Services of William McKinley, Our Martyr President*. Consequently, even though Halstead's new book sold over 700,000 copies, he received only one cent a copy in royalites, $180 in expenses, and $1,000 in cash, or only a little more than $8,000 profit.[31]

Although Halstead had sold over a million copies of his various books by 1901, because of poor contract agreements, disagreements with publishers, and numerous lawsuits, the editor never made his hoped-for fortune. The Werner Company, which published his book on Cuba, asked Henry Watterson to write a history of the Spanish-American War. The company argued that if Halstead wrote it, the public might think he had only rehashed his earlier work. Halstead then believed he had a contract with the Oldach Company of Philadelphia, and wrote a history of the war, only to discover when he finished that the company wished to change the agreed-upon terms. Consequently, he gave the book to Barber of the Dominion Company. Oldach sued and won the case.[32]

Halstead's success with the McKinley book prompted Rand McNally to ask him to write a biography of Roosevelt, this time with very favorable royalty terms. Once more, he ruined his chances for success. When Rand McNally's editors made changes in the manuscript, Halstead annulled the contract because he "wouldn't submit at all to the criticism of the University men," who, he said, "murdered and spoiled his text." Although an Akron publisher brought out the Roosevelt book in time for the 1904 campaign, the company lacked the promotional apparatus of Rand McNally, and it did not sell well. Success was important to Halstead, and he suffered bitterly in his final years. Forced by economic necessity to continue his work far beyond his seventieth birthday, every time he produced a successful book something intervened to snatch away his longed-for fortune.[33]

The editor last appeared nationally at Roosevelt's inauguration in 1905. He attended with Mrs. Halstead and their eldest daughter Jean. The death of Jean's husband brought Marshal Halstead back from his post as United States consul at Birmingham, England, to manage his sister's business affairs. Albert Halstead succeeded his brother Marshal in England. Marshal's unexpected death in January 1908 marred the editor's pleasure in having several of his children in Cincinnati during his last years.[34]

At the time of Marshal's death, Halstead's health had started to fail. By March 1908, Robert Halstead reported that his father had occasional fits of violence in which he struck his nurse. On July 2, 1908, just two months to the day short of his eightieth birthday, Halstead suffered a cerebral hemorrhage and died.[35]

Twenty years later, on the evening of November 9, 1928, seventy-five Ohio journalists and historians gathered for dinner at the Ohio State University Faculty Club. They came to inaugurate the Ohio Journalism Hall of Fame, honoring eight Ohio journalists. These eight included William Maxwell, Charles Hammond, Joseph Medill, Samuel Cox, David Ross Locke, William Dean Howells, Whitelaw Reid, and Murat Halstead. The eight represented the highest order in the history of the journalistic field in Ohio. Certainly Halstead deserved to be included in the list.

At the time of his death, Halstead's reputation had reached its lowest ebb. Strong, personal editorship no longer found an audience. Halstead's increasing partisanship, his losing battle with the senate, and his loss of a newspaper to voice his opinions regularly— all made him remembered by 1908 as a vague figure from the distant past.

Nonetheless, Murat Halstead earned his place in the Ohio Journalism Hall of Fame. He made the *Cincinnati Commercial* one of the city's largest and most respected newspapers. He also achieved a national reputation for the paper and for its editor. Halstead came to the *Commercial* in 1853 as a local reporter. In just over a decade, he became its principal owner, editor, and publisher. For the next thirty years the *Commercial* reflected his outlooks, opinions, prejudices, and personality. Halstead developed into one of the best-known of American journalists. During the Civil War and the years immediately following, when the *Commercial* had reached its prime, the earlier American hard-hitting partisan personal journalism had ended. By the late 1870s, Henry J. Raymond of the *New York Times*, James Gordon Bennett of the *New York Herald*, Horace Greeley of the *New York Tribune*, Samuel Bowles of the *Springfield Republican*, and William Cullen Bryant of the *New York Post* had all died. Al-

though this group of giants of the press had established the importance of the daily newspaper in American life, even before their
deaths a new era had begun. Halstead appeared in the forefront of
this new era. The Cincinnati editor, along with his friends Henry
Watterson, Whitelaw Reid, Horace White, Charles Dana, and Edwin
Godkin, realized the necessity of change. The war taught the reading public to be unsatisfied with a newspaper that contained the
editor's political, economic, and social views at the expense of the
news of the day. Moreover, the reader came more and more to
insist that his newspaper be current and interesting.

Halstead led in the new movement called "independent journalism." Independent journalism had many aspects, although its supporters believed that the press's primary job was the impartial
gathering and reporting of the news. Second in importance, the
independent journalist believed that editorial opinion should be
free from both partisan demands and advertisers' pressures. For
Halstead and the other independent editors, this did not mean lack
of support for a party or its candidates. It did mean freedom to
criticize when they believed that their party had erred. It also allowed them to leave their party, as in 1872, when reform seemed
necessary. Finally, independent journalism utilized the latest me-
chanical techniques, such as the telegraph and improved presses
and printing processes to bring their readers the latest and most
interesting news possible. The independent *Cincinnati Commercial*'s
growing prominence in American journalism made its editor a figure of importance on the national scene.

Independent journalism did not prove a long-lasting movement.
Within the insistence for independence and technical innovations,
the seeds had been planted that ultimately led to the growth of the
"new journalism." Technical innovations demanded costly machinery and processes that, in turn, demanded large circulations and
ever increasing advertising revenues. These demands lessened the
influence of the editor as the newspaper became a complex corpo-
rate structure.

Just as the personal journalism of the Greeleys and the elder
Bennett passed from the scene, so the independent journalism of
the Halsteads and the Danas could not keep abreast of the new
developments in American life. Although more lively than the old
personal newspapers, independent newspapers were still being
written and edited for an educated and politically motivated mid-

dle class. To gain circulation necessary to support the new journalism, newspapers had to look beyond the middle class to the growing working class. This group, often semi-literate and foreign-born, sometimes could not read the older newspapers. When they could, the newspapers contained little that appealed to them. The new journalism placed its emphasis on "the people," and tried to appeal in particular to the working class. The press became "popular" by playing up sensational news items written in simple and clear prose and by featuring sports, women's, and comic sections. The Pulitzers, Hearsts, and Scripps replaced the independents as America's leading journalists.

Although some editors made the transition to popular journalism, many, like Halstead, could not adjust. By the 1880s, Halstead had become part of the establishment. Presidents consulted him, and he regularly gave advice to senators, congressmen, and governors. As his newspaper became a big business, he became more politically conservative. In the 1870s, Halstead had been known as a reformer. Yet even then his reform views remained those of the nineteenth-century liberal. He opposed the high protective tariff, because he believed it represented government interference in the economy. By the 1880s, he supported the protective tariff, convinced that it brought prosperity to America. This argument placed him squarely behind the Republican establishment. In the 1870s, he supported civil service reform, arguing that efficiency in government demanded that the bureaucracy be staffed by well-trained professionals. By the 1880s, he joined the majority of Republican politicians in asserting that a civil service based on merit created a professional class unresponsive to the public's will and needs. Even in the 1870s, he used the columns of the *Commercial* to condemn the Greenbackers, other inflationary schemes, and the unions.

Richard Smith's *Gazette* was as business-oriented and antilabor as the *Commercial*. Thus, even with the available financing, the combined *Commercial Gazette* had little foundation on which to build a popular press. In other cities a conservative, well-edited, and responsible newspaper could find an audience, but not in Cincinnati; the *Commercial Gazette* faced competition from the Democratic *Enquirer* and *Post,* and also from Charles P. Taft's Republican *Times-Star*.

Thus, Halstead and his newspaper outlived their era. Halstead made the *Commercial* one of the leading newspapers in independent journalism; in so doing, he pioneered the movement to the new journalism, the journalism of the popular press. Halstead had a sure instinct for the news and an extraordinary talent for developing it; he could not, in temperament and on principle, continue where the movement led. So the *Commercial* and the *Commercial Gazette* could not match the pace of the new journalism, and were ultimately eliminated. The successes of the Pulitzers, the Hearsts, and the new journalism overshadowed the real accomplishments of their predecessors, and obscured the origins of the popular press in America.

Notes

CHAPTER 1

1. Murat Halstead Papers; William L. Halstead Manuscript; William L. Halstead, *The Story of the Halsteads of the United States*, passim. (The full citation for each title will be found only in its first use in each chapter.)

2. William L. Halstead MS., p. 16; Murat Halstead, "Tales and Traditions," Halstead Papers.

3. Halstead, "Tales and Traditions"; William L. Halstead MS., p. 25.

4. William L. Halstead MS., p. 26; Murat Halstead, "Pets and Sports of a Farmer Boy," *Cosmopolitan Magazine* (February 1892), pp. 472–77. Robert Herron edited and published portions of an article by Halstead found in the Halstead Papers called "Paddy's Run Papers." *Bulletin of the Historical and Philosophical Society of Ohio* (July 1957).

5. Many years later, Daniel Brown recalled Halstead's first visit to a local school. Brown, a student, remembered a very small boy sitting with the girls on the "female side" of the one-room school, who took his turn when the class read aloud and finished his passage without any corrections. Daniel Brown to M. Halstead, December 2, 1879, Halstead Papers; William Halstead MS., p. 20; *Cincinnati Commercial Gazette*, February 7, 1890.

6. William Halstead MS., p. 28. John Halstead was also to be disappointed by Murat's brother Benton, who left the farm for the profession of law. William Halstead, *The Story of the Halsteads*.

7. Samuel F. Cary, *History of College Hill and Vicinity, With a Sketch of Pioneer Life in This Part of Ohio*, pp. 19–20.

8. Murat Halstead, "Farmers' College," p. 283.

9. Ibid., p. 284; Cary, *History of College Hill*, p. 20.

10. Murat Halstead, "Farmers' College," pp. 284–85.

11. *Farmers' College Catalogue*, 1848, pp. 13–15; Robert Halstead, "Presi-

dents I Have Known," Halstead Papers; William Halstead MS., p. 32; Murat Halstead to Mrs. Benjamin Harrison, April 1, 1904, Halstead Papers; Harry J. Sievers, *Benjamin Harrison, Hoosier Warrior; Through the Civil War Years, 1833–1865,* p. 31; Murat Halstead, "Farmers' College," p. 284; James H. Rodabaugh, *Robert Hamilton Bishop,* pp. 160–66.

12. Halstead to Mrs. Benjamin Harrison, April 1, 1904, Halstead Papers.

13. Rodabaugh, *Bishop,* pp. 173–87.

14. Carl M. Becker, "The Genesis of a Copperhead," *Bulletin of the Historical and Philosophical Society of Ohio* (October 1961), p. 242.

15. Sievers, *Harrison, Hoosier Warrior,* p. 32.

16. William Halstead MS., p. 43; *Cincinnati Commercial Gazette,* June 16, 1890; *Cincinnati Commercial,* February 26, 1863, March 14, 1873; A. B. Huston, *Historical Sketch of Farmers' College,* p. 122.

17. Eugene H. Roseboom, *The Civil War Era,* p. 21; Charles Cist, *Sketches and Statistics of Cincinnati in 1851,* pp. 169–244, passim.

18. Cist, *Sketches and Statistics of Cincinnati in 1851,* pp. 74–77.

19. Murat Halstead, "Varieties of Journalism," *Cosmopolitan Magazine* (December 1892), p. 203; William Halstead MS., p. 36; Zane L. Miller, *Boss Cox's Cincinnati,* pp. 3–5.

20. Murat Halstead, "Varieties of Journalism," pp. 203–4.

21. William Halstead MS., pp. 42–44.

22. Murat Halstead, "History of the *Cincinnati Commercial,*" Halstead Papers.

23. Ibid.

24. Murat Halstead, "Varieties of Journalism," p. 205.

25. Ibid., p. 204; Murat Halstead, "Early Editorial Experiences," *Lippincott's Monthly Magazine* (June 1892), pp. 713–14.

26. James Albert Green, "The Literary Club of Cincinnati: A Centenary in Retrospect," *Bulletin of the Historical and Philosophical Society of Ohio* (January 1950), p. 51.

27. Harry Barnard, *Rutherford B. Hayes and His America,* p. 172; *The Literary Club of Cincinnati, 1849–1903, Constitution, Catalogue of Members, Etc.,* p. 12; *The Literary Club of Cincinnati, 1849–1949, Centennial Book,* p. 76.

28. Murat Halstead, "History of the *Cincinnati Commercial.*"

29. Ibid.

30. Ibid.

31. *Cincinnati Commercial,* April 29, 1856; Murat Halstead, *Trimmers, Trucklers, and Temporizers: Notes of Murat Halstead from the Political Conventions of 1856,* ed. William B. Hesseltine and Rex G. Fisher, p. v.

32. Wilfred E. Binkley, *American Political Parties, Their Natural History,* pp. 207–8; Glyndon G. Van Deusen, *Thurlow Weed; Wizard of the Lobby,* pp. 208–9; George H. Mayer, *The Republican Party, 1854-1966,* pp. 41–44.

33. *Commercial,* July–November, 1856, passim; Halstead to T.C. Day, June 30, 1856, quoted in Sarah J. Day, *The Man on a Hill Top,* p. 172.

34. Newspaper clipping, Halstead Papers.

35. *Commercial,* March 10, 1857. The delicacy which the young reporter noted in Buchanan seems to have been at least partially the result of

illness. The new president journeyed to Washington several weeks before and fell victim to the "National Hotel disease," a kind of dysentery accompanied by diarrhea brought on by a failure in the water supply of the hotel. Buchanan needed brandy and medication to settle his queasy stomach in order to get through the official ceremonies. Philip S. Klein, *President James Buchanan: A Biography*, pp. 268–72.

36. William Halstead MS., p. 70.

37. *Commercial*, October 18, 1859.

38. Ibid., October 25, 1859.

39. Ibid., December 2, 3, 1859.

40. Ibid., December 5, 1859; Jules Abel, *Man on Fire: John Brown and the Cause of Liberty*, pp. 357–67.

41. *Commercial*, December 5, 1859.

42. Ibid.

43. Ibid., December 6, 7, 8, 1859.

44. Ibid., December 5, 1859.

45. Henry H. Simms, *A Decade of Sectional Controversy, 1851–1861*, pp. 155–57; Mayer, *The Republican Party, 1854-1966*, pp. 59–60; *Commercial*, December 9, 1859.

46. *Commercial*, December 15, 1859.

CHAPTER 2

1. *Cincinnati Commercial*, January 2, 1860.

2. Ibid., April 23, 1860. Halstead's reports of the conventions can also be found in: Murat Halstead, *Caucuses of 1860*; and Murat Halstead, *Three against Lincoln: Murat Halstead Reports the Caucuses of 1860*, edited by William B. Hesseltine and Bruce Robertson.

3. *Commercial*, April 24, 26, 28, 1860.

4. Halstead, *Three against Lincoln*, p. xii.

5. *Commercial*, April 28, 30, 1860.

6. Ibid., April 30, 1860.

7. Ibid., May 2, 1860.

8. Ibid., May 8, 9, 1860.

9. Ibid., May 10, 1860.

10. Ibid., May 11, 1860.

11. Ibid., May 18, 1860.

12. Eugene H. Roseboom, *A History of Presidential Elections*, pp. 177–79; George H. Mayer, *The Republican Party, 1854–1966*, pp. 67–68.

13. *Commercial*, May 20, 1860.

14. Ibid.

15. Ibid., June 13, 1860.

16. Ibid., June 20, 1860.

17. Ibid., June 26, 1860.

18. Ibid., May 26, 1860.

19. Halstead, *Caucuses of 1860*.

20. *Cincinnati Commercial Gazette*, September 27, 1887; Halstead, *Three against Lincoln*, p. 279.

21. Eugene H. Roseboom, *The Civil War Era, 1850–1873,* p. 374; Alvin F. Harlow, *The Serene Cincinnatians,* p. 224; David M. Potter, *Lincoln and His Party in the Secession Crisis,* p. 53; Murat Halstead, "History of the Cincinnati *Commercial,*" Halstead Papers; *Commercial,* March 1861, passim.

22. Louis M. Starr, *Reporting the Civil War: The Bohemian Brigade in Action, 1861–65,* p. 9.

23. Ibid., p. 6; J. Cutler Andrews, *The North Reports the Civil War,* pp. 6–34.

24. *Commercial,* June 3, 1861.

25. Ibid., June 6, 13, 1861.

26. Ibid., June 14, 1861. In fairness to Chase, he wrote to Halstead defending Cameron, asserting that he was a patriotic man who did not receive the support he needed to carry on the work of his department. Chase to Halstead, December 25, 1861, quoted in J. W. Schuckers, *The Life and Public Services of Salmon Portland Chase, United States Senator and Governor of Ohio; Secretary of the Treasury, and Chief Justice of the United States,* p. 381.

27. *Commercial,* June 24, 1861; Burton J. Hendrick, *Lincoln's War Cabinet,* p. 264.

28. *Commercial,* June 8, 13, 1861; Andrews, *North Reports the Civil War,* p. 649; Starr, *Reporting the Civil War,* pp. 30–32.

29. *Commercial,* June 27, 1861; Starr, *Reporting the Civil War,* pp. 64–68.

30. Starr, *Reporting the Civil War,* pp. 69–70; B. H. Liddell Hart, *Sherman,* pp. 106–111; Lloyd Lewis, *Sherman: Fighting Prophet,* pp. 194–96.

31. Murat Halstead, "Recollections and Letters of General Sherman," *Independent* (June 15, 1899), 1612–13; *Commercial,* December 12, 1861. One author feels that the entire incident resulted from Villard's unfamiliarity with the American idiomatic use of the word "crazy." He states that the *Tribune* reporter used slang when telling Villard that Cameron thought Sherman was "crazy." Villard, with only a few years of English usage, believed he meant "insane." He explains the month-and-a-half delay between the time Villard told Halstead the insanity story and the *Commercial's* article by saying that as a personal friend of the Sherman family the editor wished to verify the story. Halstead felt that the facts had been proved when the general was relieved from duty. Emmet Crozier, *Yankee Reporters: 1861–1865,* pp. 176–78.

32. William T. Sherman, *Memoirs of General William T. Sherman,* 1:216.

33. Harry L. Coles, "General William T. Sherman and the Press," unpublished paper delivered before the Southern Historical Association, 1962, passim; Lewis, *Sherman,* pp. 190–91; Crozier, *Yankee Reporters,* pp. 190–91; Liddell Hart, *Sherman,* p. 103; Halstead, "Sherman," *Independent* (June 22, 1899), 1683.

34. *Commercial,* July 11, 1861.

35. Ibid., July 16, 1861.

36. Ibid., July 31, 1862.

37. Ibid., July 13, 1861; Roseboom, *Civil War,* pp. 408–9; Carl M. Becker, "The Genesis of a Copperhead," *Bulletin of the Historical and Philosophical Society of Ohio* (October 1961), p. 235.

38. *Commercial,* July 14, 1861.
39. Ibid., June 3, October 10, 1863.
40. Ibid., September 27, October 4, 14, 1862.
41. Ibid., October 6, 1862; Frank L. Klement, *The Copperheads in the Middle West,* pp. 124–25.
42. *Commercial,* October 16, 1862.
43. Ibid., October 21, 1862.
44. Klement, *Copperheads in Middle West,* pp. 87–95; Roseboom, *Civil War,* pp. 411–15; Eugene H. Roseboom and Francis P. Weisenburger, *History of Ohio,* p. 192.
45. *Commercial,* February 18, June 12, 1863.
46. Ibid., June 13, August 5, 8, September 30, October 10, 1863.
47. Ibid., October 13, 1863.
48. Ibid., October 14, 1863; Klement, *Copperheads in Middle West,* pp. 132–33.
49. *Commercial,* December 2, 4, 11, 13, 1862.
50. Ibid., November 17, 1862. Although Chase defended McClellan, in this case Halstead did not accept the secretary's judgment. Chase to Halstead, May 24, 1862, Schuckers, *Salmon Portland Chase,* p. 436.
51. William Halstead MS., p. 98; Andrews, *North Reports the Civil War,* p. 323; *Commercial,* December 18, 1862.
52. James G. Randall, *The Civil War and Reconstruction,* p. 312.
53. *Commercial,* December 17, 1862; Andrews, *North Reports the Civil War,* pp. 331–32.
54. William Halstead MS., p. 100; *Commercial,* January 27, 1863.
55. Murat Halstead, "Weakness in Journalism," Halstead Papers.
56. Harlow, *The Serene Cincinnatians,* p. 230; Sarah J. Day, *Man on the Hill Top,* p. 247; Donnal V. Smith, *Chase and Civil War Politics,* pp. 50–51. In one letter Chase stated that the war would have been more efficiently run if the cabinet members could administer their departments without constant interference, a veiled hint that Lincoln was the one interfering. Chase to Halstead, September 21, 1863, Robert B. Warden, *An Account of the Private Life and Public Services of Salmon P. Chase,* p. 549; see also Schuckers, *Salmon Portland Chase,* p. 393; William Halstead MS., p. 97.
57. Halstead to Day, June 8, 1861; Day, *Man on Hill Top,* p. 243.
58. William Henry Smith Papers; *Commercial,* December 2, 1864; Smith, *Chase and Civil War Politics,* p. 159.
59. *Commercial,* November 8, 1864.
60. Ibid., March 6, 1865.
61. Ibid., March 31, April 10, 15, 22, 1865.
62. *Ohio State Journal* (Columbus), February 14, 1888.

CHAPTER 3

1. Charles S. Diehl, *The Staff Correspondent,* p. 157.
2. Victor Rosewater, *History of Cooperative News-Gathering in the United States,* p. 115.
3. Ibid., p. 116.

4. Charles P. Taft, "The Associated Press," clipping, William H. Smith Papers; Rosewater, *Cooperative News-Gathering,* p. 118.

5. Rosewater, *Cooperative News-Gathering,* 119–21; *Commercial,* December 1, 1866.

6. Rosewater, *Cooperative News-Gathering,* pp. 126–29; Diehl, *Staff Correspondent,* p. 157.

7. Diehl, *Staff Correspondent,* p. 158; Eugene H. Kleinpell, "James M. Comly, Journalist-Politician," Ph.D. dissertation, Ohio State University, 1936, passim.

8. Lena C. Logan, "Henry Watterson and the Liberal Convention of 1872," *Indiana Magazine of History* (December 1944), p. 320.

9. Charles F. Wingate, ed., *Views and Interviews on Journalism,* pp. 123–24.

10. Ibid., pp. 118–29.

11. Ibid., p. 125.

12. Ibid., p. 119.

13. Murat Halstead, "Weakness in Journalism," Halstead Papers; *Commercial,* November 15, 1860, April 29, 1870; *Commercial Gazette,* February 18, 1889.

14. Wingate, ed., *Views and Interviews on Journalism,* pp. 126, 128.

15. Ibid., p. 116.

16. *Commercial,* July 17, October 5, 16, December 8, 21, 1865, March 1, 1866; Howard K. Beale, *The Critical Year,* p. 23; Eric L. McKitrick, *Andrew Johnson and Reconstruction,* p. 89.

17. Beale, *Critical Year,* 138; *Commercial,* March 30, April 9, July 14, 1866.

18. *Commercial,* September 1, 5, 10, 26, October 5, 10, November 24, 1866, January 5, 1867.

19. Ibid., September 2, November 21, 25, 30, December 20, 1867, February 26, April 22, 30, May 1, 16, 1868. Many moderate Republicans shared Halstead's position on Johnson's administration and the impeachment trial; see Michael Les Benedict, *A Compromise of Principle,* pp. 294–314.

20. *Commercial,* January 22, 1864.

21. Ibid., October 29, 1864; *New York Times,* October 26, 1864.

22. *Commercial,* October 23, 1865; Murat Halstead, "Varieties of Journalism," *Cosmopolitan Magazine* (December 1892), p. 207; William L. Halstead MS., p. 114.

23. *Commercial,* April 4, May 23, 1866, September 2, 1870.

24. Ibid., December 2, 1870, May 2, 1877; Murat Halstead, "History of the *Cincinnati Commercial,*" Halstead Papers.

25. Charles G. Miller, *Donn Piatt: His Work and His Ways,* pp. 214–25; Donn Piatt to Halstead, November 23, 1890, Halstead Papers.

26. Robert Halstead, "Presidents I Have Known," Halstead Papers; James E. Pollard, *The Presidents and the Press,* p. 601; Ishbel Ross, *An American Family: The Tafts, 1678–1964,* p. 67.

27. *Commercial,* June 23, 1862.

28. Ibid., June 23, 1862, January 3, March 23, 24, 1868.

29. Ibid., October 24, 25, 27, 1873.

30. Ibid., March 27, 1873.

31. Ibid., April 1, 1873. The *Commercial* printed a long and detailed ac-

count of the hearings in this issue. The Senate later ordered the official proceedings published by the Columbus firm of Nevins and Meyers: *Senate Investigation of the Little Lottery Bill. Testimony of M. Halstead, B. J. Loomis, Senator Young [and Others]*. The report of the committee, without testimony, was also placed in the appendix of the *Senate Journal*.

32. *Commercial*, April 4, 11, 13, 1873.

33. Ibid., April 18, 1874.

34. William Halstead MS., p. 147.

35. Halstead to Whitelaw Reid, January 21, 1871, Whitelaw Reid Papers.

36. *Commercial*, April 13, 1869, January 21, 1870, November 2, 1870, May 28, 1875, and May 21, 1876—all contain tax lists for the various years; William Halstead MS., p. 148. In the summer of 1960, Halstead's home at 316 West Fourth Street, as happens to so many houses in once-fashionable near-downtown districts in older cities, was razed to make room for an expressway.

37. *Commercial*, November 10, 1875. Halstead does not seem to have been a member of any church. A college classmate and lifelong friend became a Methodist bishop who officiated at several weddings for members of the editor's family and at his funeral but never seems to have converted Halstead to his faith. Although his family belonged to St. Paul's Episcopal Church, there is no evidence that Halstead was a member. William Halstead MS., p. 149; Philip Linsley, *The Chicago Tribune: Its First Hundred Years*, 2:133.

38. Henry Watterson, *"Marse Henry,": An Autobiography*, 1:162–65; Alvin F. Harlow, *The Serene Cincinnatians*, p. 252; Joseph Frazier Wall, *Henry Watterson: Reconstructed Rebel*, pp. 52–53.

39. Isaac F. Marcosson, *"Marse Henry": A Biography of Henry Watterson*, p. 243.

40. William A. Croffut, *An American Procession, 1855–1914: A Personal Chronicle of Famous Men*, p. 260; Watterson, *"Marse Henry,"* 1:128.

41. Watterson, *"Marse Henry,"* 1:130–32; Albert Bigelow Paine, *Mark Twain, A Biography: The Personal and Literary Life of Samuel Langhorne Clemens*, 1:567.

42. Samuel Bowles to Murat Halstead, June 7, 1870, Halstead Papers; "Murat Halstead," *Harper's Weekly*, [n.d.], clipping, Halstead Papers.

43. *Commercial*, August 5, 1870; Murat Halstead, "Outflanking Two Emperors," *Cosmopolitan Magazine* (August 1894), p. 424.

44. *Commercial*, August 6, 1870.

45. Ibid., August 9, 1870.

46. Halstead, "Outflanking Two Emperors," pp. 424–25; Moncure D. Conway, *Autobiography, Memories, and Experiences*, 2:219–20.

47. *Commercial*, August 20, 1870; Halstead, "Outflanking Two Emperors," pp. 426–27.

48. Moncure D. Conway, "Reminiscences of Kaiser Wilhelm," *Cosmopolitan Magazine* (April 1888), p. 146; Conway, *Autobiography*, 2:226.

49. *Commercial*, August 29, 1870; Halstead, "Outflanking Two Emperors," pp. 429–30; Conway, "Reminiscences of Kaiser Wilhelm," p. 147.

50. Conway, *Autobiography*, 2:228.

51. Halstead, "Outflanking Two Emperors," p. 433.
52. Alfred Cobban, *A History of Modern France,* 1:199.
53. Murat Halstead, "With an Invading Army," *Cosmopolitan Magazine* (September 1894), pp. 605–9; *Commercial Gazette,* November 3, 1890; Conway, *Autobiography,* 2:233–34; Murat Halstead, "Prince Bismarck," *Cosmopolitan Magazine* (August 1891), pp. 500–504; *Commercial,* September 16, 17, 23, 1870; Cobban, *A History of Modern France,* 1:200; Murat Halstead, "Current Events," *Cosmopolitan Magazine* (May 1890), p. 117.
54. Philip B. McDonald, *A Saga of the Seas: The Story of Cyrus W. Field and the Laying of the First Atlantic Cable,* pp. 233–34.
55. *Commercial,* August 4, 20, 1874; Bayard Taylor, *Egypt and Iceland in the Year 1874,* pp. 156–61.
56. Albert Shaw, "Murat Halstead, Journalist," *Review of Reviews* (April 1896), pp. 439–43.

CHAPTER 4

1. Benjamin P. Thomas, *Abraham Lincoln: A Biography,* p. 373.
2. Chase to Halstead, May 22, June 1, 1868, quoted in Robert B. Warden, *An Account of the Private Life and Public Services of Salmon Portland Chase,* pp. 698–99, 700–701; *Commercial,* May 22, November 4, 1868.
3. George S. Merriam, *The Life and Times of Samuel Bowles,* 2:154; *Commercial,* October 23, 1869.
4. Earle D. Ross, *The Liberal Republican Movement,* p. 13.
5. Eric F. Goldman, *Rendezvous with Destiny,* p. 16; Stow Persons, *The Decline of American Gentility,* pp. 157–58; John G. Sproat, *"The Best Men": Liberal Reformers in the Gilded Age,* pp. 4–10, 74–76; Eugene H. Roseboom, *A History of Presidential Elections,* pp. 224–25; Ross, *Liberal Republican Movement,* p. 52.
6. *Commercial,* October 23, 1869.
7. Ibid., August 15, 1871, July 29, October 31, 1870.
8. Ibid., December 29, 1870, March 20, December 22, 1871.
9. Ibid., January 1, 1866; Halstead to Hayes, July 6, 1866, Hayes Papers; Alvin F. Harlow, *The Serene Cincinnatians,* p. 249; Eugene H. Roseboom, *The Civil War Era, 1850–1873,* pp. 471–72.
10. Merriam, *Bowles,* 2:133.
11. Lena C. Logan, "Henry Watterson and the Liberal Convention of 1872," *Indiana Magazine of History* (December 1944), p. 320; Joseph Frazier Wall, *Henry Watterson: Reconstructed Rebel,* pp. 99–100.
12. Logan, "Henry Watterson," p. 320; *Commercial,* March 22, 1871.
13. *Commercial,* December 22, 1871; Henry Watterson, "The Humor and Tragedy of the Greeley Campaign," *Century Magazine* (November 1912), p. 34; *New York Times,* April 2, 1871; Ross, *Liberal Republican Movement,* pp. 54–55.
14. *Commercial,* January 27, 1872; Charles F. Adams, *Charles Francis Adams,* p. 390.
15. *Commercial,* March 15, 1872, November 24, 1866, April 15, 1871.

Even though Halstead had heaped scorn upon the Grant administration for at least three years, and, in return, had been completely vilified by the Grant supporters, his personal relations with many within the party remained quite cordial. In February he was even invited to a dinner party at the vice-president's home. Schuyler Colfax to Halstead, February 11, 1872, Halstead Papers; Halstead to Whitelaw Reid, December 27, 1870, Reid Papers.

16. Rollo Ogden, ed., *Life and Letters of Edwin Lawrence Godkin,* 1:255, 2:62; Murat Halstead, "Breakfasts with Horace Greeley," *Cosmopolitan Magazine* (April 1904), p. 702; Halstead to Whitelaw Reid, May 30, 1872, Reid Papers.

17. *Commercial,* March 27, April 22, 1872; Martin B. Duberman, *Charles Francis Adams, 1807–1886,* p. 361.

18. *Commercial,* August 15, 1871, April 13, 22, 1872; *New York Times,* April 30, 1872.

19. *Commercial,* March 1, 2, 1872.

20. Wall, *Henry Watterson,* p. 102.

21. Watterson, "Humor and Tragedy of Greeley Campaign," p. 30; Logan, "Henry Watterson," p. 327; Merriam, *Bowles,* 2:184.

22. William H. Hale, *Horace Greeley: Voice of the People,* p. 335; Watterson, "Humor and Tragedy of Greeley Campaign," p. 31.

23. Watterson, "Humor and Tragedy of Greeley Campaign," pp. 32, 35; Ross, *Liberal Republican Movement,* p. 77.

24. F. G. Welch, *That Convention: or Five Days a Politician,* passim.

25. Logan, "Henry Watterson," p. 331; Watterson, "Humor and Tragedy of Greeley Campaign," p. 33; Horace White, *The Life of Lyman Trumbull,* pp. 380–81; Willard L. King, *Lincoln's Manager: David Davis,* p. 281.

26. *Enquirer,* May 1, 2, 1872; *Commercial,* August 15, 1871, May 2, 1872. Traditionally leases expired on May 1, and the streets of large cities filled with movers' trucks and wagons.

27. Welch, *That Convention,* p. 87; Ben Perley Poore, *Perley's Reminiscences of Sixty Years in the National Metropolis,* 2:284; *Cincinnati Gazette,* May 1, 1872; Logan, "Henry Watterson," p. 328; *New York Times,* April 30, May 2, 3, 1872; *Commercial,* May 1, 1872; White, *Lyman Trumbull,* p. 380; George W. Julian, *Political Recollections, 1840–1872,* p. 337; Ross, *Liberal Republican Movement,* pp. 65, 92; The *Enquirer* called the *Times* reporters a "set of murderous looking pickpockets [sent] here to vilify the Cincinnati movement." *Enquirer,* May 1, 1872; Carl Schurz, *Speeches, Correspondence, and Political Papers,* 2:359.

28. Watterson, "Humor and Tragedy of Greeley Campaign," p. 34; *Commercial,* May 3, 1872.

29. *Commercial,* May 1, 4, 1872; White, *Lyman Trumbull,* p. 382; Ross, *Liberal Republican Movement,* p. 95.

30. Ross, *Liberal Republican Movement,* p. 97.

31. *Commercial,* May 4, 1872.

32. White, *Lyman Trumbull,* p. 382; Logan, "Henry Watterson," p. 335.

33. Logan, "Henry Watterson," p. 335; Watterson, "Humor and Tragedy of the Greeley Campaign," p. 39. Neither Watterson nor Miss Logan says

what these documents were, or what kind of information they contained. *Commercial,* May 4, 1872; *Enquirer,* May 4, 1872.

34. *Commercial,* May 4, 1872.

35. Ibid.

36. Ross, *Liberal Republican Movement,* pp. 99–101; Duberman, *Charles Francis Adams,* p. 363; Matthew T. Downey, "Horace Greeley and the Politicians: The Liberal Republican Convention in 1872," *Journal of American History* (March 1967), pp. 727–50. Downey supports the contention that the simple explanation that the "politicians" took control from the reformers and gave the nomination to Greeley does not do justice to the complex factors that determined the results of the convention.

37. *Commercial,* May 4, 1872; *Enquirer,* May 4, 1872; William E. Smith, *The Francis Blair Family in Politics,* 2:452.

38. *Enquirer,* May 4, 1872; *Times,* May 4, 1872.

39. Watterson, "Humor and Tragedy of Greeley Campaign," p. 40; Merriam, *Bowles,* 2:187; Logan, "Henry Watterson," p. 338; *Commercial,* May 6, 1872.

40. *Commercial,* August 28, 1872; Charles Francis Adams, Jr., to Halstead, October 5, 1872, Halstead Papers; Stanley Matthews to "a friend in Washington," May 6, 1872, quoted in Robert B. Warden, *An Account of the Private Life and Public Services of Salmon Portland Chase,* p. 732.

41. Schurz et al. to Halstead, June 6, 1872, Halstead Papers; Thomas J. McCormack, ed., *Memoirs of Gustave Koerner, 1809–1896: Life Sketches Written at the Suggestion of His Children,* 2:559; Ross, *Liberal Republican Movement,* pp. 119–25. White says that Bryant chaired the meeting but fell asleep soon after the proceedings began. White, *Trumbull,* p. 391; Logan, "Henry Watterson," p. 339.

42. Ross, *Liberal Republican Movement,* pp. 130–49; White, *Trumbull,* p. 394.

43. Halstead to Whitelaw Reid, July 14, 19, 1872, Reid Papers.

44. Murat Halstead, "Horace Greeley: A Friendly Estimate of a Great Career," *Cosmopolitan Magazine* (February 1890), p. 465; White, *Trumbull,* p. 400.

45. *Commercial,* September 7, 1872.

46. Ibid., August 6, October 9, 1872.

47. Ibid., November 5, 6, 7, 1872; Halstead to Whitelaw Reid, May 30, 1872, Reid Papers; Ross, *Liberal Republican Movement,* p. 191.

48. Sproat, *"The Best Men,"* p. 85.

49. Murat Halstead, "History of the *Cincinnati Commercial,*" Halstead Papers.

CHAPTER 5

1. Murat Halstead, "History of the *Cincinnati Commercial,*" Halstead Papers; Samuel Bowles to Halstead, November 9, 1874, Halstead Papers; Hayes to Major W. D. Bickham, June 1875, quoted in Charles Richard Williams, ed., *Diary and Letters of Rutherford Birchard Hayes, Nineteenth*

President of the United States, 3: 276; Philip D. Jordan, *Ohio Comes of Age, 1873–1900,* pp. 40–45.

2. George S. Merriam, *The Life and Times of Samuel Bowles,* 2: 244; *Cincinnati Commercial,* July 3, 15, 22, 1875; Carl Schurz, *The Reminiscences of Carl Schurz, with a Sketch of His Life and Public Services from 1809 to 1906 by Frederick Bancroft and William A. Dunning,* 3: 363; Jordan, *Ohio Comes of Age,* p. 47.

3. Schurz, *Reminiscences,* 3: 363; Earle D. Ross, *The Liberal Republican Movement,* p. 217; *Commercial,* February 2, 1875.

4. Bowles to Halstead, October 19, 1875, quoted in Merriam, *Bowles,* 2: 348; *Commercial,* May 3, 1875.

5. *Commercial,* May 3, 6, 7, 1875; *New York Times,* May 4, 1875; David S. Muzzey, *James G. Blaine: A Political Idol of Other Days,* pp. 102–3; Ross, *Liberal Republican Movement,* p. 229; Bowles to Halstead, March 4, 1876, quoted in Merriam, *Bowles,* 2: 349.

6. Muzzey, *Blaine,* p. 107.

7. Ibid., pp. 82–83; Blaine to Halstead, April 4, 1873, Halstead Papers. One Blaine letter, interestingly enough, is headed "Confidential, Destroy," Blaine to Halstead, December 31, 1873, Halstead Papers; Allan Nevins, *Abram S. Hewitt,* p. 302; Blaine to Joseph Medill, February 29, 1876, copy, Halstead Papers; Harry Barnard, *Rutherford B. Hayes and His America,* pp. 285–86. Barnard's account of the publishing of the letters is confused. He places General H. V. Boynton in Washington as the *Commercial's* correspondent, while actually he represented the *Cincinnati Gazette.* He also says that Richard Smith was publisher of the *Commercial* and Halstead editor.

8. Barnard, *Rutherford B. Hayes,* p. 286; Eugene H. Roseboom, *A History of Presidential Elections,* pp. 238–39; George H. Mayer, *The Republican Party, 1854–1966,* pp. 187–88.

9. On the eve of the balloting, Halstead republished the Mulligan letters, adding a strong editorial condemning Blaine as a "sort of broker in the stock of railroads which were affected by the legislation of Congress," and guilty of "disposing of the bonds to 'his friends in Maine,' [at] . . . a very handsome commission." *Commercial,* June 2, 1876; Schurz to Halstead, May 30, 1876, Halstead Papers; Murat Halstead, "Recollections and Letters of President Hayes," *Independent* (February 16, 1899), p. 486; Muzzey, *Blaine,* p. 102; Roseboom, *Presidential Elections,* p. 238; *Commercial,* June 17, 1876; Samuel Bowles to Halstead, June 22, 1876, Halstead Papers; Keith Ian Polakoff, *The Politics of Inertia,* pp. 65–67.

10. *Commercial,* June 17, 1876.

11. Halstead to Hayes, June 22, 1876, Hayes Papers. Later Halstead stated that "it was not a labor of love" for him to oppose Hayes, but that he liked the way Bristow "took damn scoundrels by the neck." Halstead to Hayes, September 19, 1876, Hayes Papers; Wilson J. Vance to Halstead, July 11, 1876, quoted in Charles Richard Williams, *Life of Rutherford Birchard Hayes, Nineteenth President of the United States,* 1: 471; Halstead to James M. Comly, June 18, 1876, Comly Papers.

12. Ross, *Liberal Republican Movement,* p. 231; Roseboom, *Presidential Elections,* p. 241; Polakoff, *Politics of Inertia,* p. 108.

13. *Enquirer,* September, 1976, passim; *Commercial,* October 2, 17, 1876.

14. *Commercial,* September 8, 1876; Hayes to Halstead, September 12, 18, October 14, 1876, Hayes Papers.

15. Halstead to Hayes, September 19, October 14, 1876, Hayes Papers. The Ohio State Committee distributed 160,000 copies of an earlier supplement which Halstead had written. Halstead to Hayes, September 21, 1876, Hayes Papers.

16. Barnard, *Rutherford B. Hayes,* p. 313; Hayes to Halstead, October 14, 1876, Halstead Papers; Halstead to A. T. Wikoff, October 19, 1876; Halstead to Hayes, October 23, 1876, Hayes Papers.

17. *Commercial,* October 26, 1876; Murat Halstead, "War Claims of the South."

18. *Commercial,* October 19, 30, 1876; Barnard, *Hayes,* p. 314; Elmer Davis, *History of the New York Times, 1851–1921,* p. 132. General Daniel E. Sickles may have recognized the possibilities in the southern states before either Reid or Chandler. Jerome L. Sternstein, ed., "The Sickles Memorandum: Another Look at the Hayes-Tilden Election Night Conspiracy," *Journal of Southern History* (August 1966), pp. 342–57.

19. Nevins, *Hewitt,* p. 399; Roseboom, *Presidential Elections,* pp. 243–44; Halstead to James M. Comly, November 17, 1876, Hayes Papers.

20. *Commercial,* November 10, 11, 17, 19, December 2, 1876.

21. Ibid., October 19, November 21, 1876; Roseboom, *Presidential Elections,* pp. 246–47. Henry Watterson claimed that his uncle, Stanley Matthews, told him that Republicans also wanted Davis's appointment. "Judge Davis was as safe for us as Judge Bradley. We preferred him because he carried more weight." Henry Watterson, *"Marse Henry": An Autobiography,* 1: 311. Halstead thought the commission remained safe for the Republicans with either Davis or Bradley. He saw it as a means of giving Hayes the presidency "relieved of all assumptions or mortgages and imputations." Halstead to Hayes, January 22, 1877, Hayes Papers.

22. A. Taft to Halstead, February 12, 1877, Halstead Papers; Nevins, *Hewitt,* p. 327; Mayer, *Republican Party,* pp. 196–97.

23. Halstead stated that the filibustering Democrats behaved like "idiots and lunatics." Halstead to Hayes, February 19, 1877, Hayes Papers; C. Vann Woodward, *Reunion and Reaction: the Compromise of 1877 and the End of Reconstruction,* pp. 191–92; Watterson, *"Marse Henry,"* 1: 311.

24. C. Vann Woodward, *Origins of the New South, 1877–1913,* pp. 26–30.

25. Halstead to Hayes, November 30, 1876, Hayes Papers; *Enquirer,* December 2, 1876; *Commercial,* December 3, 1876.

26. Woodward, *Reunion and Reaction,* pp. 26–27.

27. Barnard, *Hayes,* p. 360.

28. Woodward, *Origins of the New South,* pp. 28–29; William H. Smith to Whitelaw Reid, December 18, 1876, Reid Papers.

29. *Commercial,* April 28, 1877; William H. Smith to Hayes, December 14, 1876; Halstead to Hayes, December 15, 1876, Hayes Papers; W. H. Smith to Boynton, December 15, 1876, Smith Papers.

30. Watterson, *"Marse Henry,"* 1: 311; Woodward, *Reunion and Reaction,* pp. 224–25. Although Halstead believed that he and the other news-

papermen were instrumental in securing Hayes's election, Professor Polakoff states "that the diffusion of power in both major parties, and not the
machinations of a handful of journalists, was instrumental in preserving
the peace in 1877." Polakoff, *Politics of Inertia,* p. 314.

31. Woodward, *Reunion and Reaction,* pp. 218–19; Barnard, *Hayes,* pp.
394–95; *Commercial,* March 12, 1877. Halstead reported that failing all other
lines, Democrats planned to take the presidency by force. L. C. Weir to
Hayes, February 7, 1877, Hayes Papers; Barnard, *Hayes,* pp. 342–43. Even
Halstead's friend Watterson volunteered to lead an unarmed regiment
from Kentucky to force Tilden's election. Halstead called these people the
"disorderlies," saying they only showed their "childishness and cussed-
ness." *Commercial,* March 1, 1877. A *Harper's Weekly* cartoon by Thomas
Nast showed a bulky Halstead pouring water on a fire-breathing Watterson
captioned "Fire and water make vapor." *Harper's Weekly,* February 3, 1877.
Nast was a friend of both men. Halstead to Watterson, February 18, 1874,
Watterson Papers; Robert Halstead, "Presidents I Have Known," Halstead
Papers; Halstead to Hayes, February 9, 11, 1877, Hayes Papers. Samuel
Bowles sympathized with Halstead about the burden of having his state's
favorite son as a presidential candidate, declaring, "It must be wearing,
even to a man of your stubborn constitution." Bowles to Halstead, De-
cember 26, 1876, Halstead Papers; Halstead, "Hayes," *Independent,* p. 487.

32. Halstead to Hayes, February 11, 1877, William H. Smith to Richard
Smith, November 19, 1877, Hayes Papers; Halstead to Schurz, February 6,
1877, Carl Schurz, *Speeches, Correspondence, and Political Papers,* 3: 388;
Schurz, *Reminiscences,* 3: 374–75.

33. Halstead to Hayes, February 11, 13, 19, 22, 24, 1877, Hayes Papers;
Woodward, *Origins of New South,* pp. 42, 47. Eckenrode claims that Hayes
wanted to give the seat to General Joseph E. Johnston, a leading ex-
Confederate, as a grand gesture of reconciliation. General Sherman pro-
tested, and so Hayes contented himself with the lesser man. H. J. Eckenrode,
Rutherford B. Hayes: Statesman of Reunion, p. 243.

34. Halstead to Hayes, February 22, 1877, Hayes Papers; Halstead to
Benjamin Harrison, February 22, 1877, Harrison Papers; Barnard, *Hayes,*
p. 417.

35. William H. Smith to Whitelaw Reid, March 5, 1877, Reid Papers;
Barnard, *Hayes,* pp. 416–17; Eckenrode, *Hayes,* p. 242.

36. Halstead to Mrs. Hayes, January 18, 1880; Hayes to Halstead, November 26, 1880, Hayes Papers; Watt P. Marchman, ed., "The Washington
Visits of Jenny Halstead, 1879–1881: From Her Letters," *Bulletin of the
Historical and Philosophical Society of Ohio* (July 1954), pp. 179–93; *Commercial,* April 23, 1877; Halstead to Hayes, December 3, 1879, Hayes Papers.

37. *Commercial,* April 17, 22, June 30, 1877, June 15, November 16, 1878;
Hayes to Halstead, July 13, 1878, Halstead to Hayes, July 18, 1878, Hayes
Papers.

38. *Commercial,* July 11, 13, 1878; Halstead to Reid, February 25, November 7, 29, 1879, Reid Papers.

39. Halstead to Reid, December 8, 20, 1879, March 21, 1880, Reid Papers.

40. *Commercial,* March 14, 17, 1878.

41. Ibid., February 28, 1880.
42. Blaine to Halstead, April 23, 1880, Halstead Papers.
43. Ibid., May 3, 1880.
44. Eugene Roseboom, *Presidential Elections*, p. 255. Charges were made that Garfield sold Sherman out for his own gain. Stating that these were absurd, the editor declared that Garfield had told him he would "rather be 'shot with musketry than nominated' and have Sherman think he had been unfaithful to his obligations. . . ." Moreover, Halstead said that no man scheming for his own nomination could have delivered Garfield's nominating speech for Sherman. Murat Halstead, "The Tragedy of Garfield's Administration: Personal Reminiscences and Records of Conversations," *McClure's Magazine* (February 1896), p. 273.
45. *Commercial*, August 11, 1877. In 1872 Garfield presented arguments before the District of Columbia Board of Public Works for a paving company when its attorney Richard C. Parson, another congressman, was called back to his home before the case could be completed. Garfield always maintained that he acted as a member of the legal profession, not as a member of Congress. It was later learned that the paving company distributed $72,000 to gain a $700,000 contract. To many people, there seemed to be fraud involved. Theodore C. Smith, *The Life and Letters of James Abram Garfield*, 1: 556; Garfield to Hinsdale, April 30, 1874, quoted in Mary L. Hinsdale, ed., *The Garfield-Hinsdale Letters*, pp. 285–86; *Commercial*, September 16, 1872, January 7, June 8, 1880; Halstead, "Tragedy of Garfield's Administration," p. 270.
46. Halstead, "Tragedy of Garfield's Administration," p. 272; Smith, *James A. Garfield*, 2:730–31; *Commercial*, March 27, May 9, June 9, 1880; Halstead to Garfield, June 8, 1880, Garfield Papers. Privately Halstead expressed the opinion that Benjamin Harrison would have made a better choice for the party. Halstead to Harrison, June 10, 1880, Harrison Papers.
47. Halstead to Garfield, July 4, 1880, Garfield Papers.
48. Whitelaw Reid to Halstead, July 12, 1880, Halstead Papers.
49. Halstead, "Tragedy of Garfield's Administration," p. 274; Smith, *James A. Garfield*, 2: 1017.
50. *Commercial*, August 11, 1880; Halstead to Garfield, August 24, 1880, Garfield Papers.
51. *Commercial*, August 12, September 3, 1880; Halstead to Garfield, September 10, 1880, Garfield Papers.
52. Herbert J. Clancy, *The Presidential Election of 1880*, pp. 173–75; Halstead to Garfield, September 13, 1880, Garfield Papers; *Commercial*, November 3, 1880.
53. Sherman to Halstead, November 5, 1880, Halstead Papers; Halstead to Garfield, November 9, 1880, Garfield Papers.
54. Halstead to Garfield, January 8, 14, 15, February 4, 1881, Halstead to General D. G. Swain, March 3, 1881, Garfield Papers; Halstead to Blaine, January 23, 1881, Blaine Papers.
55. Halstead to Garfield, May 5, 9, 11, 1881, Garfield Papers. Halstead later asserted that he had urged Garfield to conciliate Conkling, but that Conkling did not care to be conciliated. *Commercial*, June 28, 1882; Thomas G. Reeves, *Gentleman Boss*, pp. 192–94.

56. Halstead, "The Tragedy of Garfield's Administration," pp. 277–79.

57. *Commercial,* August 10, September 23, 1881.

58. Ibid., October 15, 1881, December 29, 1882; George F. Howe, *Chester A. Arthur: A Quarter-Century of Machine Politics,* p. 158.

CHAPTER 6

1. Murat Halstead, "History of the *Cincinnati Commercial,*" *Chicago Herald,* December 29, 1883, clipping, Halstead Papers. Cincinnati's period of rapid growth ended by 1870. Census figures show that while the city's population continued to increase throughout the latter half of the century, from 1870 to 1900 the rate of growth decreased every year. See Zane L. Miller, *Boss Cox's Cincinnati: Urban Politics in the Progressive Era,* p. 5.

2. Edwin Emery, *The Press and America,* pp. 356–59.

3. *Commercial,* March 9, 1866, March 22, 1867.

4. Ibid., April 1, March 15, 1882, February 6, 10, 14, 16, 21, October 4, 8, 1876.

5. *Commercial Gazette,* January 2, 1884; Albert Shaw, "Murat Halstead, Journalist," *Review of Reviews* (April 1896), p. 441.

6. Hayes to Halstead, quoted in Charles R. Williams, ed., *Diary and Letters of Rutherford Birchard Hayes, Nineteenth President of the United States,* 4: 101; *Commercial Gazette,* January, 1884, passim. For the first few months the editorials in the new journal were signed by the initials of their authors. Halstead's reputation for impulsive action might have convinced Smith that he wanted no confusion over the authorship of an individual editorial. However, in a few months they were discontinued except for occasional denials or statements of a personal nature from one of the owners.

7. Joseph Benson Foraker, *Notes of a Busy Life,* 1: 159; Sherman to Halstead, March 13, 1884, Halstead Papers; Edward Stanwood, *James Gillespie Blaine,* p. 183; *Commercial,* February 20, 1882; Blaine to Halstead, May 28, July 14, 1882, Halstead Papers. Blaine assured Halstead that while he had a special motive for wishing to have the item inserted (a motive he could not commit to writing), it was "altogether legitimate."

8. Murat Halstead, "The Defeat of Blaine for the Presidency," *McClure's Magazine* (January 1896), pp. 160–61. Sensing a political sensation in the story Blaine told him, Halstead wrote to General Sherman asking him to send copies of the Blaine letter and his reply. Sherman answered testily that the letters were confidential and that he could not show the Blaine letter without the writer's consent. In fact, he added, "I am not sure that I would, even with his consent, because I believe the true policy is to look ahead and not behind." As to his own reply, "I will not have my letter published, as it contained certain points purely personal which the public has no right to." William T. Sherman to Halstead, November 21, 1884, ibid., p. 164.

9. Joseph B. Foraker to Halstead, May 24, 1884, Halstead Papers; Andrew D. White, *Autobiography of Andrew Dickson White,* 1: 204.

10. *Commercial Gazette,* June 7, 13, 1884; Eugene H. Roseboom, *A His-*

tory of Presidential Elections, p. 269; David S. Muzzey, *James G. Blaine: A Political Idol of Other Days,* p. 295; George H. Mayer, *The Republican Party, 1854–1966,* p. 209.

11. *Commercial Gazette,* June 17, 1884, June 20, 1884.

12. Ibid., July 9, 1884; Muzzey, *James G. Blaine,* 298.

13. *Commercial Gazette,* August 3, 1884.

14. Ibid., August 23, 1884. The scandal hit the Mugwumps harder than it did the regular Democrats, as they supported Cleveland because they believed Blaine dishonest. Now they had evidence that Cleveland's character might be unpure. The solution to the Mugwumps' dilemma is an often-told story. A group of leading Mugwumps that included Schurz, Godkin, and Henry Ward Beecher were in despair until someone suggested: "Well, from what I hear, I gather Mr. Cleveland has shown high character and great capacity in public office, but that in private life his conduct has been open to question; while, on the other hand, Mr. Blaine has been weak and dishonest in public life, while he seems to have been an admirable husband and father. The conclusion I draw from these facts is that we should elect Mr. Cleveland to the public office which he is so admirably qualified to fill, and remand Mr. Blaine to the private life which he is so eminently fitted to adorn." Quoted in Muzzey, *James G. Blaine,* p. 298.

15. Muzzey, *James G. Blaine,* pp. 310–11; *Press* (no city), August 10, 1884, clipping, Halstead Papers; *Commercial Gazette,* August 10, 1884.

16. Roseboom, *Presidential Elections,* pp. 269–70.

17. *Commercial Gazette,* October 9, 1884.

18. Ibid., October 7, 1884.

19. Roseboom, *Presidential Elections,* p. 271; Mayer, *Republican Party,* pp. 211–12.

20. Halstead to Blaine, June 17, 1884, Blaine Papers; Muzzey, *James G. Blaine,* p. 311.

21. Muzzey, *James G. Blaine,* p. 272.

22. Williams, ed., *Diary and Letters of Rutherford B. Hayes,* 4: 174; *Commercial Gazette,* November 5, 6, 7, 17, 1884; Halstead, "The Defeat of Blaine," p. 163.

23. Blaine to Halstead, November 16, 1884, quoted in Halstead, "The Defeat of Blaine," p. 169; Stanwood, *James G. Blaine,* pp. 294–95; Muzzey, *James G. Blaine,* pp. 324–25; *Commercial Gazette,* July 5, 1885.

24. *Cincinnati Evening Telegram,* October 26, 1885; *Commercial Gazette,* November 7, 1884.

CHAPTER 7

1. Philip D. Jordan, *Ohio Comes of Age, 1873–1900,* p. 183.

2. *Commercial Gazette,* December 25, 1883, January 8, 10, June 11, 1884.

3. Ibid., January 16, 21, 1884, January 12, June 15, 22, 1886.

4. Ibid., June 30, July 1, 3, 1886; *New York Times,* June 30, July 1, 1886; Henry Demarest Lloyd, *Wealth against Commonwealth,* pp. 381–83.

5. *Commercial Gazette*, June 27, 1886; Lloyd, *Wealth against Commonwealth*, pp. 383–84; Ida M. Tarbell, *The History of the Standard Oil Company*, pp. 147–48.

6. *New York Times*, July 1, 24, 1886; John Sherman, *Recollections of Forty Years in the House, Senate, and Cabinet*, 2: 946–48; *Commercial Gazette*, July 24, 1886.

7. *Commercial Gazette*, July 24, 1886.

8. Chester L. Barrows, *William M. Evarts: Lawyer, Diplomat, Statesman*, p. 448; *Commercial Gazette*, July 24, 1886; *Congressional Record*, 49th Cong., 1st sess., pp. 7265–67.

9. *Commercial Gazette*, July 24, 1886; H. V. Boynton to Halstead, July 30, 1886, Halstead Papers; Charles Foster to Halstead, April 5, 1889, Halstead Papers. The Standard Oil Company, like many giant concerns of the time, often tended to nonpartisan action when it came to elections—giving financial support to both candidates in a race. There is every reason to believe that the company supported Payne because it felt he would be a "Standard Oil senator." In fact, there is every reason to believe that Standard Oil money did buy Payne his seat as Halstead claimed. See Allan Nevins, *Grover Cleveland: A Study in Courage*, p. 344.

10. *Commercial Gazette*, December 15, 1886, January 30, 1887.

11. Ibid., May 27, 1887, April 30, June 7, 12, 1888; Murat Halstead, "The Defeat of Blaine for the Presidency," *McClure's Magazine* (January 1896), p. 170.

12. *Commercial Gazette*, June 14, 30, 1888; Joseph Foraker, *Notes of a Busy Life*, 1: 381–89; Everett Walters, *Joseph Benson Foraker: An Uncompromising Republican*, pp. 73–77; Eugene Roseboom, *A History of Presidential Elections*, pp. 279–80; Joseph Foraker to Halstead, February 11, 1889, Foraker Papers.

13. Halstead to Benjamin Harrison, June 25, July 8, 22, October 16, 21, 1888, Benjamin Harrison Papers; *Commercial Gazette*, June 26, 1888.

14. *Commercial Gazette*, August 11, September 8, 1888.

15. Roseboom, *Presidential Elections*, pp. 282–83; Halstead to Harrison, November 8, 26, December 7, 20, 1888, Harrison Papers.

16. Harrison to Halstead, December 22, 24, 1888, Halstead Papers.

17. Halstead to Harrison, January 19, 26, March 19, 1889. Halstead to J. M. Dalzell, March 8, 1889, Harrison Papers.

18. *Commercial Gazette*, March 3, 5, 24, 28, 1889. With the death of William Windom, Charles Foster, the former Ohio governor, received his post as secretary of the treasury.

19. Stanley P. Hirshson, *Farewell to the Bloody Shirt*, pp. 135–42.

20. Richard Smith to John Sherman, March 28, 1889, Smith to Sherman, n.d., Henry Watterson to Sherman, n.d., John Sherman Papers. Some commentators suggested that the editor's nomination had now become an embarrassment to Harrison and should be withdrawn before the Senate voted to reconsider, but Halstead demanded that "his flag be not hauled down under fire." Smith to Sherman, March 29, 1889, Sherman Papers.

21. *Commercial Gazette*, March 29, 1889; *New York Times*, March 29, 1889.

22. *New York Times*, March 30, 1889.

23. J. C. S. Blackburn to Halstead, March 31, 1889, Halstead Papers.

The *New York Times* suggested that Henry Watterson asserted control over Mr. Blackburn, while Call's motives could be traced to desires for patronage in Florida. Senator Quay voted as a protest against Harrison's failure to name a member of the Quay machine as postmaster at Philadelphia. *New York Times,* March 29, 31, 1889; *Commercial Gazette,* March 31, 1889; James E. Pollard, *The Presidents and the Press,* p. 543; *New York Epoch,* n.d., clipping, Halstead Papers.

24. *Commercial Gazette,* March 31, 1889.

25. Ibid., March 31, April 1, 1889.

26. Quoted ibid., March 31, April 1, 1889.

27. Quoted ibid., March 30, April 1, 7, 1889; *Nation,* April 4, 1889.

28. *Commercial Gazette,* April 5, 9, 1889; Hayes to Halstead, April 1, 4, 1889, Halstead to Hayes, April 3, 1889, Hayes Papers; Wilson Vance to Halstead, April 3, 1889, Charles Foster to Halstead, April 4, 15, 1889, Halstead Papers.

29. Halstead to Harrison, April 1, 1889, Harrison Papers. William Halstead claims that the doctor so feared for Halstead's life at the time of his relapse that they cabled Mrs. Halstead in Germany to return to Cincinnati. As Halstead wrote Harrison less then three weeks later that Mrs. Halstead and his daughters were spending the summer in Germany, it is doubtful that she returned to Cincinnati. William Halstead MS.,p. 196; Carl Schurz to Halstead, May 4, 1889, Halstead Papers; Halstead to Harrison, May 7, June 27, 1889, Harrison Papers.

30. *Commercial Gazette,* June 15, August 2, 3, 4, 5, 6, 1889; William Halstead MS., p.198; Hayes to Halstead, August 3, 1889, Halstead to Hayes, April 6, 1889, Hayes Papers.

31. Everett Walters, *Joseph Benson Foraker,* pp. 89–90; Philip Jordan, *Ohio Comes of Age: 1873–1900,* pp. 301–2.

32. Foraker, *Notes of a Busy Life,* 1: 402–3; John Sherman, *Recollections of Forty Years in the House, Senate, and Cabinet,* 2: 1053–54.

33. Foraker, *Notes of a Busy Life,* 1: 403; Walters, *Joseph Benson Foraker,* p. 92.

34. Foraker, *Notes of a Busy Life,* 1: 405.

35. Ibid.; Walters, *Joseph Benson Foraker,* p. 92.

36. Foraker, *Notes of a Busy Life,* 1: 404; *Commercial Gazette,* September 29, October 2, 3, 1889; Walters, *Joseph Benson Foraker,* pp. 93–94; *Enquirer,* October 3, 1889.

37. *Commercial Gazette,* October 3, 1889.

38. Ibid., October 4, 8, 9, 1889; *Enquirer,* October 9, 1889.

39. *Commercial Gazette,* October 11, 13, 17, 1889; *House of Representatives,* 51st Cong., 2d sess., Report 3446, p. 197; Halstead to Foraker, October 11, 1889, Foraker to Halstead, October 11, 1889, both quoted in the House Report, pp. 203–8.

40. *Commercial Gazette,* October 13, November 8, 1889.

41. Benjamin Butterworth to Halstead, October 13, 1889, Halstead Papers.

42. *Commercial Gazette,* October 14, 1889; Sherman, *Recollections of Forty Years,* 2: 1056–57.

43. *Enquirer,* November 3, 1889; Walters, *Joseph Benson Foraker,* p. 95.

44. *Commercial Gazette*, November 7, 1889.

45. Foraker, *Notes of a Busy Life*, 1: 407; *Commercial Gazette*, November 9, 1889. Several of Sherman's friends agreed with Halstead. One even went so far as to place all of the blame for the Republican defeat on Foraker's "dictatorial bearing." E. E. Wood to John Sherman, November 14, 1889, Sherman Papers.

46. Sherman to Halstead, quoted in Sherman, *Recollections of Forty Years*, 2: 1055; Warner M. Bateman to John Sherman, November 7, 1889, Sherman Papers.

47. *Commercial Gazette*, November 13, 1889.

48. H. V. Boynton to Halstead, January 5, 1890, Halstead Papers; H. R. Probasco to John Sherman, November 29, 1889, Sherman Papers.

49. *Commercial Gazette*, February 5, 1890.

50. Walters, *Joseph Benson Foraker*, p. 85; Foraker, *Notes of a Busy Life*, 1: 409–11. Foraker later published his side of the story in J. B. Foraker, *Answer of J. B. Foraker to Argument of Hon. Charles H. Grosvenor before Special Committee to Investigate Ohio Ballot Box Matter; House of Representatives*, 51st Cong., 2d sess., Report 3446, pp. 191, 215.

51. Foraker, *Notes of a Busy Life*, 1: 408–9; *House of Representatives*, Report 3446, p. 192.

52. *House of Representatives*, Report 3446, p. 210.

53. Ibid., p. 193.

54. Ibid., p. 192.

55. Ibid., pp. 191, 209. The editor wrote Sherman of his conviction that an explanation existed of the senator's signature "consistent with your character." Halstead said that although he intended to write and ask for it, he just "neglected to do so." Halstead to Sherman, November 14, 1889, Sherman Papers.

56. *House of Representatives*, Report 3446, pp. 206, 215.

57. Ibid., p. 216.

58. Ibid., pp. 192, 219; Foraker, *Notes of a Busy Life*, 1: 409; *Commercial Gazette*, November 18, 1889.

59. *House of Representatives*, Report 3446, pp. viii–x.

60. H. R. Probasco to John Sherman, November 13, 1889, Sherman Papers; Foraker to Halstead, November 10, 21, 1889, Foraker Papers.

CHAPTER 8

1. *Commercial Gazette*, February 13, 1890; "From the Editor's Window," *Cosmopolitan Magazine* (April 1890), p. 765.

2. *Commercial Gazette*, April 6, 20, 1890; William L. Halstead MS., p. 222.

3. *Commercial Gazette*, April 22, 1890; "Journalist," clipping, n.d., Halstead Papers.

4. *Commercial Gazette*, April 20, 1890.

5. Ibid., April 23, 1890.

6. William L. Halstead MS., p. 200.

7. Osman C. Hooper, *History of Ohio Journalism, 1793–1933,* p. 96; *Commercial,* August 4, 1871.

8. *Commercial Gazette,* October 25, 1885; "A Great American Journalist," clipping, n.d., Halstead Papers; Halstead to Hayes, August 21, 1877, Hayes Papers.

9. *Enquirer,* July 25, 1886.

10. *Cincinnati Evening Telegram,* October 21, 1885; *Cleveland Plain Dealer,* August 21, 1886; "Blood on the Moon's Face," clipping, n.d., Halstead Papers. William Halstead believed that the charge grew out of the difficulties Mrs. Scott suffered during menopause and said she "was entirely normal before and after." William L. Halstead MS., pp. 210–13.

11. *Enquirer,* August 6, 7, 1886; *Columbus Dispatch,* August 21, 1886; *New York Tribune,* August 20, 1886.

12. *Plain Dealer,* August 21, 1886; "Blood on the Moon's Face," Halstead Papers; Zane L. Miller, *Boss Cox's Cincinnati: Urban Politics in the Progressive Era,"* pp. 59–61; Philip D. Jordan, *Ohio Comes of Age, 1873–1900,* pp. 193–99.

13. *Evening Telegram,* August 9, 1886, declared that it had received McLean's consent to a meeting between the two men, and went on to say that if Halstead refused, he stood "branded as a shameless, slobbering slanderous coward." *Commercial Gazette,* August 20, 1886.

14. *Columbus Dispatch,* August 20, 1886; William L. Halstead MS., p. 209; *Enquirer,* August 23, September 8, 1886.

15. Halstead to William McKinley, February 18, 1898, William McKinley Papers; William L. Halstead MS., p. 216.

16. Hooper, *History of Ohio Journalism,* p. 96.

17. William Smith to Halstead, July 20, 1891, Halstead Papers; *History of Cincinnati and Hamilton County,* pp. 527–28; William L. Halstead MS., pp. 224–25.

18. A. F. Seested to Halstead, August 20, 1900, Halstead Papers.

19. Murat Halstead, *Our Cuban Relations,* pp. 420, 427.

20. Halstead to Marshal Halstead, May 10, 1898, Halstead Papers.

21. Frank L. Mott, *American Journalism: A History of Newspapers in the United States through 250 Years, 1690–1940,* p. 534; Secretary of War Alger to General Merritt, June 15, 21, 1898, Halstead Papers; Halstead to McKinley, June 28, 1898, McKinley Papers; Halstead to Albert Halstead, June 11, 1898; Halstead to Mrs. Halstead, July 25, 1898, Halstead Papers.

22. Brochure, Clayton Lyceum Bureau of Chicago, 1898, Halstead Papers.

23. *Pittsburgh Dispatch,* November 26, 1898, clipping, Halstead Papers.

24. Ibid., November 25, 1898; *Commercial Tribune,* November 29, 1898.

25. *Commercial Tribune,* November 26, 1898.

26. *New York Commercial Advertiser,* October 23, 1900, clipping, Halstead Papers.

27. Halstead to Whitelaw Reid, March 19, 1900, Whitelaw Reid Papers; Halstead to Charles Grosvenor, February 19, 1898, Halstead Papers; Halstead to McKinley, February 18, 1898, McKinley Papers; Grosvenor to Halstead, February 18, 1898, Halstead Papers; *New York Sun,* February 15, 1898, clipping, Halstead Papers.

28. Halstead to Whitelaw Reid, May 17, 1900, Reid Papers.

29. Albert Halstead to Halstead, December 9, 13, 1904, Halstead to Cornelius Bliss, January 13, 1905, Halstead Papers. Wallace put together a scissors-and-paste biography of Harrison in 1888 with Halstead's help. Harry J. Sievers, *Benjamin Harrison, Hoosier Statesman: From the Civil War to the White House, 1865–1888,* p. 371. The second volume remained the standard Harrison biography until the publication of Father Siever's work.

30. Halstead to Albert Halstead, September 29, October 2, 1901, May 26, 1904; *Boston Record,* September 17, 1900, clipping, Halstead Papers.

31. While Halstead complained bitterly about Barber's publishing the old book, calling it "a stale affair of no interest or importance" and a "fraud," the Barber edition did have an additional chapter by Albert Halstead, the editor's son. There is no mention in the letters between father and son of Albert's agreement to write the chapter. On the other hand, there is no break in the correspondence, and no evidence of Halstead's anger that Albert associated himself with the Barber venture. Halstead to [?], October 26, 1901, Halstead Papers. Amazingly, a half century passed before McKinley received an adequate biography. Halstead's work, described by one critic as a "contemporary tear-jerker which capitalized chiefly on the emotions aroused by the assassination and all its horrendous details, including the autopsy," remained the standard work. James E. Pollard, *The Presidents and the Press,* pp. 552–53.

32. G. T. Rowland to Henry Watterson, January 6, 1898, Watterson Papers; Halstead to Albert Halstead, February 7, 1900, J. J. McNanaman to Halstead, March 28, 1901, H. L. Barber to Halstead, April 5, 1901, Halstead Papers.

33. Halstead to Albert Halstead, January 2, 1902, A. J. Saalfield to Halstead, January 18, 1902, Halstead Papers.

34. Albert Halstead to Halstead, January 28, 1902, May 26, 1904, February 21, March 24, 1905, Halstead Papers; *Commercial Tribune,* January 30, 1905.

35. Robert Halstead to Albert Halstead, March 18, 1908, Halstead Papers.

Bibliography

COLLECTIONS OF LETTERS AND MANUSCRIPTS

James G. Blaine, Library of Congress
Salmon P. Chase, Library of Congress
James M. Comly, Ohio Historical Society
Jacob D. Cox, Ohio Historical Society
Joseph B. Foraker, Cincinnati Historical Society
James A. Garfield, Library of Congress
Murat Halstead, Cincinnati Historical Society
Benjamin Harrison, Library of Congress
Frederick Hassaurek, Ohio Historical Society
Rutherford B. Hayes, Rutherford B. Hayes Library
George Hoadly, Ohio Historical Society
William McKinley, Library of Congress
Stanley Matthews, Ohio Historical Society
Whitelaw Reid, Library of Congress
Jacob Schucker, Library of Congress
John Sherman, Library of Congress
William Henry Smith, Ohio Historical Society
Henry Watterson, Library of Congress

NEWSPAPERS

Columbia and Great West (Cincinnati), 1852–53
Cincinnati Commercial, 1852–83
Cincinnati Commercial Gazette, 1883–93
Cincinnati Commercial Tribune, 1893–1908
Cincinnati Enquirer, 1853–1908, passim
Cincinnati Evening Telegram, 1885–86
Cincinnati Gazette, 1853–83, passim
New York Times, 1861–1908, passim

GOVERNMENT DOCUMENTS, PRINTED CORRESPONDENCE, AND OTHER PRIMARY MATERIAL

First Annual Circular of Farmers' College. Cincinnati: R. P. Donogh, 1847.

Hinsdale, Mary L., ed. *Garfield-Hinsdale Letters.* Ann Arbor: University of Michigan Press, 1949.

Investigation Concerning the Public Works of Ohio Including the Report of the Committee and the Testimony Taken. Columbus: Nevins and Meyers, 1875.

Ohio Journalism Hall of Fame, Addresses at the Inauguration of the Hall and the Announcement of the Results of the First Election. Journalism Series, No. 7. Columbus: Ohio State University Press, 1929.

Schurz, Carl. *Speeches, Correspondence, and Political Papers of Carl Schurz,* edited by Frederic Bancroft. 6 vols. New York: G. P. Putnam's Sons, 1913.

Senate Investigations of the Little Lottery Bill. Testimony of M. Halstead, B. J. Loomis, Senator Young [and Others]. Columbus: Nevins and Meyers, 1873.

Thorndike, Rachel Sherman, ed. *The Sherman Letters: Correspondence between General and Senator Sherman from 1831 to 1891.* New York: Charles Scribner's Sons, 1894.

United States Government. "House of Representatives Report of the Committee of Investigation of the Ballot Box Forgeries in the State of Ohio." House of Representatives, 51st Congress, 2d Session, Report 3446 (1890).

United States Government. "Report of Senate Committee on Privileges and Elections on the Election of Hon. Henry B. Payne as Senator from the State of Ohio." 49th Congress, 1st Session, Report 1490 (July 15, 1886).

Williams, Charles Richard, ed. *Diary and Letters of Rutherford Birchard Hayes, Nineteenth President of the United States.* 5 vols. Columbus: The Ohio State Archaeological and Historical Society, 1922-1926.

BIOGRAPHIES, AUTOBIOGRAPHIES, AND MEMOIRS

Abels, Jules. *Man on Fire: John Brown and the Cause of Liberty.* New York: Macmillan Company, 1971.

Barnard, Harry. *Rutherford B. Hayes and His America.* Indianapolis and New York: Bobbs-Merrill Company, 1954.

Barrows, Chester L. *William M. Evarts: Lawyer, Diplomat, Statesman.* Chapel Hill: University of North Carolina Press, 1941.

Bigland, Eileen. *The Indomitable Mrs. Trollope.* London: James Barrie, 1953.

Blaine, James G. *Twenty Years of Congress: From Lincoln to Garfield.* 2 vols. Chicago: Werner Company, 1895.

Boutwell, George S. *Reminiscences of Sixty Years in Public Affairs.* 2 vols. New York: McClure, Phillips, and Company, 1902.

Bronson, S. A. *John Sherman: What He Has Said and Done, Being a History of the Life and Public Services of the Hon. John Sherman, Secretary of the Treasury of the United States.* Columbus: H. W. Derby and Company, 1880.

Bryan, William Jennings, and Jennings, Mary Baird. *The Memoirs of William Jennings Bryan.* Philadelphia: United Publishers of America, 1928.

Caldwell, Robert G. *James A. Garfield.* New York: Dodd, Mead and Company, 1931.

Carpenter, John A. *Ulysses S. Grant.* New York: Twayne Publishing, 1970.

Clay, Cassius Marcellus. *The Life of Cassius Marcellus Clay; Memoirs, Writings, and Speeches.* 2 vols. Cincinnati: J. Fletcher Brennan and Company, 1886.

Conkling, Alfred R. *The Life and Letters of Roscoe Conkling.* New York: C. L. Webster and Company, 1889.

Conway, Moncure D. *Autobiography, Memories, and Experiences.* 2 vols. New York and Boston: Houghton Mifflin and Company, 1904.

Cramer, Clarence H. *Royal Bob: The Life of Robert G. Ingersoll.* Indianapolis: Bobbs-Merrill Company, 1952.

Croffut, William A. *An American Procession, 1855–1914; A Personal Chronicle of Famous Men.* Boston: Little, Brown, and Company, 1931.

Daniels, Josephus. *Editor in Politics.* Chapel Hill: University of North Carolina Press, 1944.

Davison, Kenneth E. *The Presidency of Rutherford B. Hayes.* Westport, Conn.: Greenwood Press, 1972.

Day, Sarah J. *The Man on a Hill Top.* Philadelphia: Ware Brothers Publishing Company, 1931.

Depew, Chauncey M. *My Memories of Eighty Years.* New York: Charles Scribner's Sons, 1924.

Dodge, Mary A. [Gail Hamilton]. *Biography of James G. Blaine.* Norwich, Conn.: Henry Bill Publishing Company, 1895.

Duberman, Martin B. *Charles Francis Adams, 1807–1886.* Boston: Houghton Mifflin Company, 1961.

Durden, Robert Franklin. *James Shepherd Pike: Republicanism and the American Negro, 1850–1882.* Durham, N.C.: Duke University Press, 1957.

Eckenrode, H. J. *Rutherford B. Hayes: Statesman of Reunion.* New York: Dodd, Mead and Company, 1930.

Foraker, Joseph Benson. *Notes of a Busy Life.* 2 vols. Cincinnati: Stewart and Kidd Company, 1916.

Foraker, Julia B. *I Would Live It Again.* New York and London: Harper and Brothers Publishers, 1932.

Grant, U. S. *Personal Memoirs of U. S. Grant.* 2 vols. New York: Charles L. Webster and Company, 1885.

Hale, William H. *Horace Greeley: Voice of the People.* New York: Harper and Brothers Publishers, 1950.

Harrison, Benjamin. *Views of an Ex-President.* Indianapolis: Bowen-Merrill Company, 1901.

Hinsdale, Burke A., ed. *The World of James Abram Garfield.* 2 vols. Boston: James R. Osgood and Company, 1882.

Hoar, George F. *Autobiography of Seventy Years.* 2 vols. New York: Charles Scribner's Sons, 1903.

Holloway, Jean. *Edward Everett Hale: A Biography.* Austin: University of Texas Press, 1956.

Holzman, Robert S. *Stormy Ben Butler.* New York: Macmillan Company, 1954.

Howe, George F. *Chester A. Arthur: A Quarter-Century of Machine Politics.* New York: Frederick Ungar Publishing Company, 1957.

Hudson, William C. *Random Recollections of an Old Political Reporter.* New York: Cupples and Leon Company, 1911.

Jordan, David M. *Roscoe Conkling of New York: Voice in the Senate.* Ithaca: Cornell University Press, 1971.

Julian, George W. *Political Recollections, 1840–1872.* Chicago: Jansen, McClurg and Company, 1884.

Kerr, Winfield S. *John Sherman: His Life and Public Services.* 2 vols. Boston: Sherman, French and Company, 1908.

King, Willard L. *Lincoln's Manager: David Davis.* Cambridge, Harvard University Press, 1960.

Klein, Philip S. *President James Buchanan: A Biography.* University Park: Pennsylvania State University Press, 1962.

Krug, Mark M. *Lyman Trumbull: Conservative Radical.* New York: A. S. Barnes and Company, Inc., 1965.

Lang, Louis J. ed. *The Autobiography of Thomas Collier Platt.* New York: B. W. Dodge and Company, 1910.

Leech, Margaret. *In the Days of McKinley.* New York: Harper and Brothers, 1959.

Lewis, Lloyd. *Sherman: Fighting Prophet.* New York: Harcourt, Brace and Company, 1958.

Logsdon, Joseph. *Horace White: Nineteenth-Century Liberal.* Westport, Conn.: Greenwood Publishing Corporation, 1971.

Lyon, Peter. *Success Story: The Life and Times of S. S. McClure.* New York: Charles Scribner's Sons, 1963.

McCormack, Thomas J., ed. *Memoirs of Gustave Koerner, 1809–1896; Life Sketches Written at the Suggestion of His Children.* Cedar Rapids, Iowa: Torch Press, 1909.

McDonald, Philip B. *A Saga of the Seas: The Story of Cyrus W. Field and the Laying of the First Atlantic Cable.* New York: Wilson-Erickson, Inc., 1937.

McKitrick, Eric L. *Andrew Johnson and Reconstruction.* Chicago: University of Chicago Press, 1960.

Marcosson, Isaac F. *"Marse Henry": A Biography of Henry Watterson.* New York: Dodd, Mead and Company, 1951.

Merriam, George S. *The Life and Times of Samuel Bowles.* 2 vols. New York: Century Company, 1885.

Miller, Charles G. *Donn Piatt: His Work and His Ways.* Cincinnati: Robert Clarke and Company, 1893.

Morgan, H. Wayne. *William McKinley and His America.* Syracuse: Syracuse University Press, 1963.

Muzzey, David S. *James G. Blaine: A Political Idol of Other Days.* New York: Dodd, Mead and Company, 1934.

Nevins, Allan. *Abram S. Hewitt: With Some Account of Peter Cooper.* New York: Harper and Brothers, 1935.

———. *Grover Cleveland: A Study in Courage.* New York: Dodd, Mead and Company, 1932.

Nixon, Raymond B. *Henry W. Grady: Spokesman of the New South.* New York: Alfred A. Knopf, 1943.

Ogden, Rollo, ed. *Life and Letters of Edwin Lawrence Godkin.* 2 vols. New York: Macmillan Company, 1907.

Paine, Albert Bigelow. *Mark Twain, A Biography: The Personal and Literary Life of Samuel Langhorne Clemens.* 4 vols. New York: Harper and Brothers Publishers, 1912.

Peterson, Norman L. *Freedom and Franchise: The Political Career of B. Gratz Brown.* Columbia: University of Missouri Press, 1965.

Piatt, Donn. *Memoirs of the Men Who Saved the Union.* New York: Belford, Clarke and Company, 1887.

Pierce, Edward L., ed. *Memoirs and Letters of Charles Sumner.* 4 vols. Boston: Roberts Brothers, 1887–93.

Poore, Ben Perley. *Perley's Reminiscences of Sixty Years in the National Metropolis.* 2 vols. Philadelphia: Hubbard Brothers Publishers, 1886.

Reeves, Thomas G. *Gentleman Boss: The Life of Chester Alan Arthur.* New York: Alfred A. Knopf, 1975.

Richardson, Leon B. *William E. Chandler, Republican.* New York: Dodd, Mead and Company, 1940.

Rodabaugh, James H. *Robert Hamilton Bishop.* Columbus: Ohio State Archaeological and Historical Society, 1935.

Ross, Ishbel. *An American Family: The Tafts, 1678–1964.* Cleveland: World Publishing Company, 1964.

Royall, Margaret Shaw. *Andrew Johnson—Presidential Scapegoat: A Biographical Re-Evaluation.* New York: Exposition Press, 1958.

Schucker, J. W. *The Life and Public Services of Salmon Portland Chase, United States Senator and Governor of Ohio; Secretary of the Treasury, and Chief Justice of the United States.* New York: D. Appleton and Company, 1874.

Schurz, Carl. *The Reminiscences of Carl Schurz, with a Sketch of His Life and Public Services from 1809 to 1906 by Frederic Bancroft and William A. Dunning.* 3 vols. McClure Company, 1908.

Seitz, Don C. *The James Gordon Bennetts, Father and Son: Proprietors of the New York Herald.* Indianapolis: Bobbs-Merrill Company, 1928.

———. *Joseph Pulitzer: His Life and Letters.* Garden City: Garden City Publishing Company, Inc., 1924.

Sheridan, Philip H. *Personal Memoirs of Philip H. Sheridan, General, United States Army.* 2 vols. New York: Charles L. Webster and Company, 1888.

Sherman, John. *Recollections of Forty Years in the House, Senate, and Cabinet.* 2 vols. Chicago: Werner Company, 1895.

Sherman, William T. *Memoirs of General William T. Sherman.* 2 vols. New York: D. Appleton and Company, 1875.

Sievers, Harry J. *Benjamin Harrison, Hoosier Warrior: Through the Civil War Years, 1833–1865.* New York: University Publishers, 1952.

———. *Benjamin Harrison, Hoosier Statesman: From the Civil War to the White House, 1865–1888.* New York: University Publishers, 1959.

———. *Benjamin Harrison, Hoosier President: The White House and After.* Indianapolis: Bobbs-Merrill, 1968.

Smith, Donnal V. *Chase and Civil War Politics.* Columbus, Ohio: F. J. Heer Printing Company, 1931.

Smith, Theodore C. *The Life and Letters of James Abram Garfield.* 2 vols. New Haven: Yale University Press, 1925.

Smith, William E. *The Francis Blair Family in Politics.* New York: DaCapo Press, 1969.

Stanwood, Edward. *James Gillespie Blaine.* Boston and New York: Houghton, Mifflin and Company, 1905.

Stone, Melville E. *"M. E. S." His Book.* New York: Harper and Brothers Publishers, 1918.

Taylor, John M. *Garfield of Ohio: The Available Man.* New York: W. W. Norton and Company, Inc., 1970.

Thomas, Benjamin P. *Abraham Lincoln: A Biography.* New York: Alfred A. Knopf, 1952.

Thomas, Benjamin P., and Hyman, Harold M. *Stanton: the Life and Times of Lincoln's Secretary of War.* New York: Alfred A. Knopf, 1962.

Trefousse, H. L. *Benjamin Franklin Wade: Radical Republican from Ohio.* New York: Twayne Publishers, Inc., 1963.

Twain, Mark. *Mark Twain in Eruption, Hitherto Unpublished Pages about Men and Events.* Edited by Bernard De Voto. New York: Harper and Brothers Publishers, 1940.

Vallandigham, Rev. James Laird. *A Life of Clement L. Vallandigham.* Baltimore: Turnbull Brothers, 1872.

Van Deusen, Glyndon G. *Thurlow Weed: Wizard of the Lobby.* Boston: Little, Brown and Company, 1947.

Wall, Joseph Frazier. *Henry Watterson: Reconstructed Rebel.* New York: Oxford University Press, 1956.

Walters, Everett. *Joseph Benson Foraker: An Uncompromising Republican.* Columbus: Ohio History Press, 1948.

Warden, Robert B. *An Account of the Private Life and Public Services of Salmon Portland Chase.* Cincinnati: Wilstach, Baldwin, and Company, 1874.

Watterson, Henry. *"Marse Henry": An Autobiography.* 2 vols. New York: George H. Doran Company, 1919.

Weisenburger, Francis P. *The Life of John McLean: A Politician on the United States Supreme Court.* Columbus: Ohio State University Press, 1937.
Welch, Richard E., Jr. *George Frisbie Hoar and the Half-Breed Republicans.* Cambridge: Harvard University Press, 1971.
White, Andrew D. *Autobiography of Andrew Dickson White.* 2 vols. New York: Century Company, 1906.
White, Horace. *The Life of Lyman Trumbull.* Boston and New York: Century Company, 1906.
Williams, Burton J. *Senator John James Ingalls: Kansas' Iridescent Republican.* Lawrence: University Press of Kansas, 1972.
Williams, Charles Richard. *The Life of Rutherford Birchard Hayes, Nineteenth President of the United States.* 2 vols. Boston and New York: Houghton Mifflin Company, 1914.
Winkler, John K. *Incredible Carnegie; The Life of Andrew Carnegie (1835–1919).* New York: Vanguard Press, 1931.
Woodley, Thomas Frederick. *Thaddeus Stevens.* Harrisburg, Pa.: Telegraph Press, 1934.

GENERAL WORKS

Andrews, J. Cutler. *The North Reports the Civil War.* Pittsburgh: University of Pittsburgh Press, 1955.
Beale, Howard K. *The Critical Year: A Study of Andrew Johnson and Reconstruction.* New York: Ungar, 1958.
Benedict, Michael Les. *A Compromise of Principle: Congressional Republicans and Reconstruction, 1863–1869.* New York: W. W. Norton and Company, 1974.
Binkley, Wilfred E. *American Political Parties: Their Natural History.* New York: Alfred A. Knopf, 1943.
Blodgett, Geoffrey. *The Gentle Reformers: Massachusetts Democrats in the Cleveland Era.* Cambridge: Harvard University Press, 1966.
Boutwell, George S. *Why I Am a Republican.* Hartford: William J. Betts and Company, 1884.
Buck, Paul H. *The Road to Reunion, 1865–1900.* Boston: Little, Brown, and Company, 1937.
Cary, Samuel F. *History of College Hill and Vicinity, With a Sketch of Pioneer Life in This Part of Ohio.* Citizens of College Hill, April 1886.
Chidlaw, Rev. B. W. *"Remember the Days of Old": An Historical Sketch of Paddy's Run, Butler County, Ohio.* [n.p.], 1876.
Churchill, Allen. *Park Row.* New York: Rinehart and Company, Inc., 1958.
Clancy, Herbert J., S.J. *The Presidential Election of 1880.* Chicago: Loyola University Press, 1958.
Cobban, Alfred. *A History of Modern France.* 2 vols. Baltimore: Penguin Books, 1961.
Coleman, Charles H. *The Election of 1868; Democratic Efforts to Regain Control.* New York: Columbia University Press, 1933.
Crozier, Emmet. *Yankee Reporters, 1861–1865.* New York: Oxford University Press, 1959.
Davis, Elmer. *History of the New York Times, 1851–1921.* New York: New York Times, 1921.
De Chambrun, Clara Longworth. *Cincinnati: Story of the Queen City.* New York: Charles Scribner's Sons, 1939.
Diehl, Charles S. *The Staff Correspondent.* San Antonio, Texas: Clegg Company, 1931.
Dobson, John M. *Politics in the Gilded Age: A New Perspective on Reform.* New York: Praeger Publishers, 1972.

Duke, Basil W. *A History of Morgan's Cavalry.* Bloomington: Indiana University Press, 1960.

Emery, Edwin. *The Press in America: An Interpretative History of Mass Media.* Englewood Cliffs, N.J.: Prentice-Hall, 1972.

Foner, Eric. *Free Soil, Free Labor, Free Men: The Ideology of the Republican Party before the Civil War.* New York: Oxford University Press, 1970.

Franklin, John Hope. *Reconstruction after the Civil War.* Chicago: University of Chicago Press, 1961.

Gibson, Albert M. *A Political Crime: The History of the Great Fraud.* New York: William S. Gottsberger, Publisher, 1885.

Goldman, Eric. *Rendezvous with Destiny: A History of Modern American Reform.* New York: Alfred A. Knopf, 1952.

Goss, Rev. Charles Frederic. *Cincinnati: The Queen City, 1788–1912.* 4 vols. Chicago and Cincinnati: S. J. Clarke Publishing Company, 1912.

Graebner, Norman A., ed. *Politics and the Crisis of 1860.* Urbana: University of Illinois Press, 1961.

Harlow, Alvin F. *The Serene Cincinnatians.* New York: E. P. Dutton and Company, Inc., 1951.

Harper, Robert S. *Lincoln and the Press.* New York: McGraw–Hill Book Company, Inc., 1951.

Harrison, Harry P. *Culture under Canvas: The Story of Tent Chautauqua.* New York: Hastings House, 1948.

Hayes, Melvin L. *Mr. Lincoln Runs for President.* New York: Citadel Press, 1960.

Hendrick, Burton J. *Lincoln's War Cabinet.* New York: Doubleday and Company, 1961.

Hirshson, Stanley P. *Farewell to the Bloody Shirt: Northern Republicans and the Southern Negro, 1833–1877.* Bloomington: Indiana University Press, 1962.

History of Cincinnati and Hamilton County, Ohio. Cincinnati: S. B. Nelson and Company, 1894.

Hoogenboom, Ari. *Outlawing the Spoils: A History of the Civil Service Reform Movement, 1865–1883.* Urbana: University of Illinois Press, 1961.

Hooper, Osman C. *History of Ohio Journalism, 1793–1933.* Columbus: Spahr and Glenn Company, 1933.

Huston, A. B. *Historical Sketch of Farmers' College.* Cincinnati: Students' Association of Farmers' College, 1907.

Hyman, Harold M. *Era of the Oath: Northern Loyalty Tests during the Civil War and Reconstruction.* Philadelphia: University of Pennsylvania Press, 1954.

Jordan, Philip D. *Ohio Comes of Age, 1873–1900.* Columbus: Ohio State Archaeological and Historical Society, 1943.

Josephson, Matthew. *The Politicos, 1865–1896.* New York: Harcourt Brace and Company, 1938.

Kennedy, James H. *History of the Ohio Society of New York, 1885–1905.* New York: Grafton Press, 1906.

Kent, Frank R. *The Democratic Party: A History.* New York: Century Company, 1928.

Kinsley, Philip. *The Chicago Tribune: Its First Hundred Years.* 3 vols. Chicago: Chicago Tribune, 1945.

Klement, Frank L. *The Copperheads in the Middle West.* Chicago: University of Chicago Press, 1960.

Kleppner, Paul. *The Cross of Culture: A Social Analysis of Midwestern Politics, 1850–1900.* New York: Free Press, 1970.

Literary Club of Cincinnati, 1849–1949; Centennial Book. Cincinnati: Literary Club, 1949.

Literary Club of Cincinnati, 1849–1903; Constitution, Catalogue of Members, etc. Cincinnati: Ebbert and Richardson Company, 1903.

Lloyd, Henry Demarest. *Wealth against Commonwealth*. New York: Harper and Brothers Publishers, 1894.

Marcus, Robert D. *Grand Old Party: Political Structure in the Gilded Age, 1880–1896*. New York: Oxford University Press, 1971.

Mayer, George H. *The Republican Party, 1854–1966*. New York: Oxford University Press, 1967.

Miller, Zane L. *Boss Cox's Cincinnati: Urban Politics in the Progressive Era*. New York: Oxford University Press, 1968.

Morgan, H. Wayne. *From Hayes to McKinley: National Party Politics, 1877–1896*. Syracuse: Syracuse University Press, 1969.

————, ed. *The Gilded Age*. Syracuse: Syracuse University Press, 1970.

Mott, Frank L. *American Journalism: A History of Newspapers in the United States through 250 Years, 1690–1940*. New York: Macmillan Company, 1947.

Nevins, Allan. *Hamilton Fish: The Inner History of the Grant Administration*. New York: Dodd, Mead and Company, 1937.

————. *Ordeal of the Union*. 2 vols. New York: Charles Scribner's Sons, 1947.

Ohio Journalism Hall of Fame. Addresses at the Inauguration of the Hall and the Announcement of the Results of the First Election. Journalism Series, no. 7. Columbus: Ohio State University Press, 1929.

Persons, Stow. *The Decline of American Gentility*. New York: Columbia University Press, 1973.

Polakoff, Keith Ian. *Politics of Inertia: The Election of 1876 and the End of Reconstruction*. Baton Rouge: Louisiana State University Press, 1973.

Pollard, James E. *The Presidents and the Press*. New York: Macmillan Company, 1947.

Porter, George H. *Ohio Politics during the Civil War Period*. Columbia Studies in History, Economics and Political Law, vol. 40, no. 2. New York: Columbia University, 1911.

Potter, David M. *Lincoln and His Party in the Secession Crisis*. New Haven: Yale University Press, 1942.

Powell, Thomas E., ed. *The Democratic Party of the State of Ohio: A Comprehensive History of Democracy in Ohio from 1803–1912*. Columbus: Ohio Publishing Company, 1913.

Randall, James G. *The Civil War and Reconstruction*. Boston: D. C. Heath and Company, 1953.

————. *Constitutional Problems under Lincoln*. Gloucester, Mass.; Peter Smith, 1963.

Roseboom, Eugene H. *The Civil War Era, 1850–1873*. Columbus: Ohio State Archaeological and Historical Society, 1944.

————. *A History of Presidential Elections*. New York: Macmillan Company, 1957.

Rosewater, Victor. *History of Cooperative News-Gathering in the United States*. New York: A. Appleton and Company, 1930.

Ross, Earle D. *The Liberal Republican Movement*. New York: Henry Holt and Company, 1919.

Rothman, David J. *Politics and Power: The United States Senate, 1869–1901*. Cambridge: Harvard University Press, 1966.

Simms, Henry H. *A Decade of Sectional Controversy, 1851–1861*. Chapel Hill: University of North Carolina Press, 1942.

Smith, Joseph P., ed. *History of the Republican Party in Ohio and Memoirs of Its Representative Supporters*. 2 vols. Chicago: Lewis Publishing Company, 1898.

Smith, William C. *Queen City Yesterdays: Sketches of Cincinnati in the Eighties*. Crawford, Ind: R. E. Banta, 1959.

Sproat, John G. *"The Best Men": Liberal Reformers in the Gilded Age*. New York: Oxford University Press, 1968.

Starr, Louis M. *Reporting the Civil War: The Bohemian Brigade in Action, 1861–65*. New York: Collier Books, 1962.

Taylor, Bayard. *Egypt and Iceland in the Year 1874.* New York: G. P. Putnam's Sons, 1874.

Thomas, Harrison C., *The Return of the Democratic Party to Power in 1884.* Columbia University Studies in History, Economics and Public Law, vol. 1, no. 89. New York: Columbia University, 1919.

Trollope, Frances. *Domestic Manners of the Americans.* New York: Alfred A. Knopf, 1949.

Weisberger, Bernard A. *Reporters for the Union.* Boston: Little, Brown and Company, 1953.

Weisenburger, Francis P. *The Passing of the Frontier, 1825–1850.* Columbus: Ohio State Archaeological and Historical Society, 1941.

Welch, F. G. *That Convention: Or Five Days a Politician.* New York: F. G. Welch and Company, 1872.

Wheeler, Kenneth W., ed. *For the Union: Ohio Leaders in the Civil War.* Columbus: Ohio State University Press, 1968.

Wingate, Charles F., ed. *Views and Interviews on Journalism.* New York: F. B. Patterson, 1875.

Wittke, Carl. *The German-Language Press in America.* Lexington: University of Kentucky Press, 1957.

Woodward, C. Vann. *Origins of the New South, 1877–1913.* Baton Rouge: Louisiana State University Press, 1951.

———. *Reunion and Reaction: The Compromise of 1877 and the End of Reconstruction.* Garden City, N.Y.: Doubleday and Company, 1956.

Zornow, William F. *Lincoln and the Party Divided.* Norman: University of Oklahoma Press, 1954.

PERIODICAL ARTICLES

Becker, Carl M. "Freeman Cary and Farmers' College: An Ohio Educator and an Experiment in Nineteenth-Century 'Practical' Education." *Bulletin of the Historical and Philosophical Society of Ohio* 21 (July 1963): 151–75.

———. "The Genesis of a Copperhead." *Bulletin of the Historical Society of Ohio* 19 (October 1961): 235–53.

Carter, Clarence. "Some Notes on Ohio Historiography." *Ohio Archaeological and Historical Quarterly* 38 (January 1919): 176–85.

"The Cincinnati Convention." *The Nation* 14 (June 1872).

Clonts, Forrest W. "The Political Campaign in 1875 in Ohio." *Ohio Archaeological and Historical Quarterly* 31 (January 1922): 38–97.

Connery, T. B. "Secret History of the Garfield-Conkling Tragedy." *Cosmopolitan Magazine* 33 (June 1897): 145–62.

Conway, Moncure D. "Reminiscences of Kaiser Wilhelm." *Cosmopolitan Magazine* 5 (April 1888): 143–50.

Curl, Donald Walter. "An American Reporter and the Franco-Prussian War." *Journalism Quarterly* 49 (Autumn 1972): 480–88.

———. "The Baltimore Convention of the Constitutional Union Party." *Maryland Magazine of History* 67 (Fall 1972): 254–77.

———. "The Cincinnati *Commercial.*" *Bulletin of the Cincinnati Historical Society* 24 (July 1966): 221–35.

———. "The Cincinnati Convention of the Liberal Republican Party." *Bulletin of the Cincinnati Historical Society* 24 (April 1966): 150–63.

———. "The Long Memory of the United States Senate." *Ohio History* 76 (Summer 1967): 103–14.

Downey, Matthew T. "Horace Greeley and the Politicians: The Liberal Republican Convention in 1872." *Journal of American History* 53 (March 1967): 727–50.

"From the Editor's Window." *Cosmopolitan Magazine* 8 (April 1890): 765–67.

"A Great American Journalist." *Review of Reviews* 38 (August 1908): 191–92.

Green, James Albert. "The Literary Club of Cincinnati: A Centenary in Retrospect." *Bulletin of the Historical and Philosophical Society of Ohio* 8 (January 1950): 49–53.

Greve, Charles T. "Clubs and Club Life." *The New England Magazine* 6 (September 1888): 479–83.

Jones, Charles A. "Ohio in the Republican National Conventions." *Ohio Archaeological and Historical Quarterly* 38 (January 1929): 1–46.

Logan, Lena C. "Henry Watterson and the Liberal Convention of 1872." *Indiana Magazine of History* 40 (December 1944): 320–40.

McIntyre, Edward F. "The Men's Clubs of Ohio, The Clubs of Cincinnati." *The Ohio Illustrated Magazine* 2 (June 1907): 477–85.

Moore, Clifford. "Ohio in National Politics, 1865–1896." *Ohio Archaeological and Historical Quarterly* 37 (April 1928): 220–43.

Nichols, Jeanette P. "John Sherman and the Silver Drive of 1877–78." *Ohio Archaeological and Historical Quarterly* 46 (January 1937): 148–65.

Northrup, Milton H. "A Grave Crisis in American History." *Century Magazine* 62 (October 1901): 923–34.

"Our National Conventions." *Review of Reviews* 5 (July 1892): 709.

Sandburg, Carl. "Lincoln and Grant." *Redbook* (April 1937): 46–49.

Shaw, Albert. "Murat Halstead, Journalist." *Review of Reviews* 13 (April 1896): 439–43.

Sternstein, Jerome L., ed. "The Sickles Memorandum: Another Look at the Hayes-Tilden Election Night Conspiracy." *Journal of Southern History* 37 (August 1966): 342–57.

"A Veteran Newspaper Man." *Outlook* 89 (July 11, 1908): 548–49.

Watterson, Henry. "The Humor and Tragedy of the Greeley Campaign." *Century Magazine* 85 (November 1912): 27–45.

Weisenburger, Francis P. "Life of Charles Hammond." *Ohio Archaeological and Historical Quarterly* 43 (June 1934): 340–427.

Wittke, Carl. "Fredrick Hassaurek: Cincinnati's Leading Forty-Eighter." *Ohio Historical Quarterly* 68 (January 1959): 1–17.

UNPUBLISHED MATERIALS

Beck, Earl R. "Political Career of Joseph Benson Foraker." Ph.D dissertation, Ohio State University, 1942.

Burke, Dewayne H. "Henry B. Payne: His Congressional Career." Master's thesis, Ohio State University, 1938.

Coles, Harry L. "General William T. Sherman and the Press." Paper given at the Southern Historical Association, 1962.

Deye, Anthony H. "Archbishop John Baptist Purcell and the Civil War." Ph.D. dissertation, Notre Dame University, 1944.

DiNunzio, Mario R. "Lyman Trumbull, United States Senator." Ph.D. dissertation, Clark University, 1964.

Gray, Edgar Laughlin. "The Career of William Henry Smith, Politician–Journalist." Ph.D. dissertation, Ohio State University, 1951.

Halstead, William L. " 'Field Marshal' Murat Halstead: A Biography." Manuscript, Cincinnati Historical Society.

Hess, James W. "George F. Hoar, 1826–1884." Ph.D. dissertation, Harvard University, 1964.

Jones, James P. "John A. Logan: Politician and Soldier." Ph.D. dissertation, University of Florida, 1960.

Kleinpell, Eugene H. "James M. Comly, Journalist–Politician." Ph.D. dissertation, Ohio State University, 1936.

Krebs, Frank J. "Hayes and the South." Ph.D. dissertation, Ohio State University, 1936.

Messamore, Ford. "John A. Logan: Democrat and Republican." Ph.D. dissertation, University of Kentucky, 1939.

Neilson, James W. "The Senatorial Career of Shelby More Cullom." Ph.D. dissertation, University of Illinois, 1958.

Roske, Ralph J. "The Post Civil War Career of Lyman Trumbull." Ph.D. dissertation, University of Illinois, 1949.

Smart, James G. "Whitelaw Reid: A Biographical Study." Ph.D. dissertation, University of Maryland, 1964.

Smith, Margie A. "The Presidential Election of 1884 in Ohio." Master's thesis, Ohio State University, 1960.

Thompson, Edwin B. "Benjamin Helm Bristow: Symbol of Reform." Ph.D. dissertation, University of Wisconsin, 1940.

Wilson, Charles R. "The *Cincinnati Daily Enquirer* and Civil War Politics: A Study in 'Copperhead' Opinion." Ph.D. dissertation, University of Chicago, 1934.

BOOKS OF MURAT HALSTEAD

Aguinaldo and His Captor: The Life Mysteries of Emilio Aguinaldo and Adventures and Achievements of General Funston. Cincinnati: Halstead Publishing Company, 1901.

Briton and Boer in South Africa. Philadelphia [n.p.], 1900.

Caucuses of 1860. Columbus: Follett, Foster and Company, 1860.

Full and Official History of the War with Spain. Chicago: Dominion Company, 1899.

Galveston: The Horrors of a Stricken City. Chicago: American Publishers' Association. 1900.

The History of American Expansion and the Story of Our New Possessions. [n.c.] United Book Publishers of America, 1898.

The Illustrious Life of William McKinley: Our Martyred President. Chicago: Monarch Company, 1901.

Life and Achievements of Admiral Dewey from Montpelier to Manila. Chicago: Dominion Company, 1899.

Life and Distinguished Services of William McKinley: Our Martyr President. Chicago: Memorial Association Publishers, 1901.

Life and Public Services of Hon. Benjamin Harrison, with General Lew Wallace. [n.c.] Edgewood Publishing Company, 1892.

Life of Jay Gould: How He Made His Millions, with Frank Beale, Jr. Philadelphia: Edgewood Publishing Company, 1892.

Life of Theodore Roosevelt: Twenty-Fifth President of the United States. Akron: Saalfield Publishing Company, 1902.

One Hundred Bear Stories, Historical, Romantic, etc., edited by Murat Halstead. New York: J. S. Ogilvie Publishing Company, 1895.

Our Country in War and Relations with All Nations. [n.c.] The United Subscription Book Publishers of America, 1898.

Our New Possessions. Chicago: Dominion Company, 1898.

Pictorial History of America's New Possessions. Chicago: Dominion Company, 1898.

Pictorial History of the Louisiana Purchase and the All World's Fair at St. Louis. Philadelphia: National Publishing Company, 1904.

Three against Lincoln: Murat Halstead Reports the Caucuses of 1860. Edited by William B. Hesseltine and Bruce Robertson. Baton Rouge: Louisiana State University Press, 1960.

Trimmers, Trucklers, and Temporizers: Notes of Murat Halstead from the Political Conventions of 1856. Edited by William B. Hesseltine and Rex G. Fisher. Madison: State Historical Society of Wisconsin, 1961.

Victorious Republicanism and Lives of the Standard Bearers, McKinley and Roosevelt. Chicago: Republican National Publishing Co., 1900.

The War between Russia and Japan. Philadelphia: National Publishing Company, 1904.

The War Claims of the South. Cincinnati: Robert Clarke and Company, Printers, 1876.

The White Dollar. Philadelphia: Franklin News Company, 1895.

The World on Fire. [n.c.] International Publishing Society, 1902.

Periodical Articles of Murat Halstead

"Breakfasts with Horace Greeley." *Cosmopolitan Magazine* 36 (April 1904): 698–702.

"The Chicago Convention of 1892." *Cosmopolitan Magazine* 13 (September 1892): 585–91.

"Cincinnati." *Cosmopolitan Magazine* 71 (October 1891): 682–701.

"The City of Brooklyn." *Cosmopolitan Magazine* 15 (June 1893): 131–44.

"The City of Hamburg." *Cosmopolitan Magazine* 14 (November 1892): 35–44.

"The Convention at Minneapolis." *Cosmopolitan Magazine* 13 (August 1892): 507–12.

"The Defeat of Blaine for the Presidency." *McClure's Magazine* 6 (January 1896): 159–72.

"Do Americans Hate England?" *North American Review* 150 (June 1890): 760–64.

"Early Editorial Experiences." *Lippincott's Monthly Magazine* 49 (June 1892): 710–15.

"Electricity at the Fair." *Cosmopolitan Magazine* 15 (September 1892): 577–82.

"Historical Illustrations of the Confederacy." *Cosmopolitan Magazine* 9 (March 1890): 496–507.

"Genoa—The Home of Columbus." *Cosmopolitan Magazine* 12 (April 1892): 643–49.

"Horace Greeley: A Friendly Estimate of a Great Career." *Cosmopolitan Magazine* 9 (February 1890): 460–68.

"Increase the Standing Army." *North American Review* 146 (March 1888): 311–17.

"An Italian Camp Santo." *Cosmopolitan Magazine* 14 (March 1893): 591–99.

"Marcus A. Hanna." *Review of Reviews* 14 (October 1896): 421–26.

"The Marquis de Lafayette and President Monroe." *Cosmopolitan Magazine,* 22 (October 1897): 681–90.

"Our Cuban Neighbors and Their Struggle For Liberty." *Review of Reviews* 13 (April 1896): 419–38.

"Our National Conceits." *North American Review* 149 (November 1889): 550–59.

"Our National Political Conventions." *Cosmopolitan Magazine* 13 (June 1892): 194–201.

"Outflanking Two Emperors." *Cosmopolitan Magazine* 17 (August 1894): 424–34.

"Pets and Sports of a Farmer Boy." *Cosmopolitan Magazine* 12 (February 1892): 471–79.

"Politics of the Russian Famine." *Cosmopolitan Magazine* 13 (May 1892): 80–83.

"The Presidential Candidates: William McKinley." *Outlook* 54 (July 25, 1896): 132–34.

"Prince Bismarck." *Cosmopolitan Magazine* 11 (August 1891): 499–504.

"Recollections and Letters of General Sherman." *The Independent* 51 (June 15, 22, 1899): 1610–13, 1682–87.

"Recollections and Letters of President Hayes." *The Independent* 51 (February 9, 16, 1899): 391–92, 486–89.

"Revival of Sectionalism." *North American Review* 140 (March 1885): 237–50.

"A Silver Senator Reviewed." *North American Review* 427 (June 1892): 666–71.

"The Story of the Farmers' College." *Cosmopolitan Magazine* 21 (January 1897): 280–88.

"The Tragedy of Garfield's Administration: Personal Reminiscences and Records of Conversations." *McClure's Magazine* 6 (February 1896): 269–79.

"The Varieties of Journalism." *Cosmopolitan Magazine* 14 (December 1892): 202–10.

"With an Invading Army." *Cosmopolitan Magazine* 17 (September 1894): 603–9.

Index